Torben Wissuwa

Beweisverwertungsverbote im Besteuerungsverfahren

www.tredition.de

© 2020 Torben Wissuwa

Verlag und Druck: tredition GmbH, Halenreie 40-44, 22359 Hamburg

ISBN
Paperback: 978-3-347-17080-3
Hardcover: 978-3-347-17081-0
e-Book: 978-3-347-17082-7

Inhalt

1 Problemstellung   13

2 Beweise   15

2.1   Beweisarten   15
2.1.1   Sachverständigengutachten   16
2.1.2   Augenscheinseinnahme   21
2.1.3   Parteivernehmung   23
2.1.4   Urkunden   26
2.1.5   Zeugen   30
2.1.6   Glaubhaftmachung   34

2.2   Beweise im Strafrecht   35

2.3   Beweise im Steuerrecht   36
2.3.1   Beweisvorschriften im Besteuerungs-, Haftungs-,
Vollstreckungs-, und Rechtsbehelfsverfahren   36
2.3.2   Beweisvorschriften im finanzgerichtlichen Verfahren 47

3 Zulässige Beweisbeibringung und Verwertung   49

4 Beweisverbote   50

4.1   Beweiserhebungsverbote   51
4.1.1   Beweisthemaverbot   52
4.1.2   Beweismittelverbot   56
4.1.3   Beweismethodenverbot   59

4.2   Beweisverwertungsverbote   67
4.2.1   Relative Beweisverwertungsverbote   67

4.2.2	Absolute Beweisverwertungsverbote	70
4.2.3	Selbständige Beweisverwertungsverbote	71
4.2.4	Unselbständige Beweisverwertungsverbote	71

5 „Fruit-of-the-poisonous-tree-Theorie   **72**

6 Erweiterte Beweisverwertungsverbote in Deutschland   **79**

6.1	**Verfassungsrechtliche Beweisverbote**	**81**
6.1.1	Drei-Sphären-Theorie	81
6.1.2	Abwägungslehre	85
6.2	**Nemo-tenetur-Prinzip**	**87**
6.3	**Rechtskreistheorie**	**90**

7 Steuerrechtliche Folgen   **91**

7.1	**Situation im Steuerrecht**	**92**
7.2	**Aktuelle Entwicklung**	**98**
7.2.1	Bundesfinanzhof, Beschluss vom 26. Februar 2001	99
7.2.2	Liechtensteiner Steueraffäre	104

8 Zusammenfassung / Fazit   **123**

U.S. Supreme Court	**135**
NARDONE v. UNITED STATES, 308 U.S. 338 (1939)	135
U.S. Supreme Court	**143**
WEEKS v. U.S., 232 U.S. 383 (1914)	143
U.S. Supreme Court	**164**
SILVERTHORNE LUMBER CO. v. U S , 251 U.S. 385 (1920)	164

U.S. Supreme Court   **169**
WONG SUN v. UNITED STATES, 371 U.S. 471 (1963)   169

U.S. Supreme Court   **203**
UNITED STATES v. CECCOLINI, 435 U.S. 268 (1978)   203

U.S. Supreme Court   **223**
MIRANDA v. ARIZONA, 384 U.S. 436 (1966)   223

Abkürzungsverzeichnis

a.a.O.	am angegebenen Ort
AO	Abgabenordnung
a.A.	andere Ansicht
aF	alte Fassung
AG	Amtsgericht
Art.	Artikel (singular)
Artt.	Artikel (plural)
BFH	Bundesfinanzhof
BFH/NV	Bundesfinanzhof - nicht veröffentlichte Entscheidunger
BGBl	Bundesgesetzblatt
BGH	Bundesgerichtshof
BGHSt	Entscheidung des BGH in Strafsachen
BND	Bundesnachrichtendienst
BRD	Bundesrepublik Deutschland
BStBl	Bundessteuerblatt
BVerfG	Bundesverfassungsgericht
Diss	Dissertation
DRiZ	Deutsche Richterzeitung
DStR	Deutsches Steuerrecht (Zeitschrift)
DVDs	Digital Versatile Discs - Datenträger
EFG	Entscheidungen der Finanzgerichte
Einf	Einführung
Einl	Einleitung
et al	und Andere

FG	Finanzgericht
FGO	Finanzgerichtsordnung
FOPT	Früchte des vergifteten Baumes
FOPT-The-orie	Theorie der Früchte des vergifteten Baumes
GG	Grundgesetz
Habil	Habilitationsschrift
HFR	Humboldt Forum Recht
HZA	Hauptzollamt
idF	in der Fassung vom
iSd	im Sinne des
iVm	in Verbindung mit
KK	Kurzkommentar
lt.	laut
MDR	Monatsschrift für deutsches Recht
NStZ	Neue Strafrechtszeitung
OLG	Oberlandesgericht
PM	Pressemitteilung
PStStR	Praxis Steuerstrafrecht
RFHE	Entscheidungen des Reichsfinanzhofes
SAPUZ	5 Beweisarten (Sachverständige, Augenschein, Pa Urkunden und Zeugen)
StBp	steuerliche Betriebsprüfung
StPO	Strafprozessordnung
U.S.	United States

UFS	Unabhängiger Finanzsenat (Österreich)
UStG	Umsatzsteuergesetz
VfGH	Verfassungsgerichtshof (Österreich)
vgl.	vergleiche
vs.	versus
VwGH	Verwaltungsgerichtshof (Österreich)
zB	zum Beispiel
ZK	Zollkodex
ZPO	Zivilprozessordnung
ZStW	Zeitschrift für Strafrechtswissenschaft
ZZP	Zeitschrift für Zivilprozess

Anlagenverzeichnis

1. Nardone et al vs. United States, 308 U.S. 338 (1939)

2. Weeks vs. United States, 232 U.S. 383 (1914)

3. Silverthorne Lumber Co. vs. United States, 251 U.S. 385 (1920)

4. Wong Sun vs. United States, 371 U.S. 471 (1963)

5. United States vs. Ceccolini, 435 U.S. 268 (1978)

6. Miranda vs. Arizona, 384 U.S. 436 (1966)

7. Pressemitteilung LGT Bank vom 24. Februar 2008

1 Problemstellung

Es gibt eine Vielzahl von möglichen Beweisen und eine noch größere Vielzahl von Wegen sie zu erhalten. Manche dieser Wege sind breit und ausgetreten, andere hingegen sehr schmal, es ist leicht von diesen Wegen abzuweichen. In der Regel ist die Beweiserhebung auf den ausgetretenen Wegen weder besonders aufwändig, noch besonders anfällig für Anfechtungen. Auf den schmalen Wegen jedoch finden sich mitunter die Beweise mit der höchsten Aussagekraft, die zu erlangen kompliziert oder sogar rechtswidrig ist.

Diese Dissertationsschrift wird eine Übersicht über die Beweisarten gegeben und sich den Wegen widmen, auf denen sie erlangt werden können. Dabei wird ein besonderer Fokus auf die Beweisbeibringung und Verwertung von Beweisen im steuerlichen Kontext, unter besonderer Beachtung der Theorie der Früchte des vergifteten Baumes gelegt.

Diese Theorie ist zwar in Deutschland nur sehr begrenzt anzuwenden - gleichwohl finden sich in der strafprozessualen Lehrmeinung viele Anhänger - verdeutlicht aber auf sehr eindrucksvolle Art und Weise die mögliche Fernwirkung von erweiterten Beweisverwertungsverboten. So sind in den USA, wo diese Theorie von einem Richter des Supreme Court of the United States of America entwickelt beziehungsweise erdacht wurde, regelmäßig ganze Strafprozesse an der Fruit-of-the-poisonous-tree-Doktrin gescheitert, da die unrechtmäßig erlangten, und alle darauf aufbauenden Beweise nicht verwendet wurden durften. Des Weiteren soll diese Arbeit einen Einblick in die Möglichkeiten der Beweisanfechtung nach rechtswidriger Beweisbeibringung ermöglichen.

Bedingt durch den Datenkauf deutscher Steuerfahnder unter Mithilfe des Bundesnachrichtendienstes wurden unzählige Beweise für mögliche Steuerhinterziehung auf zumindest fragwürdigen Wegen erlangt. Da die Fragen nach der Verwertung von Beweisen ein Thema mit dauerhafter Aktualität und Brisanz ist, wird dies der Schwerpunkt dieser Arbeit werden.

Im Ziel wird diese Arbeit schlussendlich einen umfassenden Überblick über erweiterte Beweisverwertungsverbote, anhand der verschiedenen Theorien der letzten Jahre, geben, die, unter Beachtung des deutschen Steuerrechts von der Fruit-of-the-poisonous-tree-Doktrin beleuchtet werden.

2   Beweise

„Beweis ist eine Tätigkeit des Gerichts und der Parteien, die das Gericht von der Wahrheit oder der Un-
wahrheit einer Tatsachenbehauptung überzeugen soll[1]
(aber das Gericht darf erst auf Grund der Beweisaufnahme zur allein entscheidenden abschließenden
Überzeugung kommen)".[2]

Der Beweis soll also das Gericht im Verfahren von einer Be-

hauptung überzeugen, die sodann im Urteil verwendet wird.

Dies gilt ganz unabhängig davon, ob es sich hierbei um ein

zivil-, straf-, oder steuerrechtliches Verfahren handelt.

2.1   Beweisarten

Generell ist zwischen den Strengbeweisen (Sachverständi-

gengutachten, Augenscheinseinnahme, Parteivernehmung,

Urkunden und Zeugen), der Glaubhaftmachung und dem

Freibeweis zu unterscheiden[3], wobei erstere grundsätzlich

als Grundlage für die Urteilsfindung zum Beweis von Tatsa-

chen herangezogen werden dürfen. Zweck des Strengbe-

weises ist, das Gericht vollständig zu überzeugen[4], erst

---

[1] Hartmann, Beck´scher Kurzkommentar ZPO, Einf § 284 Rn 1
[2] Hartmann, Beck´scher Kurzkommentar ZPO, § 286 Rn 16
[3] Vgl. Hartmann, Beck´scher Kurzkommentar ZPO, Einf § 284 Rn
7-9
[4] Vgl. Hartmann, Beck´scher Kurzkommentar ZPO, Einf § 284 Rn
7

dann gilt der Beweis als erbracht[5]. Die Glaubhaftmachung ist vor allem in reinen Verhandlungsfragen von Bedeutung, da an sie weit geringere Ansprüche gestellt werden als an den Strengbeweis[6]. Die letzte Beweisart, der Freibeweis, hat die geringsten Anforderungen an die Überzeugungskraft vor Gericht[7]. Er dient vor allem der Feststellung des Vorliegens aller notwendigen Prozessvoraussetzungen, sowie von Erfahrungen aber auch von Regelungen mit Bezug auf ausländische Legislatur.

In den folgenden Absätzen wird gezielt auf die einzelnen Beweise eingegangen, im Besonderen auf deren Voraussetzungen im zivil- und strafrechtlichen Kontext, der vor allem für die steuerstrafrechtliche Beurteilung von Nöten ist.

2.1.1 Sachverständigengutachten

Der Beweis durch Sachverständige ist zivilrechtlich in den §§ 402 ff. ZPO geregelt. Problematisch dabei ist die Abgrenzung zwischen der Person des Sachverständigen, dem

---

[5] Vgl. Hartmann, Beck´scher Kurzkommentar ZPO, § 286 Rn 16
[6] Vgl. Hartmann, Beck´scher Kurzkommentar ZPO, Einf § 284 Rn 8
[7] Vgl. Hartmann, Beck´scher Kurzkommentar ZPO, Einf § 284 Rn 6, Rn 9

sachverständigen Zeugen und dem bloßen Zeugen. Im Gegensatz zum bloßen Zeugen[8], der sein Wissen über Tatsachen bekundet[9] und dem sachverständigen Zeugen im Sinne des § 414 ZPO nimmt der Sachverständige dem Gericht in Dingen, die die Erfahrungen des Sachverständigen auf seinem jeweiligen Fachgebiet betreffen, die Erklärung des Sachverhaltes, teilweise sogar die Deutung der zu beweisenden Tatsachen, ab[10]. Nach Hartmann bleibt dem Gericht dabei oft nur die rechtliche Würdigung der zu beweisenden Tatsachen. Dabei hat der Sachverständige die Tatsachen jedoch auf nachprüfbare Art und Weise zu belegen, bloße Vermutungen gelten also nicht als Beweis.

Neben dem Sachverständigen, der, wie oben beschrieben, Beweise begutachtet (sachverständiger Gutachter), hat noch ein weiterer Sachverständiger eine weiterreichende Bedeutung im Prozessrecht, nämlich der Sprachsachverständige oder kurz Dolmetscher. Dolmetscher dienen dem Gericht, sich fremdsprachliche Urkunden oder andere Beweise in die deutsche Sprache übersetzen zu lassen und

---

[8] Siehe unten, 2.1.5 Zeugen
[9] Vgl. Hartmann, Beck'scher Kurzkommentar ZPO, Übers § 402 Rn 4
[10] Vgl. Hartmann, Beck'scher Kurzkommentar ZPO, Übers § 402 Rn 4 A

sind in diesem Sinne auch als Sachverständige anzusehen. Die oben genannte Nachprüfbarkeit der Arbeit ist auch vom Dolmetscher zu beachten.

Zwar ist das Gericht frei in seinen Entscheidungen, insbesondere kann es seine Fachkenntnisse auch aus anderen Quellen als durch Hinzuziehung eines Sachverständigen gewinnen[11], so zum Beispiel aus Fachzeitschriften oder gar dem Internet, sollte jedoch bei der Hinzuziehung von Sachverständigen sein pflichtgemäßes Ermessen großzügig ausüben.[12]

Der Sachverständige hat nach seiner Beauftragung durch das Gericht unverzüglich zu prüfen, ob er den Auftrag zur Erstellung eines Gutachtens alleine oder nur mit Hilfe anderer Sachverständiger erfüllen kann, letzteres ist dem Gericht anzuzeigen.[13] Dabei ist er nicht befugt, den Auftrag auf andere Sachverständige zu übertragen. Sehr wohl darf er sich allerdings der Mithilfe anderer Personen bedienen, so er sie dem Gericht namhaft macht.[14] Die Hilfe von Personen, die

---

[11] Vgl. Hartmann, Beck´scher Kurzkommentar ZPO, Übers § 402 Rn 12
[12] Vgl. Broß, ZZP102, 438
[13] Vgl. § 407a I ZPO
[14] Vgl. § 407a II ZPO

untergeordnete Tätigkeiten, wie zum Beispiel Schreib-
dienste oder ähnliches übernehmen, muss dagegen dem
Gericht nicht angezeigt werden.

In diesem Zusammenhang ist es wichtig zu erwähnen, dass
auch der Gutachter eine Art von „Aussageverweigerungsrecht", nämlich das Gutachtenverweigerungsrecht besitzt,
welches analog zum Zeugnisverweigerungsrecht und aus
denselben Gründen besteht.[15] Weiters kann das Gericht
den Gutachter von seiner Verpflichtung ein Gutachten zu er-
stellen entbinden.[16] Mögliche Gründe dafür sind - neben den
Gründen für das Zeugnisverweigerungsrecht[17] - fehlende
Sachkenntnis, Überlastung des Sachverständigen und Ver-
schleppung des Gutachtens[18], letzteres alleine schon aus
dem Verfahrensbeschleunigungsgebot heraus. Darüber hinaus existiert auch eine Art Vernehmungsverbot für Sachverständige, nämlich, wenn der Sachverständige an einer richterlichen Entscheidung mitgewirkt hat, soll er nicht mehr
über Fragen, die den Gegenstand der Entscheidung bilde-
ten, vernommen werden.[19] Diese Vorschrift ist zwar eher

---

[15] Vgl. § 408 I S.1 ZPO
[16] Vgl. § 408 I S.2 ZPO
[17] Siehe auch §§ 383, 384 ZPO
[18] Vgl. Hartmann, Beck´scher Kurzkommentar ZPO, § 408 Rn 5
[19] Siehe auch § 408 III ZPO

weit auszulegen, Verstöße dagegen sind aber aus eben diesem Grunde der weiten Auslegung prozessual unbeachtlich.[20]

Eine der wichtigsten Eigenschaften des Sachverständigen ist jedoch seine Beeidigung, die ihm Unabhängigkeit gegenüber den beteiligten Parteien bescheinigt, ebenso wie die Gutachtenerstellung nach bestem Wissen und Gewissen.[21] Das Gutachten wird also nur dem Gericht gegenüber verantwortet, das es in Auftrag gegeben hat.

Nicht verwechselt werden darf das gerichtlich angeordnete Gutachten mit dem privat in Auftrag gegebenen Privatgutachten. Dies ist als substantiiertes Vorbringen vor dem erkennenden Gericht anzusehen, welches jedoch urkundlich belegt wird[22] und daher, trotz der privaten Beauftragung einen erhöhten Beweiswert gegenüber dem einfachen Vortragen hat.

---

[20] Vgl. Hartmann, Beck´scher Kurzkommentar ZPO, § 408 Rn 7
[21] Vgl. § 410 ZPO
[22] von Hardenberg, Diss Erlangen 1975, in Hartmann, KK ZPO, Übers § 402 Rn 21

2.1.2 Augenscheinseinnahme

Augenschein ist eine unmittelbare Sinneswahrnehmung des Gerichts zur Beweisaufnahme, eine Kenntnisnahme von der äußeren Beschaffenheit einer Sache, eines Menschen oder eines Vorganges."[23]

Zwar sieht Hartmann den Augenscheinsbeweis als „stets erstrangig zu bewertende Möglichkeit unmittelbarer Sinneswahrnehmung"[24], gleichzeitig betont er jedoch auch, dass der Augenscheinsbeweis oft schwierig ist, da das Gericht in der „zunehmend hochtechnisierten Welt des Riesigen, Winzigen, nur mit tausend Hilfsmitteln Hörbaren, Sichtbaren, Tastbaren"[25] immer häufiger auf das Urteil von nichtjuristischen Fachleuten angewiesen ist, um den Augenscheinsbeweis bewerten zu können. Nach Hartmann kann es nicht der Sinn sein, den Richter auch durch das Mikroskop schauen zu lassen oder im Schutzanzug in eine Druckkammer zu steigen.[26] Da es weiterhin in der Zeit von Photoshop und di-

---

[23] Vgl. Hartmann, Beck´scher Kurzkommentar ZPO, Übers § 371 Rn 4

[24] Vgl. Hartmann, Beck´scher Kurzkommentar ZPO, Übers § 371 Rn 2

[25] Vgl. Hartmann, Beck´scher Kurzkommentar ZPO, Übers § 371 Rn 2

[26] Vgl. Hartmann, Beck´scher Kurzkommentar ZPO, Übers § 371 Rn 2

gitaler Fotografie zunehmend zweifelhaft ist, ob ein Foto digital manipuliert ist oder nicht, sei es darüber hinaus eventuell sogar nicht unbedingt sinnvoll, den Augenscheinsbeweis einem Richter mit bloßem Auge zur Beweisauswertung zu überlassen; oftmals sei es wesentlich Erfolg versprechender, Augenscheinsbeweise, wie zum Beispiel eine Narbe, gleich zusammen mit dem, in diesem Falle medizinischen, Fachmann gemeinsam anzusehen und auszuwerten. Diese Ansicht spiegelt sich auch und vor allem im Wortlaut des § 372 Abs. I ZPO wieder, wonach das Prozessgericht bei der Einnahme des Augenscheins einen oder mehrere Sachverständige hinzuziehen kann.

Hartmann geht sogar so weit, dass er vom sachkundigen Auge als wesentliche Bedingung der Brauchbarkeit des Augenscheinbeweises in vielen Fällen spricht.[27] Seiner Meinung nach darf und muss das Prozessgericht in allen den Fällen einen Sachverständigen hinzuziehen, in dem es dem Gericht an Fachkenntnis mangelt[28], was aufgrund der Komplexität vieler Beweismittel auch sicher kein fehlerhafter Ermessengebrauch wäre.

---

[27] Vgl. Hartmann, Beck´scher Kurzkommentar ZPO, § 372 Rn 2
[28] Vgl. Hartmann, Beck´scher Kurzkommentar ZPO, § 372 Rn 2

Der Augenscheinsbeweis ist stets von Amts wegen zulässig und steht damit im pflichtbewussten Ermessen des Gerichts.[29]

2.1.3 Parteivernehmung

Die Parteivernehmung dient der Verwirklichung des sachlichen Rechts durch eine Erweiterung der Beweismittel zwecks möglichst umfassender Würdigung des Prozessstoffs.[30]

Das größte Problem bei der Parteivernehmung als Beweisart ist sicherlich die subjektive Sichtweise der Partei auf den Sachverhalt. Daher ist sie regelmäßig als Erweiterung der anderen Beweise anzusehen.

Die Zulässigkeit der Parteivernehmung als Beweisart unterliegt strengen Regeln, neben den allgemeinen Grundsätzen der §§ 284 ff, 355 ff ZPO ist sie zum Beispiel nur auf Antrag zulässig, und zwar die Vernehmung des Gegners des Beweisführers nur, soweit der Beweisführer keine anderen Beweismittel vorbringt oder den Beweis mit solchen nur unvollkommen oder gar nicht geführt hat.[31] Anders herum ist die

---

[29] Vgl. Hartmann, Beck´scher Kurzkommentar ZPO, Übers § 371 Rn 5
[30] Vgl. Hartmann, Beck´scher Kurzkommentar ZPO, Übers § 445 Rn 2
[31] Vgl. Hartmann, Beck´scher Kurzkommentar ZPO, Übers § 445 Rn 4

Vernehmung des Antragstellers im Einverständnis des Gegners zulässig.[32]

Allerdings ist die Parteivernehmung unabhängig von der Beweislast von Amts wegen zulässig, wenn das Gericht einigen Beweis für erbracht hält.[33]

In diesem Zusammenhang ist aber darauf hinzuweisen, dass es unzulässig ist, die Parteivernehmung zur Entkräftung einer anderen Beweisregel zu benützen, sowie im Verfahren zur Prozesskostenhilfebewilligung.[34]

Zur Vernehmung einer einzelnen Partei führt Hartmann an, dass es abweichend vom, eng verwandten, österreichischen Recht, nicht notwendig und erforderlich ist, beide Parteien zu vernehmen, da das Gesetz das Recht, die eigene Behauptung beweismäßig zu bestärken, grundsätzlich nicht dem Beweispflichtigen geben möchte.[35] Vielmehr sei für die

---

[32] S.a. § 447 ZPO
[33] Vgl. Hartmann, Beck'scher Kurzkommentar ZPO, Übers § 445 Rn 4, § 448 ZPO
[34] Vgl. Hartmann, Beck'scher Kurzkommentar ZPO, Übers § 445 Rn 4
[35] Vgl. Hartmann, Beck'scher Kurzkommentar ZPO, Übers § 445 Rn 5

Überwachung der Aussage die Parteiöffentlichkeit[36] ein ausreichendes Mittel.[37]

Der Beweis durch Parteivernehmung ist also nach geltendem Recht als Hilfsbeweis subsidiär anzuwenden,[38] deren Durchführung erst nach vergeblicher Prüfung aller anderen zulässigen Beweismittel und der sonstigen Erkenntnismöglichkeiten des Gerichtes[39] in Betracht kommt.[40]

Zwar sollte die Parteivernehmung nach Nagel öfter den Vorrang haben[41], sollte aber dennoch mit großer Vorsicht betrachtet werden, denn die eigentliche Problemstellung sieht Hartmann bei der Parteivernehmung darin, dass selbst vollkommen redliche Parteien trotz Wahrheitszwang schwerlich in der Mehrheit sind und es nicht einmal immer möglich ist,

---

[36] Vgl. § 357 ZPO

[37] Vgl. Hartmann, Beck´scher Kurzkommentar ZPO, Übers § 445 Rn 5

[38] Vgl. Hartmann, Beck´scher Kurzkommentar ZPO, Übers § 445 Rn 7

[39] zB Offenkundigkeit, § 291 ZPO

[40] Vgl. Hartmann, Beck´scher Kurzkommentar ZPO, Übers § 445 Rn 7

[41] Vgl. Bender/Röder/Nack, Nagel in Festschrift für Habscheid, 1989

in der eigenen Sache einen Sachverhalt einwandfrei wiederzugeben.[42]

Eine Möglichkeit, die Parteivernehmung in Ihrer Beweiskraft zu bestärken ist allerdings, die vernommene Partei unter Eid zu stellen,[43] wobei auch der Eid der freien Beweiswürdigung unterliegt.[44]

2.1.4 Urkunden

Urkunde, im Sinne der Zivilprozessordnung, ist die schriftliche Verkörperung eines Gedankens, demgegenüber zielt der Augenschein nur auf die Sinneswahrnehmung der Person oder Sache ab. [45]

Unter Urkundsbeweis versteht man das Belegen einer Behauptung durch öffentliche[46] oder private[47] Urkunde.

Der Urkundsbeweis galt lange Zeit als die zuverlässigste der fünf Beweisarten, im Zuge des technischen Fortschrittes ist

---

[42] Vgl. Hartmann, Beck´scher Kurzkommentar ZPO, Übers § 445 Rn 7

[43] Vgl. Hartmann, Beck´scher Kurzkommentar ZPO, Übers § 445 Rn 6

[44] Vgl. Hartmann, Beck´scher Kurzkommentar ZPO, Übers § 445 Rn 6, §§ 286, 453 ZPO

[45] Vgl. BGH 65, 301, FG Berlin, NJW 77, 2232

[46] § 415 ZPO

[47] § 416 ZPO

aber aufgrund der enorm zunehmenden Manipulationsmöglichkeiten größere Vorsicht walten zu lassen.[48]

Eine Abgrenzung zwischen Urkundsbeweis und Augenscheinsbeweis ist aufgrund der zunehmenden technischen Manipulationsmöglichkeiten daher nicht immer leicht vorzunehmen,[49] was einfach gesagt daran liegt, dass es oft eines Experten bedarf, der die Echtheit der vermeintlichen Urkunde bestätigt.

Hartmann folgert daraus, dass der „lange Zeit so einfach erkennbare Zweck gerade des Urkundsbeweises, die Wahrheit am ehesten mithilfe desjenigen zu ermitteln, was der Beweisführer „schwarz auf weiß besitzt", so fragwürdig geworden ist, dass nur eine zurückhaltende Auslegung sowohl des Urkundsbegriffs als auch der Beweiskraft der einzelnen Urkundsarten zu vertretbaren Ergebnissen führen kann."[50]

---

[48] Vgl. Hartmann, Beck´scher Kurzkommentar ZPO, Übers § 415 Rn 1
[49] Vgl. Hartmann, Beck´scher Kurzkommentar ZPO, Übers § 415 Rn 1
[50] Vgl. Hartmann, Beck scher Kurzkommentar ZPO, Übers § 415 Rn 2

Er geht sogar so weit, dass er die Werthaltigkeit des Beweismittels Urkunde an sich anzweifelt, wenn es, nicht ohne erheblichen technischen Aufwand zu betreiben, nicht erkennbar ist, ob aus einem „Ja" ein „Nein" oder aus einem „Schwarz" ein „Weiß" gemacht wurde.[51] Dies würde nicht nur bei jeder Kopie so gelten, auch manches Original sei von Manipulationen gefährdet.

Wolle man aber nicht jedermann als Urkundenfälscher bis zum Beweis des Gegenteils ansehen, müsse man daher davon ausgehen, dass strafbare Begleitumstände fehlen, wie bei jedem anderen Beweismittel auch. Dies sei alleine schon aus verfassungsrechtlichen Gesichtspunkten [52] geboten, könne doch nicht jeder Zeuge und Sachverständige von vorne herein als Lügner betrachtet werden.[53]

Ruhige Abwägung in Verbindung mit erhöhter Wachsamkeit sei also von Nöten und unumgänglich um weder übertrieben

---

[51] Vgl. Hartmann, Beck´scher Kurzkommentar ZPO, Übers § 415 Rn 3
[52] Artt. 1, 2 GG
[53] Vgl. Hartmann, Beck scher Kurzkommentar ZPO, Übers § 415 Rn 3

vertrauensselig noch allzu argwöhnisch an einen Urkunds-beweis heranzugehen.[54]

Den beiden Arten des Urkundsbeweises, öffentlich und privat wird unterschiedliche Beweiskraft zugemessen. Während die öffentliche Urkunde, die, von einer öffentlichen Behörde innerhalb der Grenzen Ihrer Amtsbefugnisse, oder von einer mit öffentlichem Glauben versehenen Person[55] innerhalb des ihr zugewiesenen Geschäftskreises, in der vorgeschriebenen Form aufgenommen wurde und über eine vor der Behörde oder Urkundsperson abgegebene Erklärung errichtet wurde, stets volle Beweiskraft entfaltet[56] und allenfalls ein Gegenbeweis über die Unrichtigkeit des beurkundeten Vorganges zulässig ist[57], beurkunden private Urkunden lediglich, dass der Inhalt von den Ausstellern abgegeben wurde, nicht den Inhalt an sich.[58]

Die Bedenken wegen Manipulationsmöglichkeiten gelten, Hartmann zu Folge bei der Privaturkunde erst recht.[59]

---

[54] Vgl. Hartmann, Beck´scher Kurzkommentar ZPO, Übers § 415 Rn 3
[55] zB ein Notar, BGH JZ 87, 522
[56] Vgl. § 415 Abs. I ZPO
[57] Vgl. § 415 Abs. II ZPO
[58] Vgl. Hartmann, Beck´scher Kurzkommentar ZPO, § 416 Rn 7
[59] Vgl. Hartmann, Beck´scher Kurzkommentar ZPO, § 416 Rn 1

2.1.5 Zeugen

Der Beweisantritt durch Einvernahme von Zeugen gilt als die mit Abstand wichtigste Beweisart, die Regeln über den allgemeinen Teil des Beweisrechts[60] gelten ebenso, wie die über die Beweiswürdigung[61].[62]

Hartmann sieht als eines der zentralen Probleme des Zeugenbeweises die Aufgabe an, durch Befragung und einem unverkrampften Umgang gerade auch dem schwierigen, störrischen Bürger gegenüber, der Wahrheit, trotz aller ihrer vielfachen Unausforschlichkeiten, wenigstens etwas näher zu kommen.[63] Dabei gebietet schon die Menschenwürde[64] dem Gericht, „den Grundsatz zumindest anfänglicher Glaubwürdigkeit eines Menschen, der sich als Zeuge vor dem Staat in Gestalt seiner dritten Gewalt äußern muss oder soll."[65]

---

[60] Vgl. §§ 355 ff. ZPO

[61] Vgl. §§ 284 ff. ZPO

[62] Vgl. Hartmann, Beck´scher Kurzkommentar ZPO, Übers § 373 Rn 1

[63] Vgl. Hartmann, Beck´scher Kurzkommentar ZPO, Übers § 373 Rn 2

[64] Artt. 1, 2 GG

[65] Vgl. Hartmann, Beck´scher Kurzkommentar ZPO, Übers § 373 Rn 2

Schwierigkeiten des Zeugenbeweises sind schon in der Abgrenzung der Begrifflichkeiten zu sehen. Danach kann regelmäßig nur Zeuge sein, wer nicht als Partei oder gesetzlicher Vertreter auskunftsverpflichtet ist.[66] Diese Ansicht folgt dem Grundsatz aus dem römischen Recht „Nemo testis in re sua", nämlich, dass niemand in eigener Sache Zeuge sein kann.[67]

Abzugrenzen ist der Zeugenbeweis außerdem vom behördlichen Zeugnis, das heißt, der zeugenähnlichen Aussage eines Amtsträgers vor dem erkennenden Gericht. Dies ist allerdings regelmäßig als Urkundsbeweis anzusehen und zu bewerten.[68]

Trotz der vielen möglichen Fehlerquellen ist der Zeugenbeweis jedoch das wichtigste Beweismittel, allerdings auch oft ein ungewisser, schlechter Beweis[69], da die Zeugenvernehmung eine nur begrenzt erlernbare Kunst darstellt.[70]

---

[66] Vgl. Hartmann, Beck´scher Kurzkommentar ZPO, Übers § 373 Rn 4
[67] Vgl. Bogisch, Beck´scher Kurzkommentar ZPO, Übers § 373 Rn 11
[68] Vgl. Hartmann, Beck´scher Kurzkommentar ZPO, Übers § 373 Rn 5
[69] So zB Kirchhoff, MDR 01, 666
[70] Vgl. Rüßmann, DRiZ 85, 41

Eine allgemeine Fehlerquelle beim Zeugenbeweis stellt nach Hartmann zum Beispiel die Schwäche der menschlichen Natur dar, vor allem aber die Unzuverlässigkeit des menschlichen Gedächtnisses (die Erinnerungsstärke nähme außerordentlich schnell ab)[71]. Selbst bei einer guten Auffassungsgabe des Zeugen sei noch nicht gesagt, dass dieser das gesehene und erlebte auch gut und richtig wiedergeben kann,[72] so könne zum Beispiel die Wahrnehmung aus einem gewissen Abstand schon einen ganz anderen Blickwinkel auf das Geschehen werfen, als die direkte Beteiligung.[73]

Als weitere Fehlerquelle ist ferner die Person des Zeugen anzusehen,[74] namentlich der Bildungsstand, das Alter, die Begabung, Erziehung, Urteilskraft oder persönliche Beziehungen zu den Parteien. „So mancher hat z.B. eine natürliche Gabe als Zeuge aufzutreten – Fest wie ein Fels."[75]

---

[71] Vgl. Kirchhoff, MDR 01, 666
[72] Vgl. Hartmann, Beck'scher Kurzkommentar ZPO, Übers § 373 Rn 7
[73] Vgl. Hartmann, Beck'scher Kurzkommentar ZPO, Übers § 373 Rn 7
[74] Vgl. Hartmann, Beck'scher Kurzkommentar ZPO, Übers § 373 Rn 8
[75] Vgl. Galsworthy, Beck'scher Kurzkommentar ZPO, Übers § 373 Rn 8

Auch sei, zum Beispiel bei der Wiederholung einer Vernehmung, die Erinnerung an frühere Formulierungen oft stärker als an die eigentlichen, zu Grunde liegenden Geschehnisse,[76] daher solle sich jeder Richter darüber im klaren sein, dass auch die Aussage des Begabtesten und gewissenhaftesten Zeugen vieler der oben genannten Fehlerquellen ausgesetzt sein kann.[77] Als Beispiel dafür führt Hartmann an, welcher Richter sich auf die Erinnerung eines Zeugen an weit zurück liegende Vorgänge verlassen könne, wenn er sich selber doch kaum an das Tatbestandsberichtigungsverfahren vor wenigen Wochen erinnert.[78]

Sehr wichtig im Zusammenhang mit dieser Arbeit ist es, noch auf ein mögliches Beweisverbot im Zusammenspiel mit dem Zeugenbeweis hinzuweisen, welches allerdings später noch einmal aufgegriffen wird: Der Aussage eines „Spitzel" als Zeuge, sofern sein Verhalten gegen das allgemeine Persönlichkeitsrecht verstoßen hat. Dann ist sowohl die Vernehmung verboten, als auch diese Aussage unverwertbar, es

---

[76] Vgl. Hartmann, Beck´scher Kurzkommentar ZPO, Übers § 373 Rn 8
[77] Vgl. Hartmann, Beck´scher Kurzkommentar ZPO, Übers § 373 Rn 9
[78] Vgl. Hartmann, Beck´scher Kurzkommentar ZPO, Übers § 373 Rn 9

sei denn ein Beweis sei anders nicht möglich, oder das Verhalten des Spitzels wird rügefrei gestellt.[79]

2.1.6 Glaubhaftmachung

Als milderes Mittel zum Strengbeweis ist die Glaubhaftmachung anzusehen:

> „Ich weiß aber, dass die Reden, die sich nur auf die Wahrscheinlichkeit stützen, Geschwätz sind und ... einen gar leicht täuschen..."[80]

Hartmann folgend ist Beweis eine an Sicherheit grenzende Wahrscheinlichkeit[81], Glaubhaftmachung aber weniger, nämlich nur eine überwiegende Wahrscheinlichkeit[82]. Zur Zulässigkeit der Glaubhaftmachung an Stelle einer Beweisführung ist zu sagen, dass die Glaubhaftmachung grundsätzlich nur in den vom Gesetz ausdrücklich genannten Fällen ausreichend und erlaubt ist.[83] § 294 ZPO sei als Ausnahme der Vollbeweisregel des § 286 ZPO daher eher streng auszulegen. Gegenstand der Glaubhaftmachung dürfen alle zulässigen Beweismittel sein, die die ZPO vorsieht

---

[79] Vgl. Hartmann, Beck´scher Kurzkommentar ZPO, Übers § 373 Rn 10

[80] Simmias, Platon Phaidon, 41, Beck´scher Kurzkommentar ZPO, § 294 Rn 1

[81] Vgl. Hartmann, Beck´scher Kurzkommentar ZPO, § 294 Rn 1

[82] Vgl. BVerfG 38, 39, BGH NJW 98, 1870

[83] Vgl. Hartmann, Beck´scher Kurzkommentar ZPO, § 294 Rn 2

(Sachverständige, Augenschein, Parteivernehmung, Urkunden und Zeugen).[84]

2.2 Beweise im Strafrecht

Strafrechtlich sind im Hauptverfahren oben genannte Strengbeweise ebenfalls zulässig.[85] Im Vorverfahren, Ermittlungsverfahren genannt, besteht, genau wie im Zivilverfahren auch, die Möglichkeit der freien Beweiswürdigung durch den Richter; Freibeweise sind also ebenfalls zulässig. Rein bedeutungstechnisch wird der Begriff „Beweis" in der Strafprozessordnung unterschiedlich gebraucht.[86] So versteht man unter Erhebung eines Beweises regelmäßig das Einbringen eines Beweis*mittels* in das Verfahren zur Verwendung eines Beweis*ergebnisses*. Beweisergebnis ist lt. Meyer-Goßner das, „was das Beweismittel an tatsächlichem Beurteilungsstoff für die Entscheidung der Beweisfrage ergibt."[87]

---

[84] Vgl. Hartmann, Beck´scher Kurzkommentar ZPO, § 294 Rn 6

[85] Vgl. Meyer-Goßner, Beck´scher Kurzkommentar StPO, Einl Rn 49

[86] Vgl. Meyer-Goßner, Beck´scher Kurzkommentar StPO, Einl Rn 48

[87] Vgl. Meyer-Goßner, a.a.O.

Alsdann muss dem Angeschuldigten oder Angeklagten die Möglichkeit gegeben werden, sich zu den Beweisergebnissen zu äußern.[88] Damit wird dem Grundrecht auf rechtliches Gehör[89] genüge getan, wonach jedermann vor Gericht Anspruch auf Anhörung hat.

2.3 Beweise im Steuerrecht

Grundsätzlich ist die Beweisthematik im Steuerrecht, wie auch in den anderen Rechtsgebieten, in den Bereich des Verfahrensrechts einzuordnen, sprich, die dafür relevanten Vorschriften befinden sich in der Abgabenordnung (AO) und der Finanzgerichtsordnung (FGO).

2.3.1 Beweisvorschriften im Besteuerungs-, Haftungs-, Vollstreckungs-, und Rechtsbehelfsverfahren

Im Großen und Ganzen gelten die Beweisvorschriften des Zivilverfahrens auch in jedem anderen Verfahren, das heißt, auch hier finden die 5 Beweisarten der SAPUZ-Formel ihre Anwendung. Allerdings sind die Verfahren mit dem Finanzamt keine Gerichts- sondern Verwaltungsverfahren und insoweit eigenständig geregelt.

---

[88] Siehe auch § 33 I StPO
[89] Siehe auch Art 103 I GG

Die zentralen Vorschriften zur Beweisthematik finden sich in den §§ 93 ff. AO, auf die im Folgenden kurz eingegangen werden soll.

Nach § 93 AO haben die Beteiligten, das heißt, die in § 78 AO aufgeführten Personen, also der Antragsteller oder Antragsgegner[90], der, an den die Finanzbehörde einen Verwaltungsakt richten will oder gerichtet hat[91] und diejenigen, mit denen die Finanzbehörde einen öffentlich rechtlichen Vertrag schließen will oder geschlossen hat[92] und andere Personen, den Finanzbehörden die zur Feststellung eines für die Besteuerung erheblichen Sachverhaltes erforderlichen Auskünfte zu erteilen.[93] Da diese Vorschrift die Gefahr birgt, gegen das Steuergeheimnis zu verstoßen, sollen in der Regel andere Personen erst dann zur Auskunft angehalten werden, wenn eine Sachverhaltsaufklärung durch die Beteiligten nicht möglich ist oder keinen Erfolg verspricht.

Brockmeyer weist darauf hin, dass die Worte „erheblichen Sachverhalts" und „erforderlichen" dahingehend auszulegen seien, dass ein konkreter Anlass einem Auskunftsersuchen

---

[90] Vgl. § 78 Nr. 1 AO
[91] Vgl. § 78 Nr. 2 AO
[92] Vgl. § 78 Nr. 3 AO
[93] Vgl. § 93 Abs I S 1 AO

zu Grunde liegen muss und eine Ermittlung ins Blaue daher nicht zulässig sei.[94] Ein hinreichender Grund für ein Auskunftsersuchen sei daher dann gegeben, wenn auf Grund konkreter Anhaltspunkte, aber auch allgemeiner Erfahrung ein solches Auskunftsersuchen angezeigt sei. [95] Nach Rechtsprechung des Bundesverfassungsgerichtes [96] darf der erforderliche konkrete Anlass aber nicht dahingehend verstanden werden, dass er so konkret ist, dass der Verdacht einer Steuerverkürzung zu rechtfertigen sei. So hat der BFH auch schon ein Auskunftsersuchen an einen Zeitungsverlag zu einer Chiffre-Anzeige für Grundstücksverkäufe[97] als zulässig erachtet.[98]

§ 93 AO ist als allgemeine Beweismittelvorschrift anzusehen und entfaltet daher nicht nur im Steuerermittlungsverfahren, sondern auch im Haftungsverfahren und im Vollstreckungsverfahren Anwendung, wird aber durch § 5 AO (Ermessen) eingeschränkt.[99] Im Rahmen dieses pflichtgemäßen Ermessensgebrauch hat die Finanzbehörde vor allen Dingen die

---

[94] Vgl. Brockmeyer, Klein, Kommentar zur AO, § 93 Rn 2
[95] Vgl. Brockmeyer, a.a.O.
[96] Vgl. BVerfG HFR 89, 440
[97] Vgl. BFH BStBl 88, 349
[98] Vgl. Brockmeyer, a.a.O.
[99] Vgl. Brockmeyer, Klein, Kommentar zur AO, § 93 Rn 5 & 6

Verhältnismäßigkeit zu prüfen, das heißt, das Auskunftsersuchen muss nicht nur notwendig und zur Sachverhaltser-
hellung geeignet sein, sondern auch verhältnismäßig im en-
geren Sinne, also erforderlich, angemessen und zumutbar
sein.[100]

Den Finanzbehörden steht gemäß § 94 AO auch die Möglichkeit offen, Zeugen eidlich zu vernehmen. Dabei hat sie
sich des für den Wohnsitz oder Aufenthaltsorts der zur Auskunft verpflichteten Person zuständigen Finanzgerichtes zu
bedienen und dort um die eidliche Vernehmung anzuhal-
ten.[101] Unter bestimmten Voraussetzungen ist auch die eidliche Vernehmung durch ein Amtsgericht zulässig.

Allerdings soll die Vereidigung stets das letzte Mittel sein,
mit dem der Auskunftspflichtige zu einer wahrheitsgemäßen
Aussage bewegt werden soll.[102] Auch ist die Vereidigung
ausschließlich auf andere Personen und nicht auf Beteiligte
anwendbar, letztere können lediglich zu einer eidesstattlichen Versicherung im Sinne des § 95 AO aufgefordert werden, dem unten näher erläuterten „Nemo-tenetur-Prinzip"

---

[100] Vgl. Brockmeyer, Klein, Kommentar zur AO, § 93 Rn 6
[101] § 94 Abs I S 1 AO
[102] Vgl. Brockmeyer, Klein, Kommentar zur AO, § 94 Rn 2

folgend, kann diese Versicherung auch nicht erzwungen werden.[103]

Sowohl bei der eidlichen als auch bei der eidesstattlichen Aussage ist zu beachten, dass sie immer nur dann gefordert werden soll, wenn andere Mittel der Erforschung der Wahrheit nicht angezeigt sind.

Die Hinzuziehung von Sachverständigen ist im § 96 AO normiert, Brockmeyer führt dazu aus, die Finanzbehörden sollen sich der Sachkundigen bedienen, soweit nicht aufgrund eigener Sachkunde Entscheidungen getroffen werden können.[104] Daher ist die Finanzbehörde nicht auf unabhängige Sachverständige angewiesen.[105]

Die Person des Sachverständigen ist den Beteiligten vorher bekannt zu machen, sie können einen Sachverständigen auch wegen der Besorgnis der Befangenheit ablehnen.[106] Allerdings soll diese Ablehnung unverzüglich erfolgen, also spätestens nach zwei Wochen nach Benennung des Sach-

---

[103] Vgl. Brockmeyer, a.a.O.
[104] Vgl. Brockmeyer, Klein, Kommentar zur AO, § 96 Rn 1
[105] Vgl. BFH/NV 95, 299; 96, 527
[106] Vgl. § 96 Abs II AO

verständigen, namentlich um zu verhindern dass der Sachverständige erst nach Erstellung eines negativen Gutachtens abgelehnt wird.[107]

Auch der Urkundsbeweis findet sich in der Abgabenordnung
wieder, geregelt ist er in § 97 AO. Demnach sind, neben den
Beteiligten, auch andere Personen, zum Beispiel Rechtsan-
wälte, Notare oder Steuerberater, vorlagepflichtig. Allerdings
können Berufsträger die Vorlage verweigern, soweit sie zur
Auskunftsverweigerung berechtigt sind[108].[109]

Der Anforderung von Urkunden ist gemäß Absatz 2 des § 97
AO dahingehend eine Schranke gesetzt, als dass regelmäßig andere Schritte, wie zum Beispiel das Verlangen von
Auskünften, der Aufforderung zur Vorlage von Urkunden vo-
rangehen sollen.[110]

Der Begriff der Urkunde ist im Steuerrecht als *„jede papier-*
mäßig verkörperte oder auf Daten- oder Bildträgern festge-

---

[107] Vgl. Brockmeyer, Klein, Kommentar zur AO, § 96 Rn 3
[108] Vgl. § 102 AO
[109] Vgl. Brockmeyer, Klein, Kommentar zur AO, § 97 Rn 1
[110] Vgl. Brockmeyer, a.a.O.

haltene Gedankenerklärung, die allgemein oder für Einge-

weihte verständlich ist und einen Urheber erkennen lässt"[111]

definiert.[112]

Nicht von untergeordnetem Interesse bei der Auslegung des § 97 AO ist, dass der Steuerpflichtige die Urkunden **vorlegen** muss, das heißt, er muss sie sich unter Umständen erst beschaffen, indem er einem Dritten (zum Beispiel seinem Rechtsanwalt oder Steuerberater) gegenüber einen Herausgabeanspruch geltend macht.[113] Dies geht aber in der Regel nur so weit, wie dem Steuerpflichtigen dieses Beschaffen auch zuzumuten ist, so sind zum Beispiel Unterlagen, die die Geschäftsführung einer Arbeitsgemeinschaft betreffen, regelmäßig nur vom Geschäftsführer dieser Arbeitsgemeinschaft zu verlangen[114]; anders wird dies erst, wenn es sich bei dem zu klärenden Sachverhalt um einen mit starkem Bezug zum Ausland handelt. Dann kann sich der Steuerpflichtige nicht darauf berufen, er sei dazu nicht in der Lage.[115]

---

[111] Vgl. Brockmeyer, Klein, Kommentar zur AO, § 97 Rn 3
[112] Vgl. FG Münster, EFG94, 590; 01, 4
[113] Vgl. Brockmeyer, a.a.O., RFHE 25, 148
[114] Vgl. Brockmeyer, a.a.O., FG Berlin, EFG 86, 426
[115] Vgl. Brockmeyer, a.a.O., § 90 Abs III AO

Auch muss der Steuerpflichtige gegebenenfalls für die Übersetzung eines in ausländischer Sprache verfassten Dokumentes Sorge tragen[116][117].

Urkunden sind grundsätzlich im Original vorzulegen, soweit dies dem Steuerpflichtigen zuzumuten und es erforderlich ist[118]. Für den Fall, dass es, für die Entscheidung über den Sachverhalt, unerheblich ist, ob ein Original oder eine Kopie vorgelegt wird, müssen sich die Finanzbehörden mit einer Kopie zufrieden stellen und diese akzeptieren.[119]

Ebenso wie bei den anderen Beweisvorschriften ist auch bei der Vorlage von Urkunden die Verhältnismäßigkeit zu wahren. So haben die Finanzbehörden zum Beispiel gegenüber Banken stets die Kontoauszüge für lediglich ein Jahr anzufordern um danach, bei vorliegen tatsächlicher Anhaltspunkte, die eine tiefere Prüfung rechtfertigen, wie zum Beispiel nicht erklärte Vermögensbildungen, die Vorlage von Kontoauszügen für weitere Jahre zu fordern.[120]

---

[116] Vgl. Brockmeyer, a.a.O., § 87 Abs II AO
[117] a.A. Tipke/Kruse, § 97 AO Rz 3 bei Vorlage von Urkunden durch Dritte
[118] Vgl. Brockmeyer, Klein, Kommentar zur AO, § 97 Rn 4
[119] Vgl. Brockmeyer, a.a.O.; BFH/NV 95, 467
[120] Vgl. Brockmeyer, Klein, Kommentar zur AO, § 97 Rn 5, BFH, BStBl 91, 277

Brockmeyer weist des Weiteren darauf hin, dass der Steuerpflichtige, bei Aufbewahrung der Urkunden auf Daten- oder Bildträgern, auf seine Kosten die geeigneten Mittel bereit stellen muss, um diese wieder lesbar zu machen, das heißt, er hat die Daten- oder Bildträger zum Beispiel gegebenenfalls auszudrucken.[121]

Der Beweis durch Augenschein ist in der Abgabenordnung im Rahmen des § 98 AO geregelt. Danach ist zum einen über die Einnahme des Augenscheins ein Aktenvermerk zu schreiben[122], zum anderen können zur Einnahme des Augenscheins auch Sachverständige hinzugezogen werden[123].

Brockmeyer führt dazu, unter Verweis auf Wenzig[124] aus, Augenschein sei *jede sinnliche Wahrnehmung"* also beispielsweise auch Geschmacks- oder Geruchsproben.[125]

Im Rahmen der Augenscheinseinnahme kann es unter Umständen erforderlich sein, dass Amtsträger und hinzugezo-

---

[121] Vgl. Brockmeyer, Klein, Kommentar zur AO, § 97 Rn 10
[122] § 98 Abs I AO
[123] § 98 Abs II AO
[124] Vgl. StBp 2000, 150: *Wenzig:* Augenschein
[125] Vgl. Brockmeyer, Klein, Kommentar zur AO, § 98

gene Sachverständige, auch gegen den Willen der Steuer-pflichtigen, Grundstücke, Räume, Schiffe oder ähnliche Einrichtungen betreten müssen. Dazu sind sie durch § 99 AO ermächtigt. Für Wohnräume gilt dies jedoch nur, soweit dies zur Verhütung dringender Gefahren für die öffentliche Sicherheit und Ordnung erforderlich ist.[126] Insoweit wird das Grundrecht auf Unverletzlichkeit der Wohnung[127] außer Kraft gesetzt, alleine deshalb ist es gemäß Absatz 2 nicht zulässig nach **unbekannten Gegenständen** zu forschen.[128]

In der Regel sollen betroffene Personen, also nicht nur die Steuerpflichtigen selbst, angemessene Zeit vorher benachrichtigt werden und das Betreten der Einrichtungen zu üblichen Geschäfts- und Arbeitszeiten erfolgen.[129] Mit betroffenen Personen sind diejenigen Personen gemeint, die die tatsächliche Sachherrschaft über die Einrichtung innehaben.[130]

Damit soll dem Betroffenen die Gelegenheit der Teilnahme gegeben werden, die das Gesetz zwar nicht ausdrücklich vorsieht, sich jedoch aus dem Recht auf Anhörung[131] ergibt.

---

[126] § 99 Abs I AO
[127] Art. 13 GG
[128] § 99 Abs II AO
[129] § 99 Abs I AO
[130] Vgl. Brockmeyer, Klein, Kommentar zur AO, § 99 Rn 6
[131] Vgl. § 91 AO

Dabei ist die Anwesenheit des Steuerpflichtigen aber nicht zwangsweise vorgeschrieben.[132]

Beim Betreten von Wohnräumen (nach einer Entscheidung des BVerfG aber auch Geschäftsräumen)[133] ist allerdings besonders zu beachten, dass die Unverletzlichkeit der Wohnung verfassungsrechtlich garantiert ist, und sie daher, gegen den Willen des Steuerpflichtigen nur zur öffentlich-rechtlichen Gefahrenabwehr betreten werden darf.[134] Diese Gefahr ist gegeben, wenn ohne ihre Abwehr wesentliche Rechtsgüter verletzt werden[135], zur öffentlichen Ordnung zählt auch das Steuerrecht.[136]

Um den Augenschein einnehmen zu können, müssen allerdings die Gegenstände, die man mit Sinnen erfassen möchte, den Finanzbehörden bekannt sein. Zum Zwecke der bloßen Ausforschung dürfen Grundstücke und vergleichbare Rechtsgüter nicht betreten werden.[137]

---

[132] Vgl. Brockmeyer, a.a.O.
[133] Vgl. BVerfGE 32, 54
[134] Vgl. Brockmeyer, Klein, Kommentar zur AO, § 99 Rn 7
[135] Vgl. Brockmeyer, a.a.O.; BVerfGE 17, 232, 251
[136] Vgl. Brockmeyer, a.a.O.
[137] Vgl. Brockmeyer, Klein, Kommentar zur AO, § 99 Rn 8

Der Augenscheinsbeweis erstreckt sich auch auf die Vorlage von Wertsachen, soweit dies im Besteuerungsinteresse notwendig ist um Feststellungen über ihre Beschaffenheit zu treffen. Dazu können gegebenenfalls auch Sachverständige hinzugezogen werden.[138] Auch hierbei darf allerdings nicht nach unbekannten Gegenständen geforscht werden; sollten Steuerfahndungsorgane im Rahmen eines Steuerstrafverfahrens im Sinne des § 208 Abs. I Nr. 2, 3 AO tätig werden und nach Gegenständen forschen wollen, die den Behörden unbekannt sind, müssen sie gegebenenfalls einen Durchsuchungs- und Beschlagnahmebeschluss nach den Vorschriften der Strafprozessordnung beantragen.[139]

2.3.2 Beweisvorschriften im finanzgerichtlichen Verfahren

Die Grundsätze der Beweisbeibringung im finanzgerichtlichen Verfahren sind im § 79 Finanzgerichtsordnung normiert. Danach kann der vorsitzende Richter oder der Berichterstatter, also der Richter des erkennenden Gerichtes,

---

[138] § 100 Abs I AO
[139] Vgl. Brockmeyer, Klein, Kommentar zur AO, § 100

der mit der Vorbereitung des Falles betraut ist, auf die gesamte Palette der SAPUZ-Formel zurückgreifen[140] um zu einer Entscheidung zu finden. Mit Inkrafttreten des FGO-Änderungsgesetzes vom 21.12.1992 [141] wurde der in § 79 Satz 3 FGO aF enthaltene Verweis auf § 273 ZPO durch eine selbständige Regelung ersetzt.[142] Koch zu Folge sollte dies der Verwirklichung der Konzentrationsmaxime, das heißt, dem Konzentrieren der Verfahrenshandlungen auf die mündliche Verhandlung in **einem** Beratungstermin dienen.[143]

Das Finanzgericht erhebt, wie alle anderen Gerichte auch, Beweis unmittelbar, das heißt, in der mündlichen Verhandlung, es sei denn es handelt sich um einen geeigneten Fall, der schon vorher eine Beweissichtung rechtfertigt.[144]

§ 82 FGO schließlich verweist, bis auf einige Besonderheiten im Steuerrecht, wie zum Beispiel das Steuergeheimnis[145], auf die Vorschriften der Zivilprozessordnung[146] bei

---

[140] Vgl. von Groll, Gräber, Kommentar zur FGO, § 76 Rn 32 ff.
[141] Vgl. BGBl I S 2109
[142] Vgl. Koch, Gräber, Kommentar zur FGO, § 79 Rn 1
[143] Vgl. Koch, a.a.O.
[144] Vgl. § 81 FGO
[145] § 30 AO
[146] S.o.

der Erlangung von Beweisen. Das bedeutet, dass die grundlegenden Beweisregeln auch im finanzgerichtlichen Verfahren Anwendung finden.

3 Zulässige Beweisbeibringung und Verwertung

Grundsätzlich ist das Verwerten zulässig gewonnener Beweise ebenfalls zulässig. Unzulässig ist die Gewinnung von Beweisen, wenn bei der Gewinnung gegen Beweiserhebungsverbote, von denen es drei Sorten[147] und zwei Arten[148] gibt, verstoßen wurde.

Das heißt, wenn ein Beweis auf rechtmäßige Art und Weise erlangt wurde, beispielsweise Informationen in einem Umsatzsteuerkarusselgeschäft, also gewerbsmäßiger Steuerhinterziehung, das gemäß §§ 26b, c UStG und 370 Absatz III Satz 2 AO strafbar ist, durch Anordnung einer Telekommunikationsüberwachung[149] eines zuständigen Gerichtes, und es werden auf Grund dessen Beweise gegen die Verdächtigen gefunden, können diese auch verwertet wer-

---

[147] Beweisthemen-(s. 4.1.1), Beweismittel-(s. 4.1.2), Beweismethodenverbote (s.4.1.3)
[148] S.u. 4.1
[149] § 100a StPO

den. Sollte sich im Rahmen der Ermittlungen jedoch herausstellen, dass keine qualifizierte, sondern „nur" eine einfache Steuerhinterziehung vorliegt, greift möglicherweise ein Verwertungsverbot, da für einfache Steuerhinterziehung diese Art der Beweisbeschaffung nicht vorgesehen ist.

4 Beweisverbote

Bei den Beweisverboten unterscheidet man grob zwischen Beweiserhebungs- und Beweisverwertungsverboten. Beweiserhebungsverbote werden vom erkennenden Gericht erlassen, wenn ein Beweis nicht auf dem Wege beschafft hätte werden dürfen auf dem er beschafft wurde. Damit soll verhindert werden, dass Ermittlungsorgane Beweise zum Beispiel durch Folter erlangen und verwerten dürfen. Das Gericht wird sich daher damit befassen müssen, inwieweit der Beweis rechtswidrig erlangt wurde und gegebenenfalls, bei Verstoß gegen Beweiserhebungsvorschriften, ein Beweisverwertungsverbot aussprechen. Allerdings führen lediglich Beweisthemaverbote[150] per se zu einem Beweisverwertungsverbot. Bei allen anderen hat eine Abwägung[151] zwischen schützenswerten Rechtsgütern einerseits und der

---

[150] S.u. 4.1.1 Beweisthemaverbot
[151] S.u. 6.1.2 Abwägungslehre

Erforschung der prozessualen Wahrheit andererseits zu erfolgen.

Beweisverwertungsverbote verbieten, wie der Name schon erkennen lässt, die Verwertung von Beweisen im Verfahren, die auf rechtswidrige Art und Weise gewonnen wurden.

4.1 Beweiserhebungsverbote

Unter Beweiserhebungsverboten versteht man das Verbot einen Beweis überhaupt zu erheben. Dabei ist zwischen den generellen Beweiserhebungsverboten und den speziellen Beweiserhebungsverboten zu unterscheiden. Generelle Beweiserhebungsverbote sind das Beweisthemaverbot[152], das Beweismittelverbot[153] und das Beweismethodenverbot[154]. Sie sollen die Parteien im Zivilverfahren, den Steuerpflichtigen im Abgaben- und Finanzgerichtsverfahren und den Angeschuldigten im Strafverfahren vor rechtswidriger Beweiserhebung schützen, indem rechtswidrig erlangte Beweise einem daraus folgenden Beweisverwertungsverbot unterliegen. Neben den generellen Beweiserhebungsverboten sind noch die speziellen Beweiserhebungsverbote zu benennen,

---

[152] S.u. 4.1.1 Beweisthemaverbot
[153] S.u. 4.1.2 Beweismittelverbot
[154] S.u. 4.1.3 Beweismethodenverbot

so zum Beispiel das Verbot im Urkundsprozess, ein besonderes, zivilrechtliches Verfahren, bei dem Beweis lediglich durch Urkunden geführt werden darf, Beweis durch zum Beispiel Parteivernehmung zu führen. Da der Urkundsprozess aber nur im Vorverfahren, also nicht im eigentlichen Prozess, geführt wird sind im darauf folgenden Haupt- oder Nachverfahren wieder alle Beweisarten zulässig. Weitaus weiter reichende Folgen als spezielle Beweiserhebungsverbote sind daher den generellen Beweiserhebungsverboten zuzurechnen, da Verstöße gegen diese in folgenden Verfahrensabschnitten gegebenenfalls nicht geheilt werden können und sie auf diesem Wege eine Art Fernwirkung entfalten können.

4.1.1   Beweisthemaverbot

Eines der Beweiserhebungsverbote ist das so genannte Beweisthemaverbot. Das bedeutet, dass Beweis über ein bestimmtes Thema im Verfahren nicht erhoben werden darf, weil dieses entweder irrelevant für die Fallentscheidung ist und dies von vorne herein abgesehen werden konnte oder aber Beweis über eine Tatsache erhoben werden soll, die nicht bewiesen werden kann, so zum Beispiel das Wetter an einem bestimmten Tag.

In der Praxis von weitaus höherer Relevanz aber ist die Aussage eines Beamten, beispielsweise eines Finanzbeamten.

Grundsätzlich haben Amtsträger das Steuergeheimnis zu wahren,[155] das heißt, sie dürfen nicht unbefugt Verhältnisse eines anderen, die ihnen im Rahmen ihrer Tätigkeit bekannt geworden sind, offenbaren oder verwerten. Allerdings ist eine Offenbarung zulässig, soweit dies für Verwaltungs-, Rechnungsprüfungs-, oder gerichtliche Steuerverfahren, sowie für Straf- oder Bußgeldverfahren notwendig, dies gesetzlich zugelassen ist, der Betroffene zustimmt oder zum Beispiel ein Strafverfahren außerhalb von Steuerangelegenheiten geführt werden soll, in dem diese Informationen benötigt werden. Darüber hinaus dürfen oben genannte Informationen offenbart werden, wenn ein zwingendes öffentliches Interesse besteht, wie zum Beispiel bei der Verfolgung von Kapitalverbrechen oder schwersten Wirtschaftsstraftaten, oder aber wenn die Offenbarung notwendig ist, um Falsche, in der Öffentlichkeit verbreitete Tatsachen, die geeignet sind, das Vertrauen in die Verwaltung erheblich zu erschüttern, richtig zu stellen.[156]

---

[155] Vgl. § 30 Abs I AO
[156] Vgl. § 30 Abs II-IV AO

Trotz allem darf ein Finanzbeamter nicht einfach zu Themen aussagen, wenn er danach gefragt wird, vielmehr bedarf es einer Aussagegenehmigung durch seinen Vorgesetzten. Im Strafverfahren, und damit auch in Steuerstrafverfahren, auf die die Vorschriften der allgemeinen Strafgesetze grundsätzlich anwendbar[157] sind, stützt sich diese Vorschrift auf § 54 StPO.[158] Durch diese Regelung wird die Verschwiegenheitspflicht, die sich für Finanzbeamte, wie oben beschrieben aus § 30 Abs. I AO ergibt, änderungsfrei auf das Strafverfahrensrecht übertragen. Allerdings schütze, Meyer-Goßner zu Folge, diese Vorschrift lediglich öffentliche Geheimhaltungsinteressen, nicht amtlich bekannt gewordene Privatgeheimnisse,[159] das Steuergeheimnis sei daher nicht davon betroffen. Eine Pflicht, das Steuergeheimnis zu wahren ergebe sich vielmehr direkt aus § 30 AO.[160] Dies sei allerdings umstritten, daher ist, zumindest begrenzt, auch § 54 StPO Bedeutung zuzumessen.

---

[157] Vgl. § 369 Abs II AO
[158] Vgl. § 54 StPO
[159] Vgl. Meyer-Goßner, Beck´scher Kurzkommentar StPO, Rn 1
[160] Vgl. Meyer-Goßner, a.a.O.

Aus oben genannten Vorschriften ergibt sich allerdings, in Verbindung mit § 161 StPO, ein Beweiserhebungsverbot.[161][162]

Demnach sei schon aufgrund des Bundes-[163] oder Landesrechts[164] die Verschwiegenheitspflicht zu den hergebrachten Grundsätzen des Berufsbeamtentums, die Verfassungsrang[165] genießen, zu zählen.[166] Angestellte des öffentlichen Dienstes sind dagegen gemäß § 9 BAT oder aber § 30 Abs. III AO ebenfalls zur Verschwiegenheit verpflichtet.[167]

Von dieser Verschwiegenheitspflicht muss der potentielle Zeuge durch Aussagegenehmigung entbunden werden, dafür zuständig ist der jeweilige Dienstvorgesetzte.[168] Die Einholung der Aussagegenehmigung darf allerdings nicht dem zu Vernehmenden aufgetragen werden, vielmehr ist dafür

---

[161] Vgl. Meyer-Goßner, a.a.O., Rn 2
[162] Vgl. Meyer-Goßner, a.a.O, § 161, Rn 5
[163] Vgl. §§ 61, 62 BBG
[164] Vgl. § 39 BRRG
[165] Vgl. Art 33 Abs V GG
[166] Vgl. Meyer-Goßner, a.a.O., § 54 Rn 4
[167] Vgl. Meyer-Goßner, a.a.O., Rn 9
[168] Vgl. Meyer-Goßner, a.a.O., Rn 19

die vernehmende Stelle zuständig, die dies in der Regel schriftlich beantragt.[169]

Eine Versagung der Genehmigung ist zwar nur zum Wohle von Bund und Ländern[170][171] zulässig, allerdings darf der Beamte auch nicht weiter aussagen, als die Aussagegenehmigung reicht. Die Folge einer Genehmigungsversagung ist, dass der Beamte als zulässiges Beweismittel ausscheidet.[172]

Eine Vernehmung als Zeuge, obwohl keine Aussagegenehmigung erteilt wurde, oder aber über die Aussagegenehmigung hinaus, zieht regelmäßig, als Beweiserhebungsverbot, ein Beweisverwertungsverbot für die aus der Aussage gezogenen Erkenntnisse nach sich.

4.1.2 Beweismittelverbot

Ein weiteres Beweiserhebungsverbot ist das so genannte Beweismittelverbot. Dabei ist ein bestimmtes Beweismittel, beispielsweise die Zeugenaussage im Urkundsprozess, kein zulässiges Beweismittel und unterliegt insoweit einem, hier

---

[169] Vgl. Meyer-Goßner, a.a.O., Rn 17
[170] Vgl. §§ 62 Abs I BBG, 39 Abs II S I BRRG
[171] Vgl. Meyer-Goßner, a.a.O., Rn 20
[172] Vgl. Meyer-Goßner, a.a.O., Rn 25

speziellen, Beweiserhebungsverbot, während aus anderen Quellen, also der Urkunde, Beweis gezogen werden darf.

Ein anderes Beweismittelverbot ist die Vernehmung von Parteien als Zeugen im Zivilprozess, allerdings hat dies eher theoretische Bedeutung, da zwar aus der Parteivernehmung als Zeugen ein Beweisverwertungsverbot folgt, aber die Partei immer noch als Partei vernommen werden kann.[173]

Relevant für das Steuerstrafrecht ist aber vor allem der so genannte Lauschangriff. Als Lauschangriff wird das Abhören von Wohnungen (großer Lauschangriff wegen des hohen Eingriffsgehalts in ein Grundrecht) und das Abhören von öffentlichen Plätzen und Anlagen (kleiner Lauschangriff) bezeichnet.

Nach einem Urteil des Bundesverfassungsgerichts[174] ist es zwar zulässig, bei besonders schweren Straftaten Wohnungen von mutmaßlichen Tätern mittels technischer Hilfsmittel abzuhören, obwohl dies eine Verletzung der Menschenwürde wäre, allerdings haben die Richter eine Reihe von

---

[173] Vgl. Parteivernehmung, 2.1.3
[174] Vgl. BVerfGE 109, 279

Vorschriften zur Durchführung eben dieses großen Lausch-angriffes als verfassungswidrig und unzulässig erklärt.

Auswirkungen auf das Steuerrecht hat insbesondere die Tatsache, dass die Höchststrafe für eine der oben genann-ten, besonders schweren Straftaten, mehr als fünf Jahre Freiheitsstrafe betragen muss, damit ein derartiger Eingriff in die Unverletzlichkeit der Wohnung und die Menschen-würde, wie bei einer akustischen Wohnraumüberwachung, zulässig ist.

Da einfache Steuerhinterziehung, oder die gewerbs- oder bandenmäßige Schädigung des Umsatzsteueraufkom-mens[175] aber in der Höchststrafe mit fünf Jahren[176] bestraft wird, entfaltet sich hierbei ein Beweismittelverbot, was den so genannten großen Lauschangriff angeht, der auch hierbei ein Beweisverwertungsverbot nach sich zieht.

Davon ausgenommen sind freilich die Spezialtatbestände der besonders schweren[177] oder aber der gewerbs- oder

---

[175] Vgl. § 26c UStG
[176] Vgl. § 370 Abs I AO
[177] Vgl. § 370 Abs III AO

bandenmäßigen Steuerhinterziehung[178], die in den Höchststrafen bei jeweils zehn Jahren Freiheitsstrafe liegen.

4.1.3 Beweismethodenverbot

Unter einem Beweismethodenverbot versteht man das illegale Beschaffen von Beweisen aufgrund einer verbotenen Methode, wie zum Beispiel Folter. Als Klassiker des Beweismethodenverbotes gilt die so genannte „custodial interrogation", also die Befragung eines Festgenommenen direkt nach seiner Festnahme, während er noch unter dem Schock der Festnahme steht und ohne ihn auf seine Rechte hinzuweisen. Das Beweismethodenverbot aufgrund einer „custodial interrogation" hat, obwohl sie auf einem US-Amerikanischen Urteil beruht[179], in Europa und Deutschland breite Anerkennung gefunden. Zu Grunde liegt eine Entscheidung des Supreme Court of the United States of America, die unter dem Namen „Miranda-Formel", nicht zuletzt durch die Filmwelt Hollywoods, weltweite Berühmtheit erlangte.

Ernesto Arturo Miranda wurde im Jahre 1963 wegen eines Raubüberfalls, Entführung und Vergewaltigung durch die Polizei festgenommen und, noch unter dem Schock der

---

[178] Vgl. § 370a AO
[179] Vgl. Miranda vs. Arizona, 384 U.S. 436 (1966)

Festnahme stehend, ohne weiteren Hinweis auf das Recht, sich nicht selbst belasten zu müssen[180] und einen Rechtsanwalt hinzuziehen zu dürfen, befragt, wobei er ein Geständnis ablegte. Im Rahmen der Gerichtsverhandlung hatte die Staatsanwaltschaft keine weiteren Beweise als das Geständnis von Miranda vorgelegt; Miranda wurde zu einer Freiheitsstrafe von 20-30 Jahren verurteilt. Gegen dieses Urteil legte der Rechtsanwalt von Miranda Berufung beim Obersten Gerichtshof des Bundesstaates Arizona ein und bezog sich auf den fünften Zusatz der US-Amerikanischen Verfassung, wonach kein Verdächtiger verpflichtet sei, sich selber zu belasten. Diese Berufung wurde abgewiesen, worauf der Anwalt das Oberste Bundesgericht, den U.S. Supreme Court unter dem Vorsitz des Richters Earl Warren anrief. Diese nahm die Revision zur Berufung an und hob in der Folge die Verurteilung Mirandas auf.

Warren, ein ehemaliger Staatsanwalt, der die Situation unter der ein Verdächtiger kurz nach seiner Festnahme steht, gut nachvollziehen konnte, urteilte:

> "The person in custody must, prior to interrogation, be clearly informed that he has the right to remain silent,

---

[180] s.u. „Nemo tenetur"-Prinzip

and that anything he says will be used against him in court; he must be clearly informed that he has the right to consult with a lawyer and to have the lawyer with him during interrogation, and that, if he is indigent, a lawyer will be appointed to represent him."[181]

Zusammengefasst lässt sich dieser Ausspruch dahingehend übersetzen, dass eine Person, die sich in Haft befindet, vor einem Verhör klar über ihr Schweigerecht und die Tatsache, dass alles, was sie in Kenntnis dieses Schweigerechtes von sich gibt, vor Gericht gegen sie verwendet werden kann und wird. Außerdem muss eine festgenommene Person klar darüber informiert werden, dass sie das Recht hat einen Anwalt zu konsultieren, der auch während eines Verhöres anwesend sein darf und dass dieser Anwalt, sollte es notwendig sein, vom Gericht gestellt werden kann.

Seit diesem Urteil gibt es die so genannte „Miranda-Warning", die einem Verdächtigen im Augenblick der Festnahme vorgetragen, und oft, um Fehler zu vermeiden, sogar von einer Karte abgelesen, wird, die fast jedermann aus dem Fernsehen kennt: *„Sie haben das Recht zu schweigen..."*

Darüber hinaus gehend wies Earl Warren darauf hin, dass es das Recht jeden Verdächtigen sei, zu jedem Zeitpunkt

---

[181] Vgl. Miranda vs. Arizona, a.a.O.

des Verhöres nach einem Anwalt zu verlangen. Von diesem Zeitpunkt an, hätten die Sicherheitsbehörden die Befragung zu unterbrechen, bis der Anwalt eintreffe und anschließend dem Verdächtigen die Gelegenheit zu geben, sich mit seinem Anwalt zu beraten, bevor das Verhör fortgesetzt werde.

Des Weiteren führte Richter Earl Warren aus, dass der Verdächtige, sollte er zu irgendeiner Zeit der Befragung den Wunsch haben für den Rest der Befragung zu schweigen, er auch das Recht dazu habe.

In Deutschland leitet sich das Recht zu schweigen und damit mittelbar auch die Verpflichtung den Angeschuldigten über dieses Recht aufzuklären aus Artikel 2 Absatz I und Artikel 1 Absatz 1 des Grundgesetzes ab und manifestiert sich in § 136 Absatz 1 StPO.

In einer wegweisenden Entscheidung legte das Oberlandesgericht Celle dem Bundesgerichtshof die Frage vor, inwieweit ein Verstoß gegen die „Miranda-Warning" auch in Deutschland zu einem Beweisverwertungsverbot führe.[182] Diese Vorlagefrage wurde vom Bundesgerichtshof positiv beschieden, eine fehlende Belehrung führe danach stets zu

---

[182] Vgl. BGHSt 38, 214

einem Beweisverwertungsverbot, wenn nicht feststeht, dass der Angeschuldigte sein Schweigerecht ohne Belehrung kennt und keinen Gebrauch davon machen will und auch in der Hauptverhandlung der Verwertung seiner Aussage nicht widerspricht.[183]

Eine weitere verbotene Methode der Beweisgewinnung ist, wie schon oben erwähnt, Folter. Unter Folter versteht man das gezielte Zufügen von physischem oder psychischem Leid zur Erzwingung einer Aussage.[184]

Je nachdem, wie weit man den Begriff fasst, lässt sich sowohl die „custodial interrogation" als auch das gezielte Drohen mit Schmerzen, wie im Falle des Bankierssohnes Jakob Metzler darunter subsumieren.

Im letzteren Falle, der unter dem Begriff „Rettungsfolter" in die deutsche Strafrechtsdogmatik einging, wies der damalige Frankfurter Vizepolizeipräsident, Wolfgang Daschner, die Ermittler an, dem Verdächtigen Magnus Gäfgen Schmerzen anzudrohen, und diese notfalls auch durchführen, um ihn, nach seinem Geständnis, den Bankierssohn entführt zu haben, dazu zu bewegen, den Aufenthaltsort des

---

[183] Vgl. BGHSt 38, 214
[184] Vgl. Brockhaus: „Folter"

Jungen zu verraten, da die Polizei glaubte er wäre noch am Leben. Gäfgen gestand sofort nach Androhung der Folter wo er den – toten – Jungen versteckt hielt, erhob aber im späteren Prozess schwere Vorwürfe gegen die Frankfurter Polizei, die letztlich zur rechtskräftigen Verurteilung Daschners und des ausführenden Beamten führten.

Herdegen verfolgt in seiner Kommentierung zum Grundgesetz[185] zwar die Ansicht, die Würde des Menschen sei in Kern- und Randbereiche aufzuteilen, wobei die Randbereiche, im Rahmen der Abwägungslehre disponibel seien. Dadurch setzte er sich der Kritik der Fachwelt aus und präzisierte seine Auffassung dahingehend, dass er zum Beispiel im Bereich der „Rettungsfolter" keine befriedigende Lösung sehe, die Menschenwürde sich aber erst aus einer Gesamtbetrachtung ergebe, der Notfalls der Schutz hochrangiger Rechtsgüter vorginge.[186] Im Ergebnis hat er mit dieser Ansicht allerdings keinen Erfolg, da das Bundesverfassungsgericht sich seiner Auffassung nicht anschloss und in

---

[185] Vgl. Herdegen, Maunz/Dürig, Kommentar zum GG, Art. 1 Abs I Rn 45
[186] Vgl. Herdegen, a.a.O.

seiner Entscheidung, das Luftsicherheitsgesetz betreffend[187] keine Abwägung der Menschenwürde gegen andere Rechtsgüter zuließ.

Beweise, die unter Androhung von Folter gewonnen wurden, sind also regelmäßig gemäß § 136a StPO nicht zu verwerten, auch wenn sie den Angeschuldigten entlasten.[188] Das Verbot setzt allerdings einen ursächlichen Zusammenhang zwischen Verstoß gegen § 136a StPO und der Aussage voraus. Dabei muss der Zusammenhang nicht erwiesen sein, es reicht, wenn er nicht auszuschließen ist.[189]

Das Verwertungsverbot hat allerdings keine Fortwirkung, das heißt, nach einer Folter, Drohung oder Täuschung kann der Angeschuldigte wieder vernommen und seine Aussage sodann verwertet werden, entscheidend ist nur, dass der Angeschuldigte sich seines freien Willens und der Möglichkeit auf die Aussage zu verzichten, bewusst war.[190]

---

[187] Vgl. BVerfG, 1 BvR 357/05 vom 15.2.2006
[188] Vgl. Meyer-Goßner, Beck'scher KK StPO, § 136a Rn 27
[189] Vgl. Meyer-Goßner, a.a.O. Rn 28
[190] Vgl. Meyer-Goßner, a.a.O. Rn 30

Die mittelbare und unmittelbare Verwertung einer Aussage, die unter einem Verstoß gegen § 136a StPO zustande gekommen ist, ist jedoch verboten, so darf zum Beispiel ein Vernehmungsprotokoll einer solchen Aussage in einer Hauptverhandlung nicht verlesen, oder bei der Vernehmung anwesende Zeugen nicht vernommen werde.[191]

Die Lehrmeinung verlangt allerdings zwischen dem Verstoß gegen § 136a und einer weiteren Vernehmung eine so genannte „qualifizierte Belehrung", die den Angeschuldigten darüber informiert, dass die vorangegangenen Angaben nicht verwertet werden dürfen.[192] Allerdings sei regelmäßig davon auszugehen, dass keine Fortwirkung mehr bestünde, wenn der zeitliche Zusammenhang nicht herzustellen sei. Ein Hinweis auf Fortwirkung des Verstoßes muss in einer Revision genau begründet werden.[193][194]

Die Frage nach einer Fernwirkung des Beweisverbotes besteht nach herrschender Meinung zwar nicht, ist allerdings

---

[191] Vgl. Meyer-Goßner, a.a.O. Rn 29
[192] Vgl. Meyer-Goßner, a.a.O. Rn 30
[193] Vgl. BGH NStZ 81, 298
[194] Vgl. Meyer-Goßner, a.a.O.

äußerst streitig. So spricht sich Beulke[195] für eine Fernwirkung aus, will aber anhand der amerikanischen „clean path doctrin"[196] eine Verwertung dann zulassen, wenn das Beweismittel auf „sauberem Weg" genauso gefunden worden wäre.[197]

Im Ergebnis ist ein Beweismethodenverbot also eine Beweisverbot, dass weder über eine besondere Fortwirkung, noch über eine Fernwirkung verfügt.

4.2 Beweisverwertungsverbote

Bei den Beweisverwertungsverboten unterscheidet man zwischen relativen und absoluten, selbständigen und unselbständigen Beweisverwertungsverboten. Alle diese Beweisverwertungsverbote haben allerdings zur Folge, dass der Beweis im fraglichen Verfahren nicht verwendet werden darf.

4.2.1 Relative Beweisverwertungsverbote

Relative Beweisverwertungsverbote ergeben sich aus zahlreichen Vorschriften, und zwar regelgemäß dann, wenn ein Beweisverwertungsverbot nachträglich „geheilt" werden

---

[195] ZStW 103, 669
[196] S.o. 3.3
[197] Vgl. Meyer-Goßner, a.a.O. Rn 31

kann, zum Beispiel durch nachträgliche Genehmigung des Angeschuldigten, wenn gegen Beweiserhebungsvorschriften verstoßen wurde, wobei im Rahmen der Dispositionsmaxime eine nachträgliche Zustimmung der Betroffenen den Verstoß heilt.

Zum Beispiel bei einem Verstoß gegen die Belehrungspflicht bei Aussageverweigerungsrechten gemäß § 55 Absatz II StPO. Diese Vorschrift dient dazu, den Zeugen vor Selbstbelastung (Nemo-tenetur-Prinzip[198]) zu schützen.[199] Wenn die Belehrung unterlassen wurde, folgt daraus zwar ein Beweisverwertungsverbot, dieses ist jedoch relativ, das heißt, es kann aufgehoben werden, wenn der Zeuge, der sich mit seiner Aussage selbst belastet hat, diese, und die damit verbundene Selbstbelastung, nachträglich genehmigt.

Als weiteres Beispiel lässt sich dies auf § 136 StPO übertragen, nämlich auf die erste richterliche Vernehmung eines Beschuldigten. Auch hierbei ist er umfangreich über seine Rechte zu belehren, und, für den Fall der Unterlassung die-

---

[198] S.u. 6.2 Nemo tenetur Prinzip
[199] Vgl. Meyer-Goßner, Beck´scher Kurzkommentar StPO, § 55 Rn 1

ser Belehrung sind die anschließend gewonnenen Erkenntnisse einem Beweisverwertungsverbot zu unterziehen. Dennoch kann auch hierbei durch die nachträgliche Genehmigung des Beschuldigten dieser Verstoß geheilt werden.[200]

Selbiges gilt auch im Ermittlungsverfahren: Der Beschuldigte ist hierbei gemäß § 163a StPO zu belehren und auch hierbei ist ein Verstoß gegen die Belehrungspflichten mit einem relativen, also heilbaren Beweisverwertungsverbot zu belegen.

Der österreichische Verwaltungsgerichtshof (VwGH) hatte in einer Entscheidung vom 25.Juni 1997[201] über die Verwertung von Beweisen in einem Finanzstrafverfahren zu entscheiden. Anders als in Deutschland sind in Österreich, bis zu einer Grenze von 50.000 EUR an hinterzogenen Abgaben, nicht die Staatsanwaltschaft und ordentliche Gerichtsbarkeit, sondern das Finanzamt und die Finanzstrafsenate des Unabhängigen Finanzsenates (UFS) für die Erst- und letztinstanzliche Verfolgung von Abgabenhinterziehungen und –Verkürzungen zuständig. Sollten dabei Fehler in der Rechtsanwendung oder Verstöße gegen die Verfassung zu

---

[200] S.o. 4.1.3 „Miranda-Urteil"
[201] Vgl. VwGH vom 25.6.97 – 96/15/0225

rügen sein, ist eine Beschwerde zum Verwaltungs- oder Verfassungsgerichtshof zulässig.

In diesem Fall hatte der VwGH eine Beschwerde eines Steuerberaters und Rechtsanwaltes zu entscheiden, bei dem im Rahmen eines Abgabenhinterziehungsverfahrens in „eigener Sache" durch die zuständige Steuerfahndung Unterlagen beschlagnahmt wurden, die einen Mandanten schwer belasteten, ebenfalls Steuern hinterzogen zu haben. Der Verwaltungsgerichtshof belegte diese, für die Information des Berufsträgers gedachten Unterlagen, mit einem relativen Beweisverwertungsverbot, welches lediglich durch die Genehmigung des betroffenen Steuersünders zur Verwertung dieser Unterlagen, aufgehoben werden könne.

4.2.2 Absolute Beweisverwertungsverbote

Als bestes Beispiel für ein absolutes Beweisverwertungsverbot lässt sich § 136a Absatz III StPO anführen, wonach regelmäßig Beweise, die unter Verstoß gegen die Freiheit der Willensentscheidung oder durch Maßnahmen die das Erinnerungsvermögen oder die Einsichtfähigkeit beeinträchtigen erlangt wurden einem Beweisverwertungsverbot unterliegen. Dazu zählen zum Beispiel Beweise, die unter Folter, durch Täuschung oder Einsatz von Drogen erlangt wurden.[202]

4.2.3 Selbständige Beweisverwertungsverbote

Ein selbständiges Beweisverwertungsverbot liegt immer dann vor, wenn das Beibringen des Beweises zwar rechtlich einwandfrei erfolgte, aber die Verwertung selbst unzulässig ist. Dies ist zum Beispiel dann der Fall, wenn bei einer rechtmäßig angeordneten Telefonüberwachung ein Beweis erlangt wurde, der allerdings Rückschluss auf eine von § 100a StPO nicht gedeckte Straftat – zum Beispiel „einfache" Steuerhinterziehung statt qualifizierter, banden- oder gewerbsmäßiger Steuerhinterziehung zulässt. In diesem Falle kann sich der Angeschuldigte auf ein selbständiges Beweisverwertungsverbot berufen, da die rechtlich nicht zu beanstandende Beweisbeibringung trotzdem zu Beweisen führte, für die diese Art der Ermittlung nicht hätte angeordnet werden dürfen.[203]

4.2.4 Unselbständige Beweisverwertungsverbote

Ein unselbständiges Beweisverwertungsverbot hat keine eigenständige Grundlage, sondern folgt aus einer anderen

---

[202] Vgl. 4.1.3 Beweismethodenverbote
[203] Vgl. Volk, Strafprozessrecht, § 28, Rn 5

Rechtsnorm. Als Beispiel dafür lässt sich wiederum das absolute Beweismethodenverbot nach § 136a StPO anführen, wonach Beweise, die nach den Regelungen des Absatzes 1 des § 136a StPO zustande gekommen sind, gemäß Absatz 3 zwingend einem Beweisverwertungsverbot unterliegen:

> „Das Verbot der Absätze 1 und 2 gilt ohne Rücksicht auf die Einwilligung des Beschuldigten. Aussagen, die unter Verletzung dieses Verbotes zustande gekommen sind, dürfen auch dann nicht verwertet werden, wenn der Beschuldigte der Verwertung zustimmt."[204]

5 „Fruit-of-the-poisonous-tree-Theorie

Unter der Fruit-of-the-poisonous-tree-Theorie oder Doktrin versteht man ein Gleichnis des US-amerikanischen Richters am Supreme Court of the United States of America, Felix Frankfurter, der in einem Verfahren gegen Frank Nardone[205] erstmals ein sehr weit reichendes Beweisverwertungsverbot erließ.

Frank Nardone, wurde in einem früheren Verfahren wegen Alkoholschmuggels verurteilt, was zum Gegenstand der

---

[204] Vgl. § 136a Abs III StPO
[205] Nardone et al vs. United States, 308 U.S. 338 (1939), siehe Anhang

Prüfung durch den Supreme Court of the United States of America wurde. Nardone wurde damals aufgrund von Beweisen verurteilt, die Bundesbeamte aufgrund von Abhörmaßnahmen gegen ihn erlangten, die allerdings gegen das Telekommunikationsgesetz von 1934 verstießen. Der Oberste Gerichtshof hob das Urteil auf und erließ ein Beweisverwertungsverbot ob der illegalen Abhörmaßnahmen, das heißt, die Beweise durften nicht mehr verwendet werden. Das Verfahren selbst wurde zurück verwiesen an die erste Instanz.

Daraufhin wurde Frank Nardone erneut angeklagt, diesmal jedoch nicht wegen Alkoholschmuggels sondern wegen Steuerbetruges, basierend auf den illegalen Schmuggelgeschäften, für die er, aufgrund des Beweisverwertungsverbotes nicht verurteilt werden konnte.

Der Richter der ersten Instanz sah kein Hindernis darin Nardone wegen Steuerbetruges zu verurteilen, da die Anklagebehörde nicht nur den Anklagevorwurf von Alkoholschmuggel auf Steuerbetrug geändert hatte, sondern auch den kompletten Tatbestand. Es wurden in dem neu aufgezogenen Verfahren komplett neue Beweise und Tatsachen vorgebracht, die allerdings auf den Erkenntnissen basierten, die durch das illegale Abhören der Telekommunikation des Frank Nardone getroffen wurden.

Nach seiner Verurteilung wegen Steuerbetruges legte Nardone wiederum Rechtsmittel ein, was den Fall erneut vor den US Supreme Court of Justice brachte.

Diesmal hatte Richter Frankfurter abzuwägen, inwieweit die, damals illegal beschafften, Beweise Grundlage sein dürfen für weitere Ermittlungsansätze und daraus resultierende Verurteilungen.

Bis zum Jahre 1914 galt in der US-amerikanischen Rechtsprechung der Ausschluss- und Sperrgrundsatz, die so genannten „exclusionary rule", wonach illegal erlangte Beweise keinen Einfluss in die Urteilsfindung des erkennenden Gerichtes finden dürfen.[206]

Durch Oliver Wendell Holmes, Jr. Entscheidung im Falle Silverthorne vs. United States, im Jahre 1920, zeigten sich die ersten Anzeichen dafür, dass das oberste Gericht der Vereinigten Staaten nicht dabei verbleiben wird einzelne Beweise

---

[206] Vgl. Weeks vs. United States, 232 U.S. 383 (1914), siehe Anhang

vom Verfahren auszuschließen, wenn sie rechtswidrig erlangt wurden, sondern darüber hinaus gänzlich verworfen zu werden und auch nicht in anderen Verfahren (beispielsweise dem Steuererhebungsverfahren) hinzugezogen werden dürfen:[207]

> „The essence of a provision forbidding the acquisition of evidence in a certain way is that not merely evidence so acquired shall not be used before the Court but that it shall not be used at all. (...)"[208]

Allerdings schien Holmes das etwas zu weit reichend, sodass, er seine Ausführungen im nächsten Satz einschränkte:

> „If knowledge of them is gained from an independent source they may be proved like any others, but the knowledge gained by the Government's own wrong cannot be used. (...)"[209]

Er führte also aus, dass dies keinesfalls bedeute, dass auf diesem Weg bekannt gewordene Tatsachen tabu und unter allen Umständen von der Verwendung ausgeschlossen seien. Vielmehr dürften sie, wenn man zu ihrer Kenntnis aus

---

[207] Vgl. Silverthorne Lumber Co. vs. United States, 251 U.S. 385 (1920), siehe Anhang

[208] Mr. Justice Oliver Wendell Holmes, Jr. Silverthorne vs. U.S., 1920

[209] Mr. Justice Oliver Wendell Holmes, Jr. Silverthorne vs. U.S., 1920

unabhängiger dritter Quelle gelange, zum Gegenstand einer Beweiserhebung gemacht werden wie alle anderen Erkenntnisse auch. Lediglich Erkenntnisse, die durch den Staat selbst rechtswidrig erlangt worden sind, dürften nicht verwendet werden.

Diese beiden Urteile bilden daher die Entscheidungsgrundlage des Richters Felix Frankfurter im Falle Nardone et al vs. United States. Frankfurter und das erkennende oberste Gericht blieb also nichts anderes übrig, als auch die zweite Verurteilung des Frank Nardone aufzuheben und die Rechtsprechung dahingehend zu präzisieren, dass rechtswidrig erlangte Beweise eine Fernwirkung haben können:

> "The burden is, of course, on the accused in the first instance to prove ... that wire-tapping was unlawfully employed. Once that is established ... the trial judge must give opportunity, however closely confined, to the accused to prove that a substantial portion of the case against him was a fruit of the poisonous tree. This leaves ample opportunity to the Government to convince the trial court that its proof had an independent origin."[210]

---

[210] Mr. Justice Felix Frankfurter, Nardone et al vs. U.S., 1939

Frankfurter führte aus, dass es zwar dem Angeklagten obliege, zu beweisen, dass seine Telekommunikation auf illegale Art und Weise abgefangen wurde, habe er (Nardone)
den Eingriff in seine Grundrechte bewiesen, obliege es ihm
weiterhin darzustellen, dass die Beweise, die gegen ihn
sprechen zu einem erheblichen Teil „Früchte des vergifteten
Baumes" seien. Dies gebe der Anklage dann die Gelegenheit, das erkennende Gericht vom Gegenteil zu überzeugen.

Dieser Teil des FOPT-Urteils wird in der amerikanischen
Rechtslehre als „clean the path", also säubern des Weges
bezeichnet. Es ist also eine materiellrechtliche, dreistufige
Prüfung durchzuführen, an deren Ende die Erlaubnis oder
das Verbot der eingebrachten Beweise steht:

1. Das Anwenden der „exclusionary rule", also das ausschließen rechtswidrig erlangter Primärbeweise aus
   dem laufenden Verfahren.

2. Der Nachweis des Angeklagten, dass gegen ihn ge-
   richtete Sekundärbeweise illegal erlangt und daher im
   Wege der Fernwirkung Früchte des vergifteten Baumes seien.

3. Der Anklagebehörde die Möglichkeit des „clean path"
   zu geben, dass heißt, es ihr zu gestatten, „den Weg

zu säubern" und nachzuweisen, dass es sich bei den Sekundärbeweisen nicht um Früchte des vergifteten Baumes handelt.

In späteren Jahren wurde die Theorie der Früchte des vergifteten Baumes weiter präzisiert, so zum Beispiel 1963 im Falle Wong Sun vs. United States[211], in welchem das erkennende Gericht ausführt, dass die Prüfung eines Sekundärbeweisverbotes nach der FOPT-Theorie in einem separaten Anhörungsverfahren ohne Hinzuziehung (und damit Beeinflussung) der Geschworenen zu erfolgen hat.

Im Jahre 1978 schlussendlich entschied der oberste Gerichtshof im Falle United States vs. Ceccolini in Sachen zeitlicher Zusammenhang der Früchte mit dem vergifteten Baum.[212]

Damals wurde ein Zeuge, der Ceccolini belasten konnte, illegal festgenommen und sagte gegen ihn aus. Monate nach seiner Entlassung wurde er erneut in der Sache befragt, ohne dass seine Festnahme damals Gegenstand der Befragung war, und belastete Ceccolini abermals. Der Tatrichter, Mr. Justice Rehnquist führte 1978 aus, dass, aufgrund der

---

[211] Vgl. Wong Sun vs. United States, 371 U.S. 471, (1963)
[212] Vgl. United States vs. Ceccolini, 435 U.S. 268, (1978)

Tatsache, dass kein zeitlicher Zusammenhang mehr gegeben sei und die Verhaftung nicht thematisiert wurde die belastenden Tatsachen weder den Baum selbst noch seine Früchte darstellen würden.[213]

6 Erweiterte Beweisverwertungsverbote in Deutschland

Wie schon eingangs erwähnt, löst die "Fruit-of-the-poisonous-tree-Theorie in Deutschland unterschiedliche Reaktionen aus. In der Lehrmeinung hoch geachtet, findet sie in der Praxis, aufgrund der unterschiedlichen Rechtsysteme in Deutschland und den Vereinigten Staaten, keine direkte Anwendung.

Um das zu verdeutlichen muss man sich das (Straf-)Rechtsystem der USA genauer vor Augen führen. In den Vereinigten Staaten findet im Strafprozess, genau wie in jedem anderen Prozess, ein Parteienverfahren Anwendung, dass heißt, die Anklageseite trägt die Anklage vor und legt dabei alle Beweise offen, die gegen den Angeklagten sprechen. Der Angeklagte wiederum versucht diese Beweise zu entkräften, indem er Gegenargumente vorlegt. Die Wahrheit im

---

[213] Vgl. Mr. Justice Rehnquist, United States vs. Ceccolini, 435 U.S. 268, (1978)

Strafprozessverfahren in den USA ist also nicht die, wie in Deutschland „ex parte"[214] durch den Staat erforschte absolute und objektive Wahrheit, sondern vielmehr eine, der Verhandlungsmaxime [215] des deutschen Zivilrechts folgende freie und einvernehmliche Disposition, das heißt, dass ausschließlich das als wahr gilt, was bewiesen wurde oder aber das, was unstrittig zwischen den beteiligten Parteien, Anklage und Verteidigung, ist. Die prozessuale Wahrheit haben im Anschluss an die Beweisaufnahme die Geschworenen zu bewerten.

Da die Fruit-of-the-poisonous-tree-Theorie dem Angeklagten, wie oben erwähnt[216], dem Angeklagten auferlegt, sich selbst zu entlasten, indem er vorträgt, was, seiner Meinung nach, gegen die Verwertung der strittigen Beweise spricht, verstößt sie somit gegen die Grundzüge des deutschen Strafprozessrechtes, namentlich gegen das „nemo-tenetur"[217]-Prinzip, nachdem der Angeklagte während des gesamten Strafprozesses und den vorherigen Ermittlungen

---

[214] ex parte = einseitig
[215] Vgl. Gottwald, Einführung zur ZPO, IV. Verfahrensgrundsätze, Tz. 2 a
[216] Siehe 3.3 – Fruit-of-the-poisonous-tree-Theorie
[217] „Nemo tenetur, se ipsum accusare." – Niemand ist gezwungen, sich selbst anzuklagen.

(als Beschuldigter) das Recht hat zu schweigen, ohne dass ihm dies negativ angerechnet werden darf.[218]

Das Bundesverfassungsgericht erkennt die Fruit-of-the-poisonous-tree-Doktrin allerdings in einigen, wenigen Fällen an, die im Folgenden beschrieben werden:

6.1 Verfassungsrechtliche Beweisverbote

Zwar erkennt das Bundesverfassungsgericht in seiner Rechtsprechung grundsätzliche keine Fernwirkung an, hat aber im Laufe der Zeit einige Theorien entwickelt, die dem Verbot illegaler Beweiserhebungen dienen. Als wichtigste dieser Theorien ist die „Drei-Sphären-Theorie" anzusehen, wonach der Kernbereich privater Lebensgestaltung in drei Sphären, die unterschiedlich vor staatlichen Eingriffen geschützt sind, aufzuteilen ist.

6.1.1 Drei-Sphären-Theorie

Das Rechtsinstitut der privaten Lebensführung ist nach Meinung des Bundesverfassungsgerichtes in drei unterschiedlich geschützte Sphären, die Geschäftsphäre, die Individualsphäre und die Intimsphäre aufzugliedern.

---

[218] Vgl. § 136 Abs. I Satz 2 StPO

Beweise, die aus der Geschäftsphäre gewonnen wurden sind regelmäßig voll verwertbar, tritt der Beschuldigte doch offen und ohne Verdeckung nach außen auf.

Die Beweise, die im Rahmen der Individual- oder auch Sozialsphäre gewonnen wurden, unterliegen ebenfalls grundsätzlich keinem Verwertungsverbot, jedoch hat hier im Einzelfall eine Abwägung zwischen den grundrechtlich geschützten Rechtsinteressen des Beschuldigten und denen der Strafrechtspflege vorgenommen zu werden[219].

Beweise, die der dritten Sphäre, der Intimsphäre des Beschuldigten, entstammen, unterliegen regelmäßig einem Beweiserhebungsverbot, da jegliche staatliche Eingriffe in die Intimsphäre, als Kernbereich privater Lebensgestaltung, durch das Grundgesetz geschützt sind. Der Kernbereich privater Lebensgestaltung ist ein Bereich absoluter staatlicher Unkenntnis.[220] So sind beispielsweise Tagebücher, Selbstgespräche oder auch die Telekommunikation vor staatlichen Eingriffen verfassungsrechtlich geschützt.

---

[219] Siehe auch 4.2 Abwägungslehre
[220] Vgl. Art. 1, Art. 2 GG

In seinen Tagebuchentscheidungen[221] hat das Bundesverfassungsgericht festgeschrieben, dass die Verwertung von Beweisen aus tagebuchähnlichen Aufzeichnungen regelmäßig dann einem Beweisverbot mit Fernwirkung unterliegt, wenn nicht schwerwiegende Straftaten, wie zum Beispiel Mord oder Totschlag entgegenstehen.

Selbstgespräche, dass heißt Gespräche, die der Beschuldigte alleine mit sich selbst geführt hat, sind nach einer Bundesgerichtshofsentscheidung aus dem Jahre 2005[222] immer dann zu Beweiszwecken unverwertbar, wenn sie dem durch Art. 13 iVm Art. 1 Abs. 1 und Art. 2 Abs. 1 GG geschützten Kernbereich der privaten Lebensgestaltung zuzurechnen sind. In dem oben genannten Fall wurde ein Mann, wegen Mordes in Tatmehrheit mit dem Besitz einer halbautomatischen Selbstladekurzwaffe, zu lebenslanger Freiheitsstrafe verurteilt. Nachdem zuerst die Ermittlungen gegen ihn ergebnislos eingestellt wurden, da die Tatwaffe nicht entdeckt wurde. Im Jahre 2003 erlitt der Angeschuldigte einen Arbeitsunfall, den die Kriminalpolizei untersuchte, wobei sie im

---

[221] Vgl. zB BVerfGE 80, 367 (370)
[222] Vgl. BGH v. 10. 8. 2005 – 1 StR 140/05

Wohnhaus des Angeschuldigten einen Schlagstock entdeckte, der als Tatwaffe in Frage käme. Daraufhin erfolgte eine akustische Überwachung des Angeschuldigten in der Rehabilitationsklinik in der er sich aufgrund des Unfalles befand, in deren Rahmen ein Selbstgespräch des Beschuldigten aufgezeichnet wurde, indem er sich mit einer alternativen Tötungsart des Opfers beschäftigte.

Nachdem die Ermittlungen gegen den Mann wieder aufgenommen wurden, als der Schlagstock entdeckt wurde, befragte die Kriminalpolizei auch eine Arbeitskollegin des mutmaßlichen Täters über dessen aggressives Verhalten, ob er Rechts- oder Linkshänder sei und ob er seine Hasen selbst schlachten würde. Die Arbeitskollegin informierte den Beschuldigten in einem Telefonat, welches auch aufgezeichnet wurde, über die Fragen der Polizei. Nach dem Telefonat führte der Angeklagte ein erregtes (und aufgezeichnetes) Selbstgespräch, in dem er mehrfach ausrief, er hätte „ihm in den Kopf schießen sollen", was die Polizei eindeutig auf das Mordopfer bezog.

Der BGH schließlich sprach ein Beweisverwertungsverbot aus, da Beweise, die aus Selbstgesprächen gewonnen wur-

den, zu den unantastbaren Kernbereichen privater Lebensgestaltung gehören und demnach gemäß Art. 13 Abs. I iVm
Art. 1 Abs. I und Art. 2 Abs. I GG und § 100c Abs. IV StPO
einem Beweisverwertungsverbot mit Fernwirkung unterliegen.

Als Folge wurde das Urteil gegen den Angeklagten die Mord-
vorwürfe aufgehoben und zur erneuten Entscheidung an die
Vorinstanz zurück verwiesen und dem Tatrichter die Entscheidung überlassen, ob der Angeklagte wegen des Mordes zur Verantwortung gezogen werden kann, ohne dass
auf den illegalen Abhörbeweis zurückzugreifen.

6.1.2 Abwägungslehre

Die Abwägungslehre wurde entwickelt um Spannungen zwischen Grundrechten mit Verfassungsrang und den allgemeinen Gesetzen zu entschärfen, indem eine Abwägung zwischen dem Grundrecht einerseits und dem, durch ein allgemeines Gesetz geschütztem Rechtsgut auf der anderen
Seite, vornehmen zu können. Erdacht hat sich die Abwägungslehre das Bundesverfassungsgericht 1980[223] in einer
Entscheidung über die karitative Krankenversorgung und

---

[223] Vgl. BVerfGE 53, 366 (392f.)

das Recht des Staates darin einzugreifen. Zum einen seien Kirche und Staat getrennt zu sehen, allerdings, was die öffentliche Krankenversorgung angehe, habe das Recht auf Krankenversorgung Vorrang vor dem Recht auf Nichteinmischung in kirchliche Angelegenheiten. Dahingehend seien also der Kirche Schranken durch die allgemeinen Gesetze gesetzt.[224]

Bei einer Abwägung nach oben genannter Lehre, zählen alle Einzelumstände und sind in die Abwägung einzubeziehen, gilt dies schon bei kleineren Fragen, dann auch in erhöhtem Maße bei Eingriffen in Grundrechte.[225]

Bei der Abwägungslehre aus beweisrechtlicher Sicht ist also eine Abwägung zwischen dem Interesse der Öffentlichkeit an der Erforschung der prozessualen Wahrheit auf der einen, und dem Interesse der Betroffenen auf Schutz Ihrer Rechtsgüter, wie zum Beispiel der Achtung der Menschenwürde oder aber dem Recht auf informationelle Selbstbe-

---

[224] Vgl. Borowski, Die Glaubens- und Gewissensfreiheit im Grundgesetz, S. 604
[225] Vgl. Michael, Jahrbuch des öffentl. Rechts, S. 172

stimmung, auf der anderen Seite vorzunehmen und, je nachdem, wie schwer die jeweiligen Seiten wiegen, zu entscheiden.

6.2 Nemo-tenetur-Prinzip

„Nemo tenetur se ipsum accusare" – niemand ist gezwungen, sich selbst anzuklagen. Dieser Grundsatz aus dem römischen Recht findet sich in der deutschen Strafrechtsdogmatik in den §§ 136 Abs. I und 243 Abs. IV StPO wieder. Nach diesem Grundsatz ist niemand verpflichtet, sich in irgendeiner Art und Weise selber zu belasten, sei es durch Aussagen oder durch Beibringung von anderen Beweisen. Das Nemo-tenetur-Prinzip hat sogar einen Niederschlag im deutschen Steuerrecht; gemäß § 90 AO sind die Beteiligten (also auch der Beschuldigte im Steuerstrafverfahren) zwar zur Mithilfe und Offenlegung aller steuerlich relevanten Tatsachen verpflichtet, aber aufgrund von § 393 Abs. I AO kann gegen den Beschuldigten eines Steuerstrafverfahrens kein Zwangsmittel im Sinne des § 328 AO festgesetzt werden.

Sollte sich ein Angeschuldigter dafür entscheiden, sich zu den gegen ihn erhobenen Vorwürfen nicht zu äußern, darf ihm daraus kein Nachteil erwachsen.

Zwar muss der vorsitzende Richter die Aussageverweigerung des Angeklagten nicht hinnehmen und darf auch nicht versuchen, den Willen in Richtung einer Aussagewilligkeit zu beeinflussen; gleichwohl ist es ihm aber erlaubt, darauf hinzuweisen, dass eine Aussageverweigerung nicht immer die zweckmäßigste Verteidigung[226] darstellt.[227]

Dem gegenüber steht die strafmildernde Wirkung des Geständnisses. Wenn niemand gezwungen werden darf, sich selbst zu belasten, wie verhält sich dann dieser „Geständnisbonus" dazu, der im Umkehrschluss ja genau das bewirkt, nämlich, dass jemand, der sich selbst belastet, mit einer milderen Strafe rechnen muss, als jemand, der während der gesamten Verhandlung von seinem Recht zu Schweigen Gebrauch macht?

In seiner Dissertation[228] beschäftigt sich Dirk Stalinski mit eben dieser Frage:

> „Sie haben die Anklage des Staatsanwalts gehört. Es steht Ihnen frei, sich zu den erhobenen Vorwürfen zu äußern oder nicht zur

---

[226] Vgl. Meyer-Goßner, Beck'scher Kurzkommentar StPO, § 136 Rn. 7
[227] Vgl. Günther, JR 78, 92
[228] Stalinski: Aussagefreiheit & Geständnisbonus, Diss, Ddorf 2000

Sache auszusagen. Falls Sie ein Geständnis ablegen, könnte das allerdings strafmildernd berücksichtigt werden. Der Angeklagte schweigt mithin auf eigenes Risiko und sieht sich so einem faktischen Geständnisdruck ausgesetzt. Die vorliegende Dissertation befasst sich mit der Frage, ob die skizzierte forensische Praxis rechtlich zulässig ist. Um das Ergebnis vorwegzunehmen: sie ist es nicht, sondern verletzt die jedem Beschuldigten garantierte Aussagefreiheit."[229]

Stalinski kommt zu dem Schluss, dass jedweder Geständnisbonus, die Aussagefreiheit des Beschuldigten verletze. Dies könne nur vermieden werden, wenn dem Aussageverhalten des Angeschuldigten jegliche Relevanz für die Strafzumessung genommen würde, sonst bliebe von der materiellen Aussagefreiheit nur die „formelle Befugnis, sich zwischen Scylla und Charybdis zu entscheiden"[230].[231]

---

[229] Vgl. Stalinski, a.a.O. "Beschreibung"
[230] Vgl. Stalinski, a.a.O. S. 166
[231] Vgl. Stalinski, a.a.O.

6.3   Rechtskreistheorie

Als weiterer Maßstab, ob ein Beweisverwertungsverbot aus-
gesprochen werden muss, ist die Rechtskreistheorie anzusehen. Nach der Rechtskreistheorie, die vor allem auf Revi-
sionsbegründungen, aber auch im allgemeinen Verfahrens-
gang, Anwendung findet, kann ein Angeklagter seine Revision ausschließlich auf Verfahrensvorschriften stützen, die
dem Schutze **seiner eigenen** Rechtsinteressen dienlich
sind. Sollte also beispielsweise der Steuerberater eines Dritten nicht ordnungsgemäß über sein Zeugnisverweigerungsrecht belehrt worden sein und alsdann eine, den Angeklagten belastende Aussage treffen, kann der Angeklagte diesen
Verfahrensfehler nicht rügen[232], da das Zeugnisverweigerungsrecht des Steuerberaters eines Dritten den Rechts-
kreis eben dieses Dritten und nicht des Angeklagten schützen soll.[233]

Zeugnisverweigerungsrechte eines Steuerberaters, Rechtsanwaltes oder Arztes schützen also regelmäßig die Rechts-

---

[232] Vgl. Meyer-Goßner, Beck´scher Kurzkommentar StPO,
§ 55 Rn. 18
[233] Sinngemäß Meyer-Goßner, Beck´scher Kurzkommentar StPO.
§ 55 Rn. 1

interessen der Mandanten bzw. Patienten eben jener Geheimnisträger, nicht jedoch die von Personen, die nicht in einem Mandats- oder Patientenverhältnis zu den Berufsträgern stehen.

7 Steuerrechtliche Folgen

Fraglich ist, welche Folgen aus den vorhergehenden Abschnitten für Beweise im Steuerrecht gezogen werden können. Zum einen haben sich die Ermittlungsorgane in steuerlichen Sachverhalten (Finanzbehörden, Finanzgerichte, Staatsanwaltschaften, Strafgerichte, etc.) den Beschränkungen des Steuergeheimnisses zu unterwerfen, andererseits trifft den Steuerpflichtigen auch eine erhöhte Mitwirkungspflicht[234]. Inwieweit dies allerdings zum Ausschluss von Beweisverwertungsverboten führen kann, sollte zumindest hinterfragt werden, da sich, für den Betroffenen, eine Menge an äußerst schwerwiegenden Folgen ergeben könnten, die, sollten sie erst einmal durch Beweisverwertung eingetreten sein, nicht mehr zu korrigieren sein könnten.

---

[234] Vgl. § 90 AO

Daher muss auch im Steuerrecht bei Ermittlungen aller Art mit dem entsprechenden Fingerspitzengefühl an Sachverhalte herangegangen werden.

7.1 Situation im Steuerrecht

Das Steuerrecht selbst hat ein explizites Beweisverwertungsverbot normiert, nämlich das in § 393 Absatz II AO niedergelegte Beweisverwertungsverbot für den Fall, dass den Ermittlungsorganen in einem Strafverfahren Tatsachen bekannt werden, die ihnen durch den Steuerpflichtigen, in Unkenntnis der Einleitung eines Strafverfahrens und in Erfüllung seiner steuerrechtlichen Pflichten mitgeteilt oder aus den Steuerakten entnommen wurden und sich auf andere als Steuerstraftaten beziehen. Kenntnisse, die auf diesem Wege erlangt wurden, dürfen regelmäßig nicht gegen den Steuerpflichtigen verwendete werden, es sei denn, dass es sich bei den Taten, die auf diesem Wege entdeckt wurden um solche von zwingendem öffentliche Interesse handelt.[235] Taten, die nicht unter diesen Begriff fallen, werden durch das Steuergeheimnis, des § 30 AO geschützt.

---

[235] Vgl. § 393 Abs II AO

Nichtsdestotrotz sieht zum Beispiel Rüsken diese Formulierung skeptisch und zu Recht als Achillesferse des Steuergeheimnisses an.[236] Er führt weiter aus, dass diese Generalklausel für den Steuerpflichtigen außerordentliche Risiken birgt[237], da der Begriff des *zwingenden öffentlichem Interesses* keinerlei feste Konturen biete und daher zur Rechtssicherheit nur wenig beitrage. Dabei sei dies umso weniger verständlich, als wichtige Fälle, bei denen die Rechtspraxis schon seit jeher eine Offenbarungspflicht vermute, einer Auflistung durchaus zugänglich seien.[238] Zwar lasse sich aus der Auflistung in § 30 Absatz IV AO durchaus die Ableitung treffen, dass beispielsweise das Informationsinteresse Einzelner regelmäßig kein zwingendes öffentliches Interesse begründe.[239] Soweit sei also nur eine Offenbarung der Daten mit dem Einverständnis des Steuerpflichtigen zulässig.

Des Weiteren sei es unproblematisch bei Kapitalverbrechen im Sinne des § 138 Abs I StGB, das heißt bei zum Beispiel

---

[236] Vgl. Rüsken, Klein, Kommentar zur AO, § 30 Rn 182
[237] Vgl. Rüsken, a.a.O.
[238] Vgl. Rüsken, a.a.O.
[239] Vgl. Rüsken, a.a.O.

Mord, Totschlag oder aber auch Geldfälschung, eine Offenbarungspflicht zu sehen. [240] Darüber hinaus sei Offenbarungspflicht auch bei schwerer Untreue, Unterschlagungshandlungen gegen den Staat, oder aber bestimmten Umweltstraftaten[241] zu bejahen, wenn sie eine konkrete Gefährdung für eine Vielzahl von Menschen mit sich brächten[242]. Keine Offenbarungspflichten werden dagegen bei lediglich abstrakter Gefährdung vermutet, was im Schluss zu einem Beweisverwertungsverbot führt.

Straftaten, die unter Ausnutzung der Verhältnisse des Wirtschaftsverkehrs begangen wurden (Wirtschaftsstraftaten), dürfen offenbart werden, allerdings muss es sich dabei um besonders schwerwiegende Wirtschaftstraftaten handeln, die geeignet sind, die wirtschaftliche Ordnung erheblich zu stören. Darunter fallen neben großen Konkursen, betrügerischen Abschreibungs- und Anlagegesellschaften auch Subventionsbetrug hinsichtlich eines außergewöhnlich hohen Betrages (hier 350.000 DM)[243].[244]

---

[240] Vgl. Rüsken, a.a.O. Rn 183
[241] Vgl. BMF v. 1.7.93 - IV A 5 - S 0130 - 41/93
[242] Vgl. Rüsken, a.a.O.
[243] Vgl. FG Niedersachsen, EFG 91, 436
[244] Vgl. Rüsken, a.a.O. Rn 185

Zwar findet Rüsken, die AO habe die Offenbarungspflichten und das damit verbundene Risiko der Selbstbelastung nicht befriedigend gelöst, da es aufgrund der weit reichenden Formulierung des zwingenden öffentlichen Interesses dazu kommen kann, dass sich ein Steuerpflichtiger, in Erfüllung seiner steuerlichen Pflichten, der Verfolgung einer Straftat aussetzt, obwohl er kein Aussageverweigerungsrecht besitzt,[245] dennoch lasse sich aus der Tatsache, dass er nicht gezwungen werden kann sich selbst zu belasten ein Aussageverweigerungsrecht ableiten, dass jedoch im Gesetz keinen Niederschlag findet.[246] Daraus schließt Rüsken, dass man zwar vom Steuerpflichtigen verlangen kann seine Einnahmen aus Wirtschaftsstraftaten oder ähnlichem zu erklären, dieser dann aber weitere Erklärungen, zum Beispiel über die Art der Einkünfte, verweigern darf.[247] Zwar habe die Verwaltung den Grundsatz der Verhältnismäßigkeit zu beachten, könne in aller Regel aber den Steuerpflichtigen von der Vorlage von Unterlagen nicht ausnehmen.[248] Bei der An-

---

[245] Vgl. Rüsken, a.a.O. Rn 201
[246] Vgl. Rüsken, a.a.O.
[247] Vgl. Rüsken, a.a.O.
[248] Vgl. Rüsken, a.a.O.

wendung des Verhältnismäßigkeitsgrundsatzes habe es jedoch eine Rolle zu spielen, in welchem Umfang der Steuerpflichtige an dem Bekannt werden der Tatsachen mitgewirkt habe.[249]

Wisser folgend[250] besteht die Möglichkeit, dass die Regelung des § 393 AO verfassungswidrig sei, da sie gegen das Nemo-tenetur-Prinzip verstoße. Die herrschende Meinung sehe darüber hinaus eine Durchbrechung des Verwertungsverbotes bei Zustimmung der Verwendung durch den Steuerpflichtigen.[251] Dies stünde im Gegensatz zu § 136a StPO, daher bestünde an sich gar kein Verwertungsverbot für auf diesem Wege erlangte Beweise.[252] Allerdings soll, Rüster folgend [253] diese Vorschrift dennoch verfassungskonform dahingehend auszulegen sein, dass erzwungene, strafrechtlich belastende, Aussagen nur unter dem Grundsatz der Verhältnismäßigkeit verwertet werden dürften. Für die Praxis habe dies darüber hinaus kaum Bedeutung, da der Umstand, dass sich ein Steuerpflichtiger, in Erfüllung seiner

---

[249] Vgl. Rüsken, a.a.O.
[250] Vgl. Wisser, Klein, Kommentar zur AO, § 393 Rn 29
[251] Vgl. Wisser, a.a.O.
[252] Vgl. Wisser, a.a.O.
[253] Vgl. Wisser, a.a.O.; Rüster, wistra 88, 56

steuerrechtlichen Pflichten, eines Deliktes der Schwerstkriminalität bezichtigt habe, kaum jemals eingetreten sei.[254] Das Bundesverfassungsgericht habe in seinem Volkszählungsurteil[255] ausgeführt, dass ein überwiegendes Allgemeininteresse, welches den freien Informationsaustausch zwischen Behörden rechtfertige, regelmäßig dann zu verneinen sei, wenn die zu Grunde liegenden Daten durch Selbstbezichtigung erlangt worden seien.[256]

Zusammenfassend lässt sich also sagen, dass als Folge der Verletzung des Steuergeheimnisses, die als Straftat nach § 355 StGB verfolgt werden kann, regelmäßig ein Beweisverwertungsverbot geltend gemacht werden kann.[257]

Darüber hinaus unterliegen alle Erkenntnisse, die die Behörden erlangten, nachdem sie den Steuerpflichtigen rechtswidrig und im Verstoß gegen § 393 Absatz I Satz 2 und 3 dennoch zur Mitwirkung gezwungen haben ebenso einem Beweisverwertungsverbot.[258]

---

[254] Vgl. Wisser, a.a.O. Rn 29
[255] Vgl. BVerfGE 65, 1ff.
[256] Vgl. Wisser, a.a.O. Rn 29
[257] Vgl. Rüsken, a.a.O. Rn 223
[258] Vgl. Wisser, Klein, Kommentar zur AO, § 393 Rn 17

7.2 Aktuelle Entwicklung

In den letzten Jahren hat es einige Bahn brechende Entwicklungen zum Thema Beweisverwertungsverbote aus steuerrechtlicher Sicht gegeben. Neben einem Beschluss des Bundesfinanzhofes, der, abweichend von der bisherigen Praxis, Beweisverwertungsverbote aus steuerrechtlicher Sicht erstmalig bejahte tauchten auch im Rahmen der so genannten Liechtensteiner Steueraffäre einige Fragen über die Verwertung von Beweisen im Besteuerungs- und Strafverfahren auf.

In der Vergangenheit sah die Rechtsprechung Beweisverwertungsverbote eher als Ausnahme denn als Regel an. Im Jahre 1983 zum Beispiel, urteilte der Bundesfinanzhof in einem Verfahren[259] über die Verwertung von rechtswidrig erlangten Ergebnissen einer Außenprüfung dahingehend, dass diese nur insoweit vom Verfahren ausgeschlossen werden dürften, wie erfolgreich gegen die Rechtswidrigkeit der betroffenen Prüfungsmaßnahme vorgegangen worden ist.

---

[259] Vgl. BFH v. 27.7.83 – I R 210/79

Mit Beschluss vom 26. Februar 2001[260] hat der Bundesfinanzhof einen Beschluss zum Eingriff in das Grundrecht der Telekommunikationsfreiheit verabschiedet. Darin beschäftigten sich die Richter des siebten Senates mit der Frage, inwieweit Erkenntnisse, die die Ermittlungsorgane im Rahmen einer Telefonüberwachung bei einem einer Straftat verdächtigten gewonnen haben, im Besteuerungsverfahren Verwendung finden dürfen.

In dem zu Grunde liegenden Verfahren ging es um ein Ehepaar, dessen Telefone aufgrund einer rechtmäßigen richterlichen Anordnung abgehört wurden, weil der Ehemann, gemeinsam mit zwei anderen Beschuldigten und einigen, nicht identifizierten Mittätern, der Einfuhr und dem Handel mit Betäubungsmitteln, Menschenhandel, Zigarettenschmuggel und anderen Straftaten der Gewinnerzielung aus schweren Straftaten verdächtigt wurde.

Das zuständige Amtsgericht bewilligte aufgrund der schwere der Vorwürfe die Überwachung der Telekommunikation ge-

---

[260] Vgl. BFH v. 26.2.01 – VII B 265/00

gen das Ehepaar gemäß §§ 100a und 100b StPO, da hinsichtlich des, auf die Ehefrau eingetragenen, Telefonanschlusses zu erwarten sei, dass der Ehemann diesen mitbenutze und Erkenntnisse über die Straftaten auf diesem Wege zu gewinnen seien. Daraufhin wurde der Telefonanschluss überwacht und alle Gespräche, die über ihn geführt wurden, aufgezeichnet.[261]

Im Weitergang des Verfahrens erließ das zuständige Hauptzollamt eine auf Artikel 57 des Zollkodex[262], sowie § 324 AO gestützte Arrestanordnung.

Der dingliche Arrest in das Vermögen der Ehefrau wurde angeordnet, um die Einfuhrabgaben in bestimmter Höhe zu sichern, weil zu befürchten wäre, dass andernfalls deren Beitreibung vereitelt oder wesentlich erschwert werden könnte. Die Ehefrau gehöre nach den Erkenntnissen der ermittelnden Polizeibehörde, die sich auf die telefonischen Überwachungsmaßnahmen stützte, zu einer Tätergruppe, die unverzollte und unversteuerte Zigaretten aus Drittländern in das Gemeinschaftsgebiet eingeschmuggelt habe.[263]

---

[261] Vgl. BFH, a.a.O. Tz 1
[262] Verordnung (EWG) Nr. 2913/92 - ZK
[263] Vgl. BFH, a.a.O. Tz 2

Nach den Regelungen des Zollkodexes sei sie daher als Zollschuldnerin anzusehen, da sie entweder als Täterin[264] oder aber Hilfsweise als Person, die die Zigaretten zeitweise in Besitz gehabt habe[265] für die Einfuhrabgaben einzustehen habe. Darüber hinaus müsse damit gerechnet werden, dass die Ehefrau Vermögen beiseite schafft um die Beitreibung zu verhindern.[266]

Dagegen wehrte sich die Ehefrau im Rahmen des Einspruchsverfahrens gegen die Arrestanordnung und führte aus, dass sie mit den vorgeworfenen Taten weder etwas zu tun habe noch Kenntnis davon erlangt oder sich in irgendeiner Weise an dem Zigarettenschmuggel beteiligt habe.[267]

Weder der Einspruch noch der Antrag auf Aufhebung der zwischenzeitlich erfolgten Vollziehung wurde durch das Hauptzollamt bearbeitet, so dass die Ehefrau Klage zum zuständigen Finanzgericht erhob, mit der Begründung, die Beweise, die zu der Arrestanordnung führten seien als Erkenntnisse aus der Telefonüberwachung nach § 100a StPO mit dem Makel behaftet, dass sie lediglich im Straf- und nicht im

---

[264] Art 202 Abs I a ZK
[265] Art 202 Abs III 2. Spiegelstrich ZK
[266] Vgl. BFH, a.a.O. Tz 4
[267] Vgl. BFH, a.a.O. Tz 5

Besteuerungsverfahren verwendet werden dürften und machte insoweit ein Beweisverwertungsverbot geltend.

Das Finanzgericht gab der Klage der Ehefrau statt und hob die Vollziehung wieder auf, wogegen das Hauptzollamt sich mit zugelassener Beschwerde zum Bundesfinanzhof wehrte und ausführte, dass der in den Überwachungsbeschlüssen des Amtsgerichtes angeführte Zigarettenschmuggel eine Steuerstraftat im Sinne des § 370 AO darstelle und die Erkenntnisse daher keine Zufallsfunde seien, sondern genau das bestätigten, was die Ermittler vermutet hätten. Daher sei ein Verwertungsverbot nicht gerechtfertigt. Darüber hinaus bestehe kein Verwertungsverbot von Erkenntnissen, die aus einem Strafverfahren in ein Besteuerungsverfahren übernommen würden.[268]

Zum einen lasse sich aus Artikel 10 Grundgesetz kein allgemeines Verwertungsverbot ableiten, zum anderen sei es den Finanzbehörden schon gemäß § 92 Satz 1 AO erlaubt sich aller erforderlichen Beweismittel zu bedienen, hierzu gehöre insbesondere, gemäß § 92 Satz 2 Nr. 3 AO das hinzuziehen staatsanwaltlicher Ermittlungsakten. Außerdem

---

[268] Vgl. BFH, a.a.O. Tz 9

gebe es eine entsprechende Norm auch im Zollkodex, nämlich Art. 14 ZK.[269]

Der Bundesfinanzhof hatte sich also mit der Frage zu beschäftigen, inwieweit Artikel 10 GG ein Beweisverwertungsverbot von in einem Strafverfahren gewonnenen Erkenntnissen für das Besteuerungsverfahren ausweist.

In der Folge kam der BFH zu der Erkenntnis, dass das Erfassen von bestimmten Fernmeldevorgängen (Telefonüberwachung) durch Strafverfolgungsbehörden und die Weitergabe von daraus gewonnenen Informationen an die Finanzverwaltung zur Durchführung des Besteuerungsverfahrens
in den durch Artikel 10 Abs. 1 GG geschützten Bereich ein-
greife.[270]

Des Weiteren habe das Verwertungsverbot, das sich aus Artikel 10 Abs. 1 GG ergebe keine zulässige Durchbrechung
erfahren, das heißt, die Informationsweitergabe war rechtswidrig. Zwar sei eine Durchbrechung aufgrund von
§ 100a StPO grundsätzlich zulässig, jedoch nur für Strafverfolgungsbehörden. Die Abgabenordnung enthalte weder
eine Erlaubnis zur Verletzung des Fernmeldegeheimnisses,

---

[269] Vgl. BFH, a.a.O. Tz 10 f.
[270] Vgl. BFH, a.a.O. Leitsatz 1

noch eine Vorschrift, die die Verwertung von Beweisen zulasse, die auf dem oben geschilderten Wege erlangt wurden.[271]

Für Aufzeichnungen, die unmittelbar aus einer Telefonüberwachung in einem Strafverfahren resultierten, bestehe folglich im Besteuerungsverfahren ein Verwertungsverbot, das gleichermaßen für Sicherungsmaßnahmen - wie den dinglichen Arrest – gelte.[272]

7.2.2 Liechtensteiner Steueraffäre

Im Jahre 2002 stahl der Bankmitarbeiter Heinrich Klieber seinem Arbeitgeber, der Liechtensteinischen LGT Bank, 4.527 Datensätze mit sensiblen Kundendaten, die ca. 1.200 Kunden, 600 davon aus Deutschland, betrafen, die bei der LGT Bank und der LGT Treuhand Stiftungen unterhielten.[273]

Diese Datensätze bot Klieber, der in der Zwischenzeit für seinen Diebstahl von der LGT Bank angezeigt und durch die liechtensteinische Strafgerichtsbarkeit auch verurteilt wurde, dem Bundesnachrichtendienst zum Kauf an. Zuvor hatte er versucht, mit den Datensätzen den Landesfürsten von

---

[271] Vgl. BFH, a.a.O. Leitsatz 2
[272] Vgl. BFH, a.a.O. Leitsatz 3
[273] Vgl. PM LGT Bank

Liechtenstein zu erpressen, was jedoch nicht gelang. Stattdessen wurde er wegen Urkundenunterdrückung, schweren Betrugs, Nötigung und gefährlicher Drohung zu vier Jahren Haft verurteilt und gab die gestohlenen DVDs vermeintlich zurück. Vom Verbrechen der Auskundschaftung eines Geschäfts- und Betriebsgeheimnisses sprach das Gericht Klieber aber frei, da es davon ausging, dass er nicht die Absicht gehabt hat, die Daten Ausländern zugänglich zu machen.[274]

Der Bundesnachrichtendienst kaufte die Datensätze, die ihm angeboten wurden schließlich zum Preis von einigen Millionen Euro an und leitete sie an die Finanzbehörden in Deutschland weiter.

Kurz darauf teilten die Finanzbehörden der Öffentlichkeit und der Presse mit, dass sie aufgrund von Ermittlungen des BND in den Besitz von Daten gekommen seien, die Rückschlüsse auf eine Vielzahl an Steuerstraftaten und Steuernachforderungen in mehrstelliger Millionenhöhe zuließen.

Ihren Höhepunkt fand die so genannte Steueraffäre dann in der medienwirksam aufgemachten Durchsuchung bei Dr. Klaus Zumwinkel, dem damaligen Vorstandsvorsitzenden

---

[274] Vgl. PM LGT Bank

der Deutschen Post AG, der ebenfalls Vermögen in liechtensteinische Stiftungen investiert und aus den Erträgen profi-
tiert haben soll, ohne dies dem deutschen Fiskus zu erklären.

Dieses Vorgehen der deutschen Finanzbehörden wirft eine
Menge an Fragen auf.

Die Tatsache, dass Beweismittel durch Privatpersonen in
strafbarer Weise erlangt wurden, führt zwar nicht zwingend
zu einem Beweisverwertungsverbot[275], jedoch wurden hier
diese Straftaten aus deutschen Steuermitteln „belohnt".

Professor Salditt erörtert diese in einem Aufsatz in der Zeit-
schrift „Praxis Steuerstrafrecht" unter dem Blickwinkel mög-
licher Beweisverwertungsverbote aufgrund des Vorgehens
des BND und der Finanz- und Ermittlungsbehörden. Dabei
trifft er einige interessante Feststellungen, die in den Prozes-
sen der Steuersünder zu erörtern wären.

Einführend hinterfragt Salditt die Rolle des BND in der Liechtensteiner Steueraffäre, der, so Salditt, aus gutem Grund die
Rolle als Bote spielt. Aufgabe des BND sei es, Erkenntnisse

---

[275] Vgl. OLG Frankfurt v. 20.12.1995 – 3 VAs 25-26/95

über das Ausland zu gewinnen, die außen- und sicherheits-politische Bedeutung haben. Personenbezogene Daten an Staatsanwaltschaft oder Polizei (dazu zählt auch die Steuer-fahndung) darf der BND nur aufgrund von Staatsschutzde-likten oder sonstigen Straftaten, die grundlegende Schutz-güter des Bestandes, der Sicherheit oder auswärtigen Be-lange der Bundesrepublik Deutschland bedrohen übermit-teln, wozu Steuerhinterziehung nicht gehöre.[276]

Auch habe der BND nicht die Befugnis, der Steuerfahndung Amtshilfe zu leisten, da gemäß § 112 Absatz II AO die er-suchte Behörde nur Hilfe leisten darf, soweit sie aus rechtli-chen Gründen dazu in der Lage ist. Der reine Transport ei-nes Päckchens mit Daten sei hingegen keine Amtshilfe, be-gründe aber auch keinen Anspruch auf Kostenübernahme für die Bezahlung gemäß § 115 Absatz I Satz 2 AO. Dage-gen sei das Verhandeln mit dem Lieferanten über Bezahlung und das Ausstellen einer neuen Identität zwar eventuelle Amtshilfe, jedoch dem BND untersagt, wenn er dies für Strafverfolgungs- oder Finanzbehörden unternehme.[277]

---

[276] Vgl. Salditt, PStStR 04/08, S. 84 ff.
[277] Vgl. Salditt, a.a.O.

Das Bundesverfassungsgericht[278] schränkte die Befugnis des BND zur Auslandsaufklärung dahingehend ein, dass, wenn die Verhütung und Verfolgung von Straftaten überhaupt betroffen sei, dies nur zum Schutz hochrangiger Gemeinschaftsgüter erlaubt sei, deren Verletzung schwere Schäden für den inneren oder äußeren Frieden und für Rechtsgüter einzelner zur Folge hätte. Dem Urteil folgend reiche dafür nicht einmal Geldfälschung im Ausland aus, der BND sei erst dann zuständig, wenn durch die Geldfälschung die Währungsstabilität der BRD derart gefährdet sei dass es den normierten Großgefahren (Katalogtatbestände des § 100a StPO) gleichkomme.[279]

Salditt zu Folge dürften nur bei Zufallsfunden von Straftaten diese an Strafverfolgungsbehörden weitergeleitet werden. Da in dem hier vorliegenden Fall die Ermittlung (Kauf der Datenträger) allerdings als geplante Hauptsache dastehe, müsse diese an § 100a StPO gemessen werden, das heißt, die aufgedeckte Straftat müsse einer der Katalogtatbe-

---

278 BVerfG vom 14.7.99, NJW 00, 55
279 Vgl. Salditt, a.a.O.

stände des § 100a StPO sein, was für die einfache Steuerhinterziehung des Normalfalls des § 370 AO nicht zutreffe.[280]

Zwar sei damit noch nicht festgestellt dass die Daten strafrechtlich als Beweismittel einem Verwertungsverbot unterlägen, allerdings ließe das oben genannte Urteil des Bundesverfassungsgerichtes[281] Rückschluss auf einen „amtshilfefesten Schutz gegen Zweckentfremdung durch Weitergabe und Verwertungsverbote" zu.[282]

Die geheimdienstliche Beschaffung von Datensätzen, die die Privatsphäre von mehr als 1.000 Bürgern betreffe und die Übergabe an Strafverfolgungs- und Steuerbehörden verletze daher in jedem Falle das Grundrecht auf informationelle Selbstbestimmung und das Grundrecht auf Wahrung der Menschenwürde[283].[284]

Dazu käme noch die Tatsache, dass alle diese Daten mit den jeweiligen Steuerakten abgeglichen werden müssten, ob überhaupt ein, anfangs nur vermuteter, Anfangsverdacht

---

[280] Vgl. Salditt, a.a.O.
[281] BVerfG vom 14.7.99, a.a.O.
[282] Vgl. Salditt, a.a.O.
[283] Vgl. Art 2 Abs I GG iVm Art 1 Abs I GG
[284] Vgl. Salditt, a.a.O.

bestehe. Diese oben genannten Punkte ließen nur den Rückschluss zu, dass die Daten im Rahmen einer geheimdienstlichen Operation gewonnen wurden, die sich in jedem Falle an den Schranken des § 100a StPO zu orientieren habe. Sollte dies nicht der Fall sein ergebe sich für § 370 AO in analoger Anlehnung an § 100b Absatz V StPO ein Beweisverwertungsverbot, dass die Finanz- und Strafverfolgungsbehörden daran hindere, die erwischten Steuersünder auf der Grundlage von „Zufallsfunden" zu verurteilen und Steuern nachzufordern. Ein Verstoß gegen § 100a StPO hat aber, wie schon in den vorgehenden Kapiteln beschrieben, ebenfalls ein Verwertungsverbot zur Folge.[285]

Allerdings seien Beweisverwertungsverbote mit Vorsicht zu genießen. Zwar dürfen Beweise, die einem Verwertungsverbot unterliegen nicht Grundlage eines Schuldspruchs sein, wohl aber eines Ermittlungsansatzes.[286] Danach reichen solche Beweise dafür aus, einen Anfangsverdacht zu wecken, der eventuell zu Durchsuchungsbeschlüssen und Festnahmen führt, bei der weitere Beweismittel gefunden

---

[285] Vgl. Salditt, a.a.O.
[286] Vgl. BGHSt 34, 362

werden, die den Voraussetzungen für eine Verurteilung genügen.[287]

Stahl und Demuth[288] führen darüber hinaus in Ihrem Aufsatz „Strafrechtliches Verwertungsverbot bei Verletzung des Steuergeheimnisses"[289] noch einen interessanten Blickwinkel ein. Demnach sei die Verletzung des Steuergeheimnisses in der Sphäre staatlicher Quellen erfolgt, was sich auch mit Salditts Ansicht deckt, der, wie oben erwähnt, den BND mittelbar verantwortlich macht. Aus dieser Tatsache resultiere eine Garantiepflicht der Ermittler, die Verletzung des Steuergeheimnisses nicht auszunutzen.

Die Duldung einer Verletzung des Steuergeheimnisses könne unter keinen Umständen eine zulässige Ermittlungsmethode sein. Ließe sich also zum Ermittlungsschluss nicht mit Sicherheit eine Verletzung des Steuergeheimnisses ausschließen, welches zu einer für den Steuerpflichtigen belastenden Situation, die die Willensbildung beeinflusst habe geführt haben könne, die Verletzung des Steuergeheimnisses

---

[287] Vgl. Salditt, a.a.O.
[288] Vgl. DStR 13/2008, 603
[289] Vgl. DStR a.a.O.

(durch Information der Medien) also als quasi ermittlungs-
taktische Maßnahme billigend in Kauf genommen wurde,
gebiete schon das Rechtstaatsprinzip ein umfassendes Verwertungsverbot.[290]

Daher, so Stahl und Demuth, hätte die „custodial interrogation", also die Vernehmung vor Ort unter dem Eindruck der
Ermittlungen und Öffentlichkeit durch die Medien, genauso
wenig statt finden dürfen, wie die Vernehmung später, als
die Zwangslage immer noch fortwirkte.

Dadurch, dass der Steuerpflichtige trotzdem vernommen
wurde, wurde die, aus der Sphäre der Behörden stam-
mende, Verletzung des Steuergeheimnisses benützt um,
durch öffentliches anprangern, den Steuerpflichtigen zu vor-
schnellen Aussagen zu verleiten, was in jedem Falle zu einem umfassenden Verwertungsverbote führen würde.[291]

Durch die jüngst durch den BFH[292] ergangene Entscheidung
zu nach §93 Abs. 1 S. 3 AO angeforderten Kontoauszügen

---

[290] Vgl. DStR a.a.O.
[291] Vgl. Stahl & Demuth, DStR, 13/2008, 604
[292] BFH v. 29.08.2017 – VIII R 17/13

bekam die Frage nach Beweisverwertung im Steuerrecht noch einmal eine höhere Aktualität.

In dem hier vom Bundesfinanzhof entschiedenen Streitfall begründete der Kläger ein Verwertungsverbot der angefochtenen Feststellungen des Finanzamts zu den streitigen zusätzlichen Betriebseinnahmen damit,

- die dafür ausgewerteten Bankauszüge seien unter Verstoß gegen § 93 Abs. 1 Satz 3 AO von den Banken angefordert worden,

- eine Belehrung nach § 393 Abs. 1 Satz 4 AO sei unterblieben,

- die Außenprüfung sei trotz eindeutigen Anfangsverdachts am ersten Prüfungstag nicht gemäß § 10 Abs. 1 Satz 3 BpO 2000 abgebrochen worden und

- eine fortlaufende und zeitnahe Unterrichtung über die Prüfungsfeststellungen und den daraus abgeleiteten Verdacht auf Steuerhinterziehung (§ 199 Abs. 2 AO) sei nicht erfolgt.

Diesen Einwendungen vermochte der Bundesfinanzhof durchgreifende rechtliche Hindernisse für die Verwertung der Prüferfeststellungen nicht zu entnehmen:

Entgegen der Auffassung des Klägers war die Anforderung der Bankunterlagen ohne Verstoß gegen § 93 Abs. 1 Satz 3 AO schon deshalb gerechtfertigt, weil der Kläger diese Unterlagen weder auf die Anfrage der Außenprüfung vom 10.02.2010 noch auf die mit einer Belehrung über ein Aussageverweigerungsrecht versehene- Anforderung der Bußgeld- und Strafsachenstelle des Finanzamts Stadt A vom 22.02.2010 vorgelegt hatte. Denn bei verweigerter Mitwirkung des Steuerpflichtigen ist die Finanzverwaltung berechtigt, Dritte bei der Sachverhaltsaufklärung gemäß § 93 AO heranzuziehen.

Zu Recht hat das Finanzgericht auch entschieden, dass das Finanzamt an der Berücksichtigung der noch streitigen zusätzlichen Betriebseinnahmen nicht wegen behaupteter verspäteter Einleitung des Strafverfahrens oder fehlender Unterrichtung des Klägers gehindert war.

Nach der Rechtsprechung des Bundesfinanzhofs[293] bewirkt grundsätzlich weder ein Verstoß gegen die Belehrungspflicht des § 393 Abs. 1 Satz 4 AO noch gegen die Unterbre-

---

[293] BFH v. 08.01.2014 . X B112, 113/13 u.a.

chungspflicht des § 10 Abs. 1 Satz 3 BpO 2000, dass Erkenntnisse aus einer solchen Außenprüfung im Besteuerungsverfahren einem Verwertungsverbot unterliegen; eine gegen diese Rechtsprechung eingelegte Verfassungsbeschwerde hat das Bundesverfassungsgericht nicht zur Entscheidung angenommen[294].

Danach können Verfahrensverstöße im Rahmen einer Außen- oder Steuerfahndungsprüfung eine Verwertung der im Rahmen jener Verfahren gewonnenen Erkenntnisse im Besteuerungsverfahren nur dann ausschließen, wenn die Verfahrensverstöße schwerwiegend waren oder bewusst oder willkürlich begangen wurden[295]. Fehlt es an einem derart schwerwiegenden Verfahrensmangel, insbesondere an einem grundrechtsrelevanten Verstoß einer unmittelbaren Ermittlungsmaßnahme, so ist es bei der gebotenen Abwägung zwischen den Individualinteressen von Steuerpflichtigen, nicht aufgrund verfahrensfehlerhafter Ermittlungsmaßnahmen mit einer materiell-rechtlich an sich zutreffenden Steuer belastet zu werden, und der Pflicht des Staates, eine gesetz-

---

[294] U.a. BVerfG v. 09.11.2010, 2 BvR 2101/09
[295] BVerfG v. 07.04.2016 – 2 BvR 2237/15

mäßige und gleichmäßige Steuerfestsetzung zu gewährleisten, gerechtfertigt, eine Fernwirkung eventueller Verwertungsverbote auf spätere, rechtmäßig erlangte Ermittlungsergebnisse zu verneinen[296].

Nach diesen Grundsätzen sind im vorliegenden Fall die Voraussetzungen für einen qualifizierten Verfahrensverstoß nicht erfüllt, weil ein solcher Verstoß nach der Rechtsprechung grundsätzlich nicht in einer fehlenden Belehrung nach § 393 Abs. 1 Satz 4 AO oder in der Unterlassung einer Unterbrechung nach § 10 Abs. 1 Satz 3 BpO 2000 zu sehen ist[297] und besondere Umstände für die Annahme einer besonderen Schwere des Verfahrensverstoßes nicht ersichtlich sind.

Für die behauptete Verletzung der Unterrichtungspflicht nach § 199 Abs. 2 AO kann nichts anderes gelten, so dass

---

[296] 5.　　　BFH, Urteile vom 04.12 2012 – VIII R 5/10, BFHE 239, 19, BStBl II 2014, 220; in BFHE 215, 12, BStBl II 2007, 227[↵]
[297] 6.　　　BFH, Beschluss in BFH/NV 2014, 487, unter Hinweis auf BFH, Urteil in BFHE 198, 7, BStBl II 2002, 328, sowie BFH, Beschluss in BFH/NV 2012, 956[↵]

nach allgemeiner Auffassung insoweit ebenfalls kein Verwertungsverbot hinsichtlich der Tatsachen ausgelöst wird, über die der Steuerpflichtige nicht unterrichtet wurde[298].

Die Frage, ob im Streitfall das Finanzamt den Kläger im Rahmen der Außen- oder Steuerfahndungsprüfung hinreichend belehrt hat, bedarf ebenfalls keiner Entscheidung, weil es im Besteuerungsverfahren wie bereits ausgeführt- kein allgemeines gesetzliches Verwertungsverbot für Tatsachen gibt, die unter Verletzung von Verfahrensvorschriften ermittelt wurden[299]. Deshalb führt auch eine Verletzung der Belehrungspflicht des § 393 Abs. 1 Satz 4 AO im Besteuerungsverfahren grundsätzlich zu keinem Verwertungsverbot[300].

---

[298] 7.   Schallmoser in Hübschmann/Hepp/Spitaler, § 199 AO Rz 36; Klein/Rüsken, AO, 13. Aufl., § 199 Rz 3, unter Hinweis auf BFH, Beschluss vom 26.06.1997 – XI B 174/96, BFH/NV 1998, 17; Seer in Tipke/Kruse, Abgabenordnung, Finanzgerichtsordnung, § 199 AO Rz 22; Koenig/Intemann, Abgabenordnung, 3. Aufl., § 199 Rz 20
[299] 8.   vgl. z.B. BFH, Beschluss vom 30.10.2008 – VIII B 146/07 m.w.N
[300] 9.   BFH, Urteile in BFHE 198, 7, BStBl II 2002, 328; vom 28.10.2009 – I R 28/08, BFH/NV 2010, 432, sowie BFH, Beschluss vom 03.04.2007 – VIII B 110/06, BFH/NV 2007, 1273

Explizit auf den Fall der angekauften Steuerdaten aus Drittländern stellte das FG Köln[301] klar, dass die fehlende Begründung und die erlassene Anhörung vor Erlass von Änderungsbescheiden nach Erwerb von sog. Steuer-CDs nicht geeignet seine, die Rechtswidrigkeit von Bescheiden zu begründen.

Dem Beschuldigten sei ausreichend Gelegenheit gegeben worden, zu den der Besteuerung zugrunde liegenden Tatsachen Stellung zu nehmen. Eine mögliche Verletzung von § 121 Abs. 1 AO und § 91 Abs. 1 AO sei damit gemäß § 126 Abs. 1 Nr. 2 und 3, Abs. 2 AO geheilt und folglich unbeachtlich. Vielmehr sei der Beschuldigte seiner erhöhten Mitwirkungspflicht gemäß § 90 Abs. 2 AO nicht nachgekommen, denn durch Vorlage von Kontounterlagen hätte der Sachverhalt transparent gemacht werden können. Er habe solche Vorgänge aufzuklären und die erforderlichen Beweismittel zu beschaffen und hierbei alle für ihn bestehenden rechtlichen und tatsächlichen Möglichkeiten auszuschöpfen. Dar-

---

[301] FG Köln v 15.12.2019 – 14 V 2484/19

über hinaus sei eine Überschreitung des Schätzungsrahmens durch das Finanzamt nicht feststellbar, da diese auf einer nicht unangemessenen Verzinsung von 5 % beruhe.

Ferner liege auch kein steuerlich zu beachtendes Verwertungsverbot für die Daten einer aus der Schweiz herrührenden CD vor. Ein steuerliches Verwertungsverbot liege nach dem BFH nur bei sog. qualifizierten materiell-rechtlichen Verstößen und nicht bei bloßen Verfahrensrechtlichen Mängeln vor. Unter Berufung auf das BVerfG[302] führt das FG aus, dass kein Mangel vorliege, der zu einem steuerlichen Verwertungsverbot führe.

Der Beschuldigte war auf einer Steuer-CD/Steuerdaten-CD mit Daten über Kapitalanlagen der Schweizer Bank Credit Suisse benannt. Daraufhin wurde bei ihm eine Hausdurchsuchung durchgeführt, die jedoch keine Hinweise auf ein Konto bei der besagten Bank ergab. Das Finanzamt änderte am 05.07.2010 die Einkommensteuer des Beschuldigten und seiner Ehefrau für die Jahre 1999 bis 2008 durch eine

---

[302] BVerfG v. 09.11.2010, 2 BvR 2101/09

Hinzuschätzung von Kapitalerträgen und teilte dem Beschuldigten nachträglich zur Begründung mit, dass er seit 18.09.1991 ein Konto bei der Credit Suisse unterhalten habe und er bei der Durchsuchung mehrfach aufgefordert wurde, Unterlagen der Bank anzufordern und vorzulegen. Dieser Aufforderung sei er nicht nachgekommen. Die Schätzung sei auf Grundlage eines Kontostandes im Jahr 2007 erfolgt, der 1.841.000 CHF betragen habe. Bei der Hinzuschätzung sei von einer durchschnittlichen Verzinsung von 5 % pro im Jahr ausgegangen worden.

Hiergegen wandte sich der Beschuldigte mit diversen Argumenten. Er rügte die steuerliche Verwertbarkeit der Daten und bemängelt, dass bei Erlass der Bescheide keine nachprüfbare Begründung der Besteuerungsgrundlagen bestanden habe, denn eine Begründung befinde sich weder in den Bescheiden noch anderorts. Die Begründung erschöpfe sich in dem Hinweis auf die Ermittlungen der Steuerfahndung. Ferner sei kein ausreichendes rechtliches Gehör gewährt worden. Nachdem der Aussetzungsantrag des Beschuldigten

Bei den Fragen, ob die CD mit den Kontodaten einem steuerlichen Verwertungsverbot unterliegt, ob die Bescheide ausreichend begründet und dem Antragsteller ausreichend rechtliches Gehör gewährt wurde, handelt es sich nach Auffassung des FG um Nebenkriegsschauplätze. In der sog. Lichtensteiner Steueraffäre hat bereits das LG Bochum[303] die strafrechtliche Verwertung der Daten zugelassen. Dazu hat das BVerfG[304] trotz Nichtannahmebeschlusses Stellung genommen und ausgeführt, dass die Ablehnung eines Beweisverwertungsverbotes nicht zu beanstanden sei. Ebenso hat das LG Düsseldorf[305] in den Credit Suisse Fällen ein strafrechtliches Beweisverwertungsverbot abgelehnt.

Im Kern geht es in der Entscheidung daher um die Reichweite der Anwendung des strafrechtlichen Grundsatzes „in dubio pro reo" und des sog. „nemo tenetur"-Prinzips im Besteuerungsverfahren. Im Streitfall lagen dem Finanzamt nur Unterlagen vor, die auf eine Kontoeröffnung im Jahre 1991 schließen lassen. Ferner war ein Kontostand aus dem Jahre 2007 bekannt. Über weitere Informationen, insbesondere darüber, ob und in welcher Höhe steuerpflichtige Erträge angefallen sind, verfügte das Finanzamt nicht. Dieser Kernproblematik widmet sich das FG nur am Rande mit wenigen

---

[303] LG Bochum 2 Qs 10/08 und 2 Qs 2/09
[304] 2 BvR 2101/09
[305] LG Düsseldorf, 014 Qs – 131 Js, 150/10 – 60/10

Sätzen, ohne sich mit der Rechtsprechung in diesem Bereich[306] oder der Literatur auch nur ansatzweise zu beschäftigen. Es darf bezweifelt werden, ob das FG die Problematik und die damit in Zusammenhang stehenden Fragen der notwendigen Unterscheidung zwischen Beweismaß und Beweislast, überhaupt erkannt hat. Die Entscheidung ist mithin alles andere als überzeugend. Dennoch nutzen die Finanzämter und die Strafverfolgungsbehörden den Beschluss, um Druck auf die Betroffenen auszuüben und die Vorlage von Unterlagen zu verlangen.

---

[306] vgl. BFH, 2.7.1998, BStBl 1999, II 28; BFH, 7.11.2006, VIII R 81/04

8 Zusammenfassung / Fazit

Zusammenfassend lässt sich daher sagen, dass es auch im deutschen Steuerrecht Beweisverwertungsverbote geben kann, gerade auch im Hinblick auf Steuerstrafverfahren.

Grundlage für ein Beweisverwertungsverbot ist zu aller erst einmal ein Beweis, der in Form der fünf Beweisarten (Sachverständige, Augenschein, Parteivernehmung, Urkunden und Zeugen), dessen Grundlagen im Zivilrecht liegen und sowohl vom Steuer- als auch vom Strafverfahrensrecht übernommen wurden, erhoben werden muss.

Solange der Beweis auf zulässige Art und Weise beigebracht wird, entstehen keine Probleme bei der Erforschung der prozessualen Wahrheit. Sollten bei der Beweiserhebung jedoch Fehler im Sinne von rechtswidriger Beweisbeschaffung unterlaufen sein, ist ein Beweisverbot möglich.

Beweisverbote werden unterteilt in Beweiserhebungs- und Beweisverwertungsverbote, welche wiederum in mehrere Arten zu unterteilen sind. Bei den Erhebungsverboten unterscheidet man zwischen Beweismethoden-, Beweismittel-, und Beweisthemaverboten, die in den oberen Kapiteln ausführlich erläutert wurden.

Beweisverwertungsverbote untergliedern sich in relative und absolute, selbständige und unselbständige Beweisverwertungsverbote, je nachdem, ob das Beweisverwertungsverbot endgültig (absolut) oder disponibel (relativ), in einer eigenen Norm aufgeführt (selbständig) oder aus einer anderen resultiert (unselbständig).

Fernwirkende Beweisverwertungsverbote sind in der Lehrmeinung höchst angesehen, in der Praxis allerdings hart umstritten. Das wichtigste Beweisverwertungsverbot mit Fernwirkung ist sicherlich die Theorie der Früchte des vergifteten Baumes (Fruit-of-the-poisonous-tree-Doktrin) von Richter Felix Frankfurter am Supreme Court of the United States of America. Frankfurter war der Erste, der ein Beweisverwertungsverbot mit Fernwirkung normierte, allerdings ist seine Theorie aufgrund der Unterschiede vom deutschen zum angloamerikanischen Recht auf die deutschen Verhältnisse nicht direkt anwendbar. In den USA werden nämlich auch Strafprozesse als Parteienprozesse geführt, im Gegensatz zu Deutschland, wo die Erforschung der absoluten Wahrheit im Vordergrund eines Strafprozesses steht.

Beweisverwertungsverbote mit Fernwirkung kennt das deutsche Recht nur in sehr eingeschränktem Maße, so zum Beispiel im Rahmen der Drei-Sphären-, der Rechtskreistheorie oder der Abwägungslehre. In diesem Zusammenhang darf auch das Nemo-tenetur-Prinzip nicht vergessen werden, welches, bei Verstoß hiergegen, zu einem relativen, selbständigen Beweisverwertungsverbot mit eingeschränkter Fernwirkung führt.

Alle diese oben genannten Grundsätze und Folgen lassen sich auch auf das deutsche Steuerrecht übertragen, was, im Hinblick auf die aktuelle Entwicklung sicher zu einigen interessanten Sachverhaltskonstellationen führen könnte.

Abgesehen von der methodischen Fragwürdigkeit grundrechtsmotivierter Rechtsfortbildung im Steuerrecht ist auch problematisch, dass die Abwägung häufig nur darauf bezogen wird, ob aus der Rechtswidrigkeit der Beweisbeschaffung ein Verwertungsverbot folgt. Logisch vorrangig ist aber die Prüfung, ob die Beschaffung eines Beweismittels überhaupt als rechtswidrig anzusehen ist; nur dann stellt sich die Frage der Verwertbarkeit. Richtigerweise darf die Rechtswidrigkeit der Beschaffung eines Beweismittels aber nicht vorschnell bejaht werden. Etwa ein Verstoß gegen das zivilrechtliche Persönlichkeitsrecht kann, da es sich um ein Rahmenrecht handelt, erst nach einer Interessenabwägung angenommen werden. Darüber hinaus liegt bei Notwehr kein rechtswidriger Eingriff vor (§ 227 I BGB). Gerade letzterem Aspekt trägt die Rechtsprechung häufig nicht Rechnung. Zwar fristet die „notwehrähnliche Lage" (zu Unrecht) ein Schattendasein, gleichwohl lassen sich im öffentlichen Recht – zu dem das Steuerrecht zählt – Notwehrlagen kaum seriös darstellen, da hier Situationen in denen der Staat sich gegenüber dem Steuerbürger nicht denkbar sind.

Allerdings ist zu sagen, dass das Berufen auf ein Beweisverwertungsverbot regelmäßig einen Gang vor die Höchstgerichte mit sich bringen wird, also einen langen Atem erfordert.

Gerade die Entwicklungen aufgrund der Bedrohungen durch den internationalen Terrorismus können in Zukunft dazu führen, dass immer mehr Bürgern Eingriffe in Ihre verfassungsrechtlich garantierten Grundrechte durch Überwachungsmaßnahmen des Staates drohen, bei denen eventuell Beweise für Abgabenverkürzungen gefunden werden. Im Rahmen des Nemo-tenetur-Prinzips und den allgemeinen Grundsätzen der Bundesrepublik Deutschland als Rechtstaat zu Folge, sollte allerdings peinlich darauf geachtet werden, diese Grundrechte nicht mehr zu dehnen, als es zur Abwehr von Katalogstraftaten, die als so genannte „Großgefahren" Eingang in die Rechtsdogmatik gefunden haben, notwendig und erforderlich ist, da Beweisverwertungsverbote vor allem dazu gedacht sind, den Bürger vor überschießenden Ermittlungseingriffen des Rechtstaates zu schützen, indem solche Ermittlungshandlungen mit Beweisverwertungsverboten belegt werden, die gegen rechtstaatliche Prinzipien verstoßen.

Problematisch ist auch die immer wieder geäußerte Ansicht, dass die für die Verwertbarkeit maßgebliche Abwägung „im Regelfall" zum Nachteil des Beweisführers ausfalle und eine Verwertung „nur in Ausnahmefällen" möglich sei. Mit dieser

Abwägungsregel wird das Verwertungsverbot zum Automatismus, obwohl doch dem grundrechtlich geschützten Persönlichkeitsrecht das gleichrangige Recht auf richterliches Gehör aus Art. 103 I GG gegenüber steht. De lege lata ist ein Rangverhältnis zwischen den konkurrierenden Rechten der Prozessparteien Finanzverwaltung / Staat vs. Steuerbürger nicht begründbar. Statt einer abstrakten Bewertung ist daher eine Einzelfallprüfung erforderlich, die sowohl die Intensität der Persönlichkeitsbeeinträchtigung als auch die Beweisinteressen berücksichtigt.

Beweisverwertungsverbote stellen eine erhebliche Belastung für den Beweisführer bei der Verwirklichung seiner materiellen Rechtspositionen dar und greifen in das grundrechtsgleiche Recht aus Art. 103 I GG ein. Vor diesem Hintergrund ist bereits bei der Annahme Vorsicht geboten, ein bestimmtes Beweismittel sei rechtswidrig erlangt. Dabei ist auf den konkreten Einzelfall abzustellen, wie schon die Rechtsprechung der Höchstgerichte zeigt: Nicht jeder Eingriff in das Recht am eigenen Wort ist auch rechtswidrig, und nach der hier vertretenen Ansicht ist selbst im Falle einer

notwehrähnlichen Lage die Rechtmäßigkeit der Beweisbeschaffung und damit die Verwertbarkeit zu bejahen. Auch
wird eine Rechtfertigung nach § 227 I BGB bzw. auf Grund
einer „notwehrähnlichen Lage" zumindest zu erörtern sein.
Dabei wird man nicht nur der Intensität des Eingriffs, sondern auch dem Umstand Bedeutung beimessen dürfen, ob
der Beweisführer für die Art und Weise der Beweisbeschaffung einen nachvollziehbaren Anlass hatte und es um Straftaten geht, die praktisch nicht anders aufgeklärt werden
können. Selbst wenn ein Beweismittel rechtswidrig erlangt
sein sollte, ist zu fragen, ob im Einzelfall der Eingriff in das
Persönlichkeitsrecht so schwer wiegt, dass es gerechtfertigt
ist, den Beweisführer der Gefahr des Verlusts materieller
Rechte auszusetzen.

Die Entscheidung zu den Steuer-CD-Fällen sind meist unzureichend begründet und überzeugen bereits aus diesem
Grunde nicht. Den Entscheidungen kann oft entnommen
werden, dass das „Klima" zwischen dem Antragsteller und
dem Gericht aus diversen Gründen ganz erheblich belastet

war. In geeigneten Fällen sollte der Beschluss eines FG Betroffene nicht davon abhalten, den Rechtsweg bei einem anderen Senat/Gericht zu beschreiten.

Die weit verbreitete Praxis, bei vermuteter Steuerhinterziehung Steuerschätzungen durchzuführen ist in vielen Fällen unzulässig bzw. unzureichend begründet. Lediglich dann, wenn die Tatbestandsvoraussetzungen der Steuerhinterziehung dem Grunde nach mit an Sicherheit grenzender Wahrscheinlichkeit feststehen, ist eine Schätzung der Steuern der Höhe nach erlaubt. Unabhängig hiervon kann aber – je nach Fallgestaltung - eine Vorlage von Unterlagen und eine Einigung mit den Ermittlungsbehörden durchaus sinnvoll sein.

Literaturverzeichnis

A. Monographien, Handbücher, Sammelwerken, Artikel in Periodika

Baumbach/ Lauterbach/ Albers/ Hartmann, Beck´scher Kurzkommentar Zivilprozessordnung, 61. Aufl., München 2003

Borowski, Martin, Die Glaubens- und Gewissensfreiheit des Grundgesetzes, Habilitationsschrift, Kiel, 2004

Brockhaus in 15 Bänden, Brockhaus Verlag, Mannheim 2001

Gottwald, Peter, Prof. Dr., Einführung zur ZPO, Beck-Texte im DTV Zivilrechtssammlung, 41. Aufl., München 2006

Gräber, Fritz, Finanzgerichtsordnung Kommentar, 3. Auflage, Verlag C.H. Beck, München 1993

Häberle, Peter, Jahrbuch des öffentlichen Rechts, Band 48, Verlag Mohr Siebeck, Tübingen 2001

Klein, Franz, Abgabenordnung Kommentar, 8. Aufl., Verlag C.H. Beck, München 2003

Maunz/ Dürig, Grundgesetz, Loseblatt-Kommentar, 47. Ergänzungslieferung, Stand 03/2006

Meyer-Goßner, Lutz, Beck´scher Kurzkommentar Strafprozessordnung, 50. Aufl., München 2007

Salditt, Franz, Praxis Steuerstrafrecht, Verwertungsverbot – Liechtenstein: Fragen und Argumente, Vogel IWW, Ausgabe 4/2008 Seite 84ff.

Stahl, Rudolf & Demuth, Dr. Ralf, Strafrechtliches Verwertungsverbot bei Verletzung des Steuergeheimnisses, Steuerrecht Praxisforum, DStR 13/2008

Stalinski, Dirk, „Aussagefreiheit und Geständnisbonus", Dissertation, Juristische Fakultät der Heinrich-Heine-Universität, Düsseldorf 2000

Volk, Klaus, Strafprozessrecht, 2. Aufl., München 2001

Wenzig, Herbert, Steuerliche Betriebsprüfung, Verlag Erich Fleischer, 8. Auflage, Aachen 2000

B.   Internetquellen

Wikipedia – Früchte des vergifteten Baumes – Hintergrundrecherche

http://de.wikipedia.org, Zugriffsdatum 30. März 2020

LGT Bank, Liechtenstein – Hintergrund Datendiebstahl durch Heinrich Klieber

http://www.lgt.com, Zugriffsdatum 11. Mai 2008

C.   Entscheidungen oberster Gerichte

I.   Internationale Höchstgerichte

Supreme Court of the United States of America, Miranda vs. Arizona, 384, U.S. 436 (1966)

Supreme Court of the United States of America, Nardone et al vs. United States, 308 U.S. 338 (1939)

Supreme Court of the United States of America, Weeks vs. United States, 232 U.S. 383 (1914)

Supreme Court of the United States of America, Silverthorne Lumber Co. vs. United States, 251 U.S. 385 (1920)

Supreme Court of the United States of America, Wong Sun vs. United States, 371 U.S. 471 (1963)

Supreme Court of the United States of America, United States vs. Ceccolini, 435 U.S. 268 (1978)

Verwaltungsgerichtshof der Republik Österreich, Urteil vom 25. Juni 1997, 96/15/0225

II. Deutsche Höchstgerichte

Bundesverfassungsgericht, Urteil vom 15. Februar 2006 - 1 BvR 357/05 –

Bundesverfassungsgericht, Urteil vom 15. Dezember 1983 - 1 BvR 209, 269, 362, 420, 440, 484/83

Bundesverfassungsgericht, Urteil vom 03. März 2004 – 1 BvR 2378/98, 1 BvR 1084/99

Bundesverfassungsgericht, Urteil vom 14. Juli 1999 – 1 BvR 226/94; 2420/95; 2437/95

Bundesgerichtshof, Urteil vom 10. August 2005 – 1 StR 140/05

Bundesverfassungsgericht, Beschluss vom 25. März 1980 – 2 BvR 208/76

Bundesverfassungsgericht, Beschluss vom 14. September 1989 – 2 BvR 1062/87

Bundesgerichtshof, Beschluss vom 27. Februar 1992 - 5 StR 190/91

Bundesfinanzhof, Urteil vom 27.07.1983 – I R 210/79

Bundesfinanzhof, Beschluss vom 26. Februar 2001 – VII B 265/00

Oberlandesgericht Frankfurt am Main, Urteil vom 20. Dezember 1995, 3 VAs 25-26/97

Bundesfinanzhof, 2.7.1998, BStBl 1999, II 28; BFH, 7.11.2006, VIII R 81/04

Bundesverfassungsgericht v. 09.11.2010, 2 BvR 2101/09

Bundesfinanzhof v. 08.01.2014 . X B112, 113/13

D. Verwaltungsanweisungen

Verordnung EWG 2913/92 – Zollkodex

BMF-Schreiben vom 01. Juli 1993, IV A 5 - S 0130 - 41/93

Anlage 1:

U.S. Supreme Court

NARDONE v. UNITED STATES, 308 U.S. 338 (1939)

308 U.S. 338

NARDONE et al.
v.
UNITED STATES.
No. 240.

Argued Nov. 14, 1939.
Decided Dec. 11, 1939.

Mr. David V. Cahill, of New York City, for petitioner Nardone.

Mr. Jesse Climenko, of New York City, for petitioner Hoffman.

Mr. Louis Halle, of New York City, for petitioner Gottfried.

O. John Rogge, Asst. Atty. Gen., for respondent. [308 U.S. 338, 339]

Mr. Justice FRANKFURTER delivered the opinion of the Court.

We are called upon for the second time to review affirmance by the Circuit Court of Appeals for the Second Circuit of petitioners' convictions under an indictment for frauds on the revenue. In Nardone v. United States, 302 U.S. 379 , 58 S.Ct.

275, this Court reversed the convictions on the first trial because they were procured by evidence secured in violation of 605 of the Communications Act of 1934, c. 652, 48 Stat. 1064, 1103; 47 U.S.C., 605, 47 U.S.C.A. 605. For details of the facts reference is made to that case. Suffice it here to say that this evidence consisted of intercepted telephone messages, constituting 'a vital part of the prosecution's proof'.

Conviction followed a new trial, and 'the main question' on the appeal below is the only question open here-namely, 'whether the (trial) judge improperly refused to allow the accused to examine the prosecution as to the uses to which it had put the information' which Nardone v. United States, supra, found to have vitiated the original conviction. Though candidly doubtful of the result it reached, the Circuit Court of Appeals limited the scope of 605 to the precise circumstances before this Court in the first Nardone case, and ruled that 'Congress had not also made incompetent testimony which had become accessible by the use of unlawful 'taps', for to divulge that information was not to divulge an intercepted telephone talk.' 2 Cir., 106 F.2d 41, 44.

The issue thus tendered by the Circuit Court of Appeals is the broad one, whether or no 605 merely interdicts the introduction into evidence in a federal trial of intercepted telephone conversations, leaving the prosecution free to make every other use of the proscribed evidence. Plainly, this presents a far-reaching problem in [308 U.S. 338, 340] the administration of federal criminal justice, and we therefore brought the case here for disposition. 308 U.S. 539 , 60 S.Ct. 103, 84 L.Ed. --.

Any claim for the exclusion of evidence logically relevant in criminal prosecutions is heavily handicapped. It must be justified by an over-riding public policy expressed in the Constitution or the law of the land. In a problem such as that before us now, two opposing concerns must be harmonized: on the one hand, the stern enforcement of the criminal law; on the other, protection of that realm of privacy left free by Constitution and laws but capable of infringement either through zeal or design. In accommodating both these concerns, meaning must be given to what Congress has written, even if not in explicit language, so as to effectuate the policy which Congress has formulated.

We are here dealing with specific prohibition of particular methods in obtaining evidence. The result of the holding below is to reduce the scope of 605 to exclusion of the exact words heard through forbidden interceptions, allowing these interceptions every derivative use that they may serve. Such a reading of 605 would largely stultify the policy which compelled our decision in Nardone v. United States, supra. That decision was not the product of a merely meticulous reading of technical language. It was the translation into practicality of broad considerations of morality and public well-being. This Court found that the logically relevant proof which Congress had outlawed, it outlawed because 'inconsistent with ethical standards and destructive of personal liberty.' 302 U.S. 379, 384, 58 S.Ct. 275, 277. To forbid the direct use of methods thus characterized but to put no curb on their full indirect use would only invite the very methods deemed 'inconsistent with ethical standards and destructive of personal liberty.' What was said in a different context in Silverthorne Lumber Co. v. United States, 251 U.S. 385, 392, 40 S.Ct. 182, 183, 24 A.L.R. 1426, is pertinent here: 'The essence of a pro- [308 U.S. 338, 341] vision forbidding the acquisition of evidence in a certain way is that not merely evidence so acquired shall not be used before the Court but that it shall not be used at all.' See Gouled v. United States, 255 U.S. 298, 307 , 41 S.Ct. 261, 264. A decent respect for the policy of Congress must save us from imputing to it a self-defeating, if not disingenuous purpose.

Here, as in the Silverthorne case, the facts improperly obtained do not 'become sacred and inaccessible. If knowledge of them is gained from an independent source they may be proved like any others, but the knowledge gained by the Government's own wrong cannot be used by it' simply because it is used derivatively. 251 U.S. 385, 392 , 40 S.Ct. 182, 183, 24 A.L.R. 1426

In practice this generalized statement may conceal concrete complexities. Sophisticated argument may prove a causal connection between information obtained through illicit wiretapping and the Government's proof. As a matter of good sense, however, such connection may have become so attenuated as to dissipate the taint. A sensible way of dealing with such a situation-fair to the intendment of 605, but fair also to the purposes of the criminal law-ought to be within the reach of experienced trial judges. The burden is, of course, on the accused in the first instance to prove to the trial court's satisfaction that wire-tapping was unlawfully employed. Once that is established-as was plainly done here-the trial judge must give opportunity, however closely confined, to the accused to prove that a substantial portion of the case against him was a fruit of the poisonous tree. This leaves ample opportunity to the Government to convince the trial court that its proof had an independent origin.

Dispatch in the trial of criminal causes is essential in bringing crime to book. Therefore, timely steps must be taken to secure judicial determination of claims of illegality on the part of agents of the Government in obtain- [308 U.S. 338, 342] ing testimony. To interrupt the course of the trial for such auxiliary inquiries impedes the momentum of the main proceeding and breaks the continuity of the jury's attention. Like mischief would result were tenuous claims sufficient to justify the trial court's indulgence of inquiry into the legitimacy of evidence in the Government's possession. So to read a Congressional prohibition against the availability of certain evidence would be to subordinate the need for rigorous administration of justice to undue solicitude for potential and, it is to be hoped, abnormal disobedience of the law by the law's officers. Therefore claims that taint attaches to any portion of the Government's case must satisfy the trial court with their solidity and not be merely a means of eliciting what is in the Government's possession before its submission to the jury. And if such a claim is made after the trial is under way, the judge must likewise be satisfied that the accused could not at an earlier stage have had adequate knowledge to make his claim. The civilized conduct of criminal trials cannot be confined within mechanical rules. It necessarily demands the authority of limited direction entrusted to the judge presiding in federal trials, including a well-established range of judicial discretion, subject to appropriate review on appeal, in ruling upon preliminary questions of fact. Such a system as ours must, within the limits here indicated, rely on the learning, good sense, fairness and courage of federal trial judges.

We have dealt with this case on the basic issue tendered by the Circuit Court of Appeals and have not indulged in a finicking appraisal of the record, either as to the issue of the time limit of the proposed inquiry into the use to which the Government had put its illicit practices, or as to the existence of independent sources for the Government's proof. Since the Circuit Court of Appeals did [308 U.S. 338, 343] not question its timeliness, we shall not. And the hostility of the trial court to the whole scope of the inquiry reflected his own accord with the rule of law by which the Circuit Court of Appeals sustained him, and which we find erroneous.

The judgment must be reversed and remanded to the District Court for further proceedings in conformity with this opinion.

REVERSED.

Mr. Justice McREYNOLDS is of opinion that the Circuit Court of Appeals reached the proper conclusion upon reasons there adequately stated and its judgment should be affirmed.

Mr. Justice REED took no part in the consideration or decision of this case.

Anlage 2:

U.S. Supreme Court

WEEKS v. U.S., 232 U.S. 383 (1914)

232 U.S. 383

FREMONT WEEKS, Plff. in Err.,
v.
UNITED STATES.
No. 461.

Argued and submitted December 2 and 3, 1913.
Decided February 24, 1914.

[232 U.S. 383, 384]   Mr. Martin J. O'Donnell for plaintiff in error.

[232 U.S. 383, 385]   Assistant Attorney General Denison and Solicitor General Davis for defendant in error.

[232 U.S. 383, 386]

Mr. Justice Day delivered the opinion of the court:

An indictment was returned against the plaintiff in error, defendant below, and herein so designated, in the district court of the United States for the western district of Missouri, containing nine counts. The seventh count, upon which a conviction was had, charged the use of the mails for the purpose of transporting certain coupons or tickets representing chances or shares in a lottery or gift enterprise, in violation of 213 of the Criminal Code [35 Stat. at L. 1129, chap. 321, U. S. Comp. Stat. Supp. 1911, p. 1652]. Sentence of fine and imprisonment was imposed. This writ of error is to review that judgment.

The defendant was arrested by a police officer, so far as the record shows, without warrant, at the Union Station in Kansas City, Missouri, where he was employed by an express company. Other police officers had gone to the house of the defendant, and being told by a neighbor where the key was kept, found it and entered the house. They searched the defendant's room and took possession of various papers and articles found there, which were afterwards turned over to the United States marshal. Later in the same day police officers returned with the marshal, who thought he might find additional evidence, and, being admitted by someone in the house, probably a boarder, in response to a rap, the marshal searched the defendant's room and carried away certain letters and envelops found in the drawer of a chiffonier. Neither the marshal nor the police officer had a search warrant. [232 U.S. 383, 387] The defendant filed in the cause before the time for trial the following petition:

Petition to Return Private Papers, Books, and Other Property.

Now comes defendant and states that he is a citizen and resident of Kansas City, Missouri, and that he resides, owns, and occupies a home at 1834 Penn street in said city:

That on the 21st day of December, 1911, while plaintiff was absent at his daily vocation, certain officers of the government whose names are to plaintiff unknown, unlawfully and without warrant or authority so to do, broke open the door to plaintiff's said home and seized all of his books, letters, money, papers, notes, evidences of indebtedness, stock, certificates, insurance policies, deeds, abstracts, and other muniments of title, bonds, candies, clothes, and other property in said home, and this in violation of 11 and 23 to the Constitution of Missouri, and of the 4th and 5th Amendments to the Constitution of the United States;

That the district attorney, marshal, and clerk of the United States court for the western district of Missouri took the above-described property so seized into their possession, and have failed and refused to return to defendant portion of same, to wit:

One (1) leather grip, value about $7; one (1) tin box valued at $3; one (1) Pettis county, Missouri, bond, value $500; three (3) mining stock certificates which defendant is unable to more particularly describe, valued at $12,000; and certain stock certificates in addition thereto, issued by the San Domingo Mining, Loan, & Investment Company; about $75 in currency; one (1) newspaper published about 1790, an heirloom; and certain other property which plaintiff is now unable to describe.

That said property is being unlawfully and improperly [232 U.S. 383, 388]   held by said district attorney, marshal, and clerk, in violation of defendant's rights under the Constitution of the United States and the state of Missouri.

That said district attorney purposes to use said books, letters, papers, certificates of stock, etc., at the trial of the above-entitled cause, and that by reason thereof and of the facts above set forth defendant's rights under the amendments aforesaid to the Constitution of Missouri and the United States have been and will be violated unless the court order the return prayed for;

Wherefore, defendant prays that said district attorney, marshal, and clerk be notified, and that the court direct and order said district attorney, marshal, and clerk, to return said property to said defendant.

Upon consideration of the petition the court entered in the cause an order directing the return of such property as was not pertinent to the charge against the defendant, but denied the petition as to pertinent matter, reserving the right to pass upon the pertinency at a later time. In obedience to the order the district attorney returned part of the property taken, and retained the remainder, concluding a list of the latter with the statement that, 'all of which last above described property is to be used in evidence in the trial of the above-entitled cause, and pertains to the alleged sale of lottery tickets of the company above named.'

After the jury had been sworn and before any evidence had been given, the defendant again urged his petition for the return of his property, which was denied by the court. Upon the introduction of such papers during the trial, the defendant objected on the ground that the papers had been obtained without a search warrant, and by breaking open his home, in violation of the 4th and 5th Amendments to the Constitution of the United States, which objection was overruled by the court. Among the papers retained and put in evidence were a number of [232 U.S. 383, 389] lottery tickets and statements with reference to the lottery, taken at the first visit of the police to the defendant's room, and a number of letters written to the defendant in respect to the lottery, taken by the marshal upon his search of defendant's room.

The defendant assigns error, among other things, in the court's refusal to grant his petition for the return of his property, and in permitting the papers to be used at the trial.

It is thus apparent that the question presented involves the determination of the duty of the court with reference to the motion made by the defendant for the return of certain letters, as well as other papers, taken from his room by the United States marshal, who, without authority of process, if any such could have been legally issued, visited the room of the defendant for the declared purpose of obtaining additional testimony to support the charge against the accused, and, having gained admission to the house, took from the drawer of a chiffonier there found certain letters written to the defendant, tending to show his guilt. These letters were placed in the control of the district attorney, and were subsequently produced by him and offered in evidence against the accused at the trial. The defendant contends that such appropriation of his private correspondence was in violation of rights secured to him by the 4th and 5th Amendments to the Constitution of the United States. We shall deal with the 4th Amendment, which provides:

'The right of the people to be secure in their persons, houses, papers, and effects, against unreasonable searches and seizures, shall not be violated, and no warrants shall issue but upon probable cause, supported by oath or affirmation, and particularly describing the place to be searched, and the persons or things to be seized.'

The history of this Amendment is given with particularity in the opinion of Mr. Justice Bradley, speaking for [232 U.S. 383, 390] the court in Boyd v. United States, 116 U.S. 616 , 29 L. ed. 746, 6 Sup. Ct. Rep. 524. As was there shown, it took its origin in the determination of the framers of the Amendments to the Federal Constitution to provide for that instrument a Bill of Rights, securing to the American people, among other things, those safeguards which had grown up in England to protect the people from unreasonable searches and seizures, such as were permitted under the general warrants issued under authority of the government, by which there had been invasions of the home and privacy of the citizens, and the seizure of their private papers in support of charges, real or imaginary, make against them. Such practices had also received sanction under warrants and seizures under the so-called writs of assistance, issued in the American colonies. See 2 Watson, Const. 1414 et seq. Resistance to these practices had established the principle which was enacted into the fundamental law in the 4th Amendment, that a man's house was his castle, and not to be invaded by any general authority to search and seize his goods and papers. Judge Cooley, in his Constitutional Limitations, pp. 425, 426, in treating of this feature of our Constitution said: 'The maxim that 'every man's house is his castle' is made a part of our constitutional law in the clauses prohibiting unreasonable searches and seizures, and has always been looked upon as of high value to the citizen.' 'Accordingly,' says Lieber in his work on Civil Liberty and Self-Government, 62, in speaking of the English law in this respect, 'no man's house can be forcibly opened, or he or his goods be carried away after it has thus been forced, except in cases of felony; and then the sheriff must be furnished with a warrant, and take great care lest he commit a trespass. This principle is jealously insisted upon.' In Ex parte

Jackson, 96 U.S. 727, 733 , 24 S. L. ed. 877, 879, this court recognized the principle of protection as applicable to letters and sealed packages in the mail, and held that, consistently [232 U.S. 383, 391]   with this guaranty of the right of the people to be secure in their papers against unreasonable searches and seizures, such matter could only be opened and examined upon warrants issued on oath or affirmation, particularly describing the thing to be seized, 'as is required when papers are subjected to search in one's own household.'

In the Boyd Case, supra, after citing Lord Camden's judgment in Entick v. Carrington, 19 How. St. Tr. 1029, Mr. Justice Bradley said (630):

'The principles laid down in this opinion affect the very essence of constitutional liberty and security. They reach farther than the concrete form of the case then before the court, with its adventitious circumstances; they apply to all invasions on the part of the government and its employees of the sanctity of a man's home and the privacies of life. It is not the breaking of his doors and the rummaging of his drawers that constitutes the essence of the offense; but it is the invasion of his indefeasible right of personal security, personal liberty, and private property, where that right has never been forfeited by his conviction of some public offense,-it is the invasion of this sacred right which underlies and constitutes the essence of Lord Camden's judgment.'

In Bram v. United States, 168 U.S. 532 , 42 L. ed. 568, 18 Sup. Ct. Rep. 183, 10 Am. Crim. Rep. 547, this court, in speaking by the present Chief Justice of Boyd's Case, dealing with the 4th and 5th Amendments, said (544):

'It was in that case demonstrated that both of these Amendments contemplated perpetuating, in their full efficacy, by means of a constitutional provision, principles of humanity and civil liberty which had been secured in the mother country only after years of struggle, so as to implant them in our institutions in the fullness of their integrity, free from the possibilities of future legislative change.'

The effect of the 4th Amendment is to put the courts [232 U.S. 383, 392] of the United States and Federal officials, in the exercise of their power and authority, under limitations and restraints as to the exercise of such power and authority, and to forever secure the people, their persons, houses, papers, and effects, against all unreasonable searches and seizures under the guise of law. This protection reaches all alike, whether accused of crime or not, and the duty of giving to it force and effect is obligatory upon all intrusted under our Federal system with the enforcement of the laws. The tendency of those who execute the criminal laws of the country to obtain conviction by means of unlawful seizures and enforced confessions, the latter often obtained after subjecting accused persons to unwarranted practices destructive of rights secured by the Federal Constitution, should find no sanction in the judgments of the courts, which are charged at all times with the support of the Constitution, and to which people of all conditions have a right to appeal for the maintenance of such fundamental rights.

What, then, is the present case? Before answering that inquiry specifically, it may be well by a process of exclusion to state what it is not. It is not an assertion of the right on the part of the government always recognized under English and American law, to search the person of the accused when legally arrested, to discover and seize the fruits or evidences of crime. This right has been uniformly maintained in many cases. 1 Bishop. Crim. Proc. 211; Wharton, Crim. Pl. & Pr. 8th ed. 60; Dillon v. O'Brien, 16 Cox, C. C. 245, I. R. L. R. 20 C. L. 300, 7 Am. Crim. Rep. 66. Nor is it the case of testimony offered at a trial where the court is asked to stop and consider the illegal means by which proofs, otherwise competent, were obtained,-of which we shall have occasion to treat later in this opinion. Nor is it the case of burglar's tools or other proofs of guilt found upon his arrest within his control. [232 U.S. 383, 393] The case in the aspect in which we are dealing with it involves the right of the court in a criminal prosecution to retain for the purposes of evidence the letters and correspondence of the accused, seized in his house in his absence and without his authority, by a United States marshal holding no warrant for his arrest and none for the search of his premises. The accused, without awaiting his trial, made timely application to the court for an order for the return of these letters, as well or other property. This application was denied, the letters retained and put in evidence, after a further application at the beginning of the trial, both applications asserting the rights of the accused under the 4th and 5th Amendments to the Constitution. If letters and private documents can thus be seized and held and used in evidence against a citizen accused of an offense, the protection of the 4th Amendment, declaring his right to be secure against such searches and seizures, is of no value, and, so far as those thus placed are concerned, might as well be stricken from the Constitution. The efforts of the courts and their officials to bring the guilty to punishment, praiseworthy as they are, are not to be aided by the sacrifice of those great principles established be years of endeavor and suffering which have resulted in their embodiment in the fundamental law of the land. The United States marshal could only have invaded the house of the accused when armed with a warrant issued as required by the Constitution, upon sworn information, and describing with reasonable particularity the thing for which the search was to be made. Instead, he acted without sanction of law, doubtless prompted by the desire to bring further proof to the aid of the government, and under color of his office undertook to make a seizure of private papers in direct violation of the constitutional prohibition against such action. Under such circumstances, without sworn information and particular description, not even an order of court would [232 U.S. 383, 394]   have justified such procedure; much less was it within the authority of the United States marshal to thus invade the house and privacy of the accused. In Adams v. New York, 192 U.S. 585 , 48 L. ed. 575, 24 Sup. Ct. Rep. 372, this court said that the 4th Amendment was intended to secure the citizen in person and property against unlawful invasion of the sanctity of his home by officers of the law, acting under legislative or judicial sanction. This protection is equally extended to the action of the government and officers of the law acting under it. Boyd Case, 116 U.S. 616 , 29 L. ed. 746, 6 Sup. Ct. Rep. 524. To sanction such proceedings would be to affirm by judicial decision a manifest neglect, if not an open defiance, of the prohibitions of the Constitution, intended for the protection of the people against such unauthorized action.

The court before which the application was made in this case recognized the illegal character of the seizure, and ordered the return of property not in its judgment competent to be offered at the trial, but refused the application of the accused to turn over the letters, which were afterwards put in evidence on behalf of the government. While there is no opinion in the case, the court in this proceeding doubtless relied upon what is now contended by the government to be the correct rule of law under such circumstances, that the letters having come into the control of the court, it would not inquire into the manner in which they were obtained, but, if competent, would keep them and permit their use in evidence. Such proposition, the government asserts, is conclusively established by certain decisions of this court, the first of which is

Adams v. New York, supra. In that case the plaintiff in error had been convicted in the supreme court of the state of New York for having in his possession certain gambling paraphernalia used in the game known as policy, in violation of the Penal Code of New York. At the trial certain papers, which had been seized by police officers executing a search warrant for the discovery and [232 U.S. 383, 395]   seizure of policy slips, and which had been found in addition to the policy slips, were offered in evidence over his objection. The conviction was affirmed by the court of appeals of New York (176 N. Y. 351, 63 L.R.A. 406, 98 Am. St. Rep. 675, 68 N. E. 636), and the case was brought here for alleged violation of the 4th and 5th Amendments to the Constitution of the United States. Pretermitting the question whether these Amendments applied to the action of the states, this court proceeded to examine the alleged violations of the 4th and 5th Amendments, and put its decision upon the ground that the papers found in the execution of the search warrant, which warrant had a legal purpose in the attempt to find gambling paraphernalia, was competent evidence against the accused, and their offer in testimony did not violate his constitutional privilege against unlawful search or seizure, for is was held that such incriminatory documents thus discovered were not the subject of an unreasonable search and seizure, and in effect that the same were incidentally seized in the lawful execution of a warrant, and not in the wrongful invasion of the home of a citizen, and the unwarranted seizure of his papers and property. It was further held, approving in that respect the doctrine laid down in 1 Greenleaf, Ev. 254a, that it was no valid objection to the use of the papers that they had been thus seized, and that the courts in the course of a trial would not make an issue to determine that question, and many state cases were cited supporting that doctrine.

The same point had been ruled in People v. Adams, 176 N. Y. 351, 63 L. R.A. 406, 98 Am. St. Rep. 675, 68 N. E. 636, from which decision the case was brought to this court, where it was held that if the papers seized in addition to the policy slips were competent evidence in the case, as the court held they were, they were admissible in evidence at the trial, the court saying (p. 358): 'The underlying principle obviously is that the court, when engaged in trying a criminal cause, will not take notice of [232 U.S. 383, 396] the manner in which witnesses have possessed themselves of papers, or other articles of personal property, which are material and properly offered in evidence.' This doctrine thus laid down by the New York court of appeals and approved by this court, that a court will not, in trying a criminal cause, permit a collateral issue to be raised as to the source of competent testimony, has the sanction of so many state cases that it would be impracticable to cite or refer to them in detail. Many of them are collected in the note to State v. Turner, 136 Am. St. Rep. 129, 135 et seq. After citing numerous cases the editor says: 'The underlying principle of all these decisions obviously is, that the court, when engaged in the trial of a criminal action, will not take notice of the manner in which a witness has possessed himself of papers or other chattels, subjects of evidence, which are material and properly offered in evidence. People v. Adams, supra. Such an investigation is not involved necessarily in the litigation in chief, and to pursue it would be to halt in the orderly progress of a cause, and consider incidentally a question which has happened to cross the path of such litigation, and which is wholly independent thereof.'

It is therefore evident that the Adams Case affords no authority for the action of the court in this case, when applied to in due season for the return of papers seized in violation of the Constitutional Amendment. The decision in that case rests upon incidental seizure made in the execution of a legal warrant, and in the application of the doctrine that a collateral issue will not be raised to ascertain the source from which testimony, competent in a criminal case, comes.

The government also relies upon Hale v. Henkel, 201 U.S. 43 , 50 L. ed. 652, 26 Sup. Ct. Rep. 370, in which the previous cases of Boyd v. United States, and Adams v. New York, supra; Interstate [232 U.S. 383, 397]   Commerce Commission v. Brimson, 154 U.S. 447 , 38 L. ed. 1047, 4 Inters. Com. Rep. 545, 14 Sup. Ct. Rep. 1125, and Interstate Commerce Commission v. Baird, 194 U.S. 25 , 48 L. ed. 860, 24 Sup. Ct. Rep. 563, are reviewed, and wherein it was held that a subpoena duces tecum requiring a corporation to produce all its contracts and correspondence with no less than six other companies, as well as all letters received by the corporation from thirteen other companies, located in different parts of the United States, was an unreasonable search and seizure within the 4th Amendment, and it was there stated that (p. 76) 'an order for the production of books and papers may constitute an unreasonable search and seizuer within the 4th Amendment. While a search ordinarily implies a quest by an officer of the law, and a seizure contemplates a forcible dispossession of the owner, still, as was held in the Boyd Case, the substance of the offense is the compulsory production of private papers, whether under a search warrant or a sub-poena duces tecum, against which the person, be he individual or corporation, is entitled to protection.' If such a seizure under the authority of a warrant supposed to be legal, constitutes a violation of the constitutional protection, a fortiori does the attempt of an officer of the United States, the United States marshal, acting under color of his office, without even the sanction of a warrant, constitute an invasion of the rights within the protection afforded by the 4th Amendment.

Another case relied upon is American Tobacco Co. v. Werckmeister, 207 U.S. 284 , 52 L. ed. 208, 28 Sup. Ct. Rep. 72, 12 Ann. Cas. 595, in which it was held that the seizure by the United States marshal in a copyright case of certain pictures under a writ of replevin did not constitute an unreasonable search and seizure. The other case from this court relied upon is Holt v. United States, 218 U.S. 245 , 54 L. ed. 1021, 31 Sup. Ct. Rep. 20, 20 Ann. Cas. 1138, in which it was held that testimony tending to show that a certain blouse which was in evidence as incriminating him, had been put upon the prisoner, and fitted him, did not violate his constitutional right. We [232 U.S. 383, 398]   are at a loss to see the application of these cases to the one in hand.

The right of the court to deal with papers and documents in the possession of the district attorney and other officers of the court, and subject to its authority, was recognized in Wise v. Henkel, 220 U.S. 556 , 55 L. ed. 581, 31 Sup. Ct. Rep. 599. That papers wrongfully seized should be turned over to the accused has been frequently recognized ognized in the early as well as later decisions of the courts. 1 Bishop, Crim. Proc. 210; Rex v. Barnett, 3 Car. & P. 600; Rex v. Kinsey, 7 Car. & P. 447; United States v. Mills, 185 Fed. 318; United States v. McHie, 194 Fed. 894, 898.

We therefore reach the conclusion that the letters in question were taken from the house of the accused by an official of the United States, acting under color of his office, in direct violation of the constitutional rights of the defendant; that having made a seasonable application for their return, which was heard and passed upon by the court, there was involved in the order refusing the application a denial of the constitutional rights of the accused, and that the court should have restored these letters to the accused. In holding them and permitting their use upon the trial, we think prejudicial error was committed. As to the papers and property seized by the policement, it does not appear that they acted under any claim of Federal authority such as would make the amendment applicable to such unauthorized seizures. The record shows that what they did by way of arrest and search and seizure was done before the finding of the indictment in the Federal court; under what supposed right or authority does not appear. What remedies the defendant may have against them we need not inquire, as the 4th Amendment is not directed to individual misconduct of such officials. Its limitations reach the Federal government and its agencies. Boyd Case, 116 U.S. 616 , 29 L. ed. 746, 6 Sup. Ct. Rep. 524, and see Twining v. New Jersey, 211 U.S. 78 , 53 L. ed. 97, 29 Sup. Ct. Rep. 14. [232 U.S. 383, 399] It results that the judgment of the court below must be reversed, and the case remanded for further proceedings in accordance with this opinion.

Reversed.

Anlage 3:

U.S. Supreme Court

SILVERTHORNE LUMBER CO. v. U S , 251 U.S. 385 (1920)

251 U.S. 385

SILVERTHORNE LUMBER CO., Inc., et al.
v.
UNITED STATES.
No. 358.

Argued Dec. 12, 1919.
Decided Jan. 26, 1920.

Messrs. Frederic D. McKenney and Myer Cohen, both of Washington, D. C ., and William D. Guthrie, of New York City, for plaintiffs in error.

Mr. Assistant Attorney General Stewart, for the United States.[Silverthorne Lumber Co. v. U S 251 U.S. 385 (1920)]

[251 U.S. 385, 390]

Mr. Justice HOLMES delivered the opinion of the Court.

This is a writ of error brought to reverse a judgment of the District Court fining the Silverthorne Lumber Company two hundred and fifty dollars for contempt of court and ordering Frederick W. Silverthorne to be imprisoned until he should purge himself of a similar contempt. The contempt in question was a refusal to obey subpoenas and an order of Court to produce books and documents of the company before the grand jury to be used in regard to alleged violation of the statutes of the United States by the said Silverthorne and his father. One ground of the refusal was that the order of the Court infringed the rights of the parties under the Fourth Amendment of the Constitution of the United States.

The facts are simple. An indictment upon a single specific charge having been brought against the two Silverthornes mentioned, they both were arrested at their homes early in the morning of February 25, and were detained in custody a number of hours. While they were thus detained representatives of the Department of Justice and the United States marshal without a shadow of authority went to the office of their company and made a clean sweep of all the books, papers and documents found there. All the employes were taken or directed to go to the office of the District Attorney of the United States to which also the books, &c., were taken at once. An application was made as soon as might be to the District [251 U.S. 385, 391]   Court for a return of what thus had been taken unlawfully. It was opposed by the District Attorney so far as he had found evidence against the plaintiffs in error, and it was stated that the evidence so obtained was before the grand jury. Color had been given by the District Attorney to the approach of those concerned in the act by an invalid subpoena for certain documents relating to the charge in the indictment then on file. Thus the case is not that of knowledge acquired through the wrongful act of a stranger, but it must be assumed that the Government planned or at all events ratified the whole performance. Photographs and copies of material papers were made and a new indictment was framed based upon the knowledge thus obtained. The District Court ordered a return of the originals but impounded the photographs and copies. Subpoenas to produce the originals then were served and on the refusal of the plaintiffs in error to produce them the Court made an order that the subpoenas should be complied with, although it had found that all the papers had been seized in violation of the parties' constitutional rights. The refusal to obey this order is the contempt alleged. The Government now, while in form repudiating and condemning the illegal seizure, seeks to maintain its right to avail itself of the knowledge obtained by that means which otherwise it would not have had.

The proposition could not be presented more nakedly. It is that although of course its seizure was an outrage which the Government now regrets, it may study the papers before it returns them, copy them, and then may use the knowledge that it has gained to call upon the owners in a more regular form to produce them; that the protection of the Constitution covers the physical possession but not any advantages that the Government can gain over the object of its pursuit by doing the forbidden act. Weeks v. United States, 232 U.S. 383 , 34 Sup. Ct. 341, L. R. A. 1915B, 834, Ann. Cas. 1915C, 1177, to be sure, had established that laying the papers directly before the grand jury was [251 U.S. 385, 392] unwarranted, but it is taken to mean only that two steps are required instead of one. In our opinion such is not the law. It reduces the Fourth Amendment to a form of words. 232 U.S. 393 , 34 Sup. Ct. 341, L. R. A. 1915B, 834, Ann. Cas. 1915C, 1177. The essence of a provision forbidding the acquisition of evidence in a certain way is that not merely evidence so acquired shall not be used before the Court but that it shall not be used at all. Of course this does not mean that the facts thus obtained become sacred and inaccessible. If knowledge of them is gained from an independent source they may be proved like any others, but the knowledge gained by the Government's own wrong cannot be used by it in the way proposed. The numberous decisions, like Adams v. New York, 192 U.S. 585 , 24 Sup. Ct. 372, holding that a collateral inquiry into the mode in which evidence has been got will not be allowed when the question is raised for the first time at the trial, are no authority in the present proceeding, as is explained in Weeks v. United States, 232 U.S. 383, 394 , 395 S., 34 Sup. Ct. 341, L. R. A. 1915B, 834, Ann. Cas. 1915C, 1177. Whether some of those decisions have gone too far or have given wrong reasons it is unnecessary to inquire; the principle applicable to the present case seems to us plain. It is stated satisfactorily in Flagg v. United States, 233 Fed. 481, 483, 147 C. C. A. 367. In Linn v. United States, 251 Fed. 476, 480, 163 C. C. A. 470, it was thought that a different rule applied to a corporation, on the ground that it was not privileged from producing its books and papers. But the rights of a corporation against unlawful search and seizure are to be protected even if the same result might have been achieved in a lawful way.

Judgment reversed.

The CHIEF JUSTICE and Mr. Justice PITNEY dissent.

Anlage 4:

U.S. Supreme Court

WONG SUN v. UNITED STATES, 371 U.S. 471 (1963)

371 U.S. 471

WONG SUN ET AL. v. UNITED STATES.
CERTIORARI TO THE UNITED STATES COURT OF APPEALS FOR THE NINTH CIR-
CUIT.
No. 36.
Argued March 29 and April 2, 1962. Restored to calendar for reargument June 4,
1962. Reargued October 8, 1962.
Decided January 14, 1963.

In a trial in a Federal District Court without a jury, petitioners were convicted of fraudulent and knowing transportation and concealment of illegally imported heroin, in violation of 21 U.S.C. 174. Although the Court of Appeals held that the arrests of both petitioners without warrants were illegal, because not based on "probable cause" within the meaning of the Fourth Amendment nor "reasonable grounds" within the meaning of the Narcotics Control Act of 1956, it affirmed their convictions, notwithstanding the admission in evidence over their timely objections of (1) statements made orally by petitioner Toy in his bedroom at the time of his arrest; (2) heroin surrendered to the agents by a third party as a result of those statements; and (3) unsigned statements made by each petitioner several days after his arrest, and after being lawfully arraigned and released on his own recognizance. The Court of Appeals held that these items were not the fruits of the illegal arrests, and, therefore, were properly admitted in evidence. Held:

1. On the record in this case, there was neither reasonable grounds nor probable cause for Toy's arrest, since the information upon which it was based was too vague and came from too untested a source to accept it as probable cause for the issuance of an arrest warrant; and this defect was not cured by the fact that Toy fled when a supposed customer at his door early in the morning revealed that he was a narcotics agent. Pp. 479-484.

2. On the record in this case, the statements made by Toy in his bedroom at the time of his unlawful arrest were the fruits of the agents' unlawful action, and they should have been excluded from evidence. Pp. 484-487.

3. The narcotics taken from a third party as a result of statements made by Toy at the time of his arrest were likewise fruits of the unlawful arrest, and they should not have been admitted as evidence against Toy. Pp. 487-488. [371 U.S. 471, 472]

4. After exclusion of the foregoing items of improperly admitted evidence, the only proofs remaining to sustain Toy's conviction are his and his codefendant's unsigned statements; any admissions of guilt in Toy's statement require corroboration; no reference to Toy in his codefendant's statement constitutes admissible evidence corroborating any admission by Toy; and Toy's conviction must be set aside for lack of competent evidence to support it. Pp. 488-491.

5. In view of the fact that, after his unlawful arrest, petitioner Wong Sun had been lawfully arraigned and released on his own recognizance and had returned voluntarily several days later when he made his unsigned statement, the connection between his unlawful arrest and the making of that statement was so attenuated that the unsigned statement was not the fruit of the unlawful arrest and, therefore, it was properly admitted in evidence. P. 491.

6. The seizure of the narcotics admitted in evidence invaded no right of privacy of person or premises which would entitle Wong Sun to object to its use at his trial. Pp. 491-492.

7. Any references to Wong Sun in his codefendant's statement were incompetent to corroborate Wong Sun's admissions, and Wong Sun is entitled to a new trial, because it is

not clear from the record whether or not the trial court relied upon his codefendant's statement as a source of corroboration of Wong Sun's confession. Pp. 492-493.

288 F.2d 366, reversed and cause remanded.

Edward Bennett Williams, acting under appointment by the Court, 368 U.S. 973 , reargued the cause and filed a supplemental brief for petitioners. Sol A. Abrams also filed a brief for petitioners.

J. William Doolittle reargued the cause for the United States. On the brief were Solicitor General Cox, Assistant Attorney General Miller, Beatrice Rosenberg and J. F. Bishop.

MR. JUSTICE BRENNAN delivered the opinion of the Court.

The petitioners were tried without a jury in the District Court for the Northern District of California under a two-count indictment for violation of the Federal Narcotics [371 U.S. 471, 473] Laws, 21 U.S.C. 174. 1 They were acquitted under the first count which charged a conspiracy, but convicted under the second count which charged the substantive offense of fraudulent and knowing transportation and concealment of illegally imported heroin. The Court of Appeals for the Ninth Circuit, one judge dissenting, affirmed the convictions. 288

F.2d 366. We granted certiorari. 368 U.S. 817 . We heard argument in the 1961 Term and reargument this Term. 370 U.S. 908 .

About 2 a. m. on the morning of June 4, 1959, federal narcotics agents in San Francisco, after having had one Hom Way under surveillance for six weeks, arrested him and found heroin in his possession. Hom Way, who had not before been an informant, stated after his arrest that he had bought an ounce of heroin the night before from one known to him only as "Blackie Toy," proprietor of a laundry on Leavenworth Street.

About 6 a. m. that morning six or seven federal agents went to a laundry at 1733 Leavenworth Street. The sign [371 U.S. 471, 474] above the door of this establishment said "Oye's Laundry." It was operated by the petitioner James Wah Toy. There is, however, nothing in the record which identifies James Wah Toy and "Blackie Toy" as the same person. The other federal officers remained nearby out of sight while Agent Alton Wong, who was of Chinese ancestry, rang the bell. When petitioner Toy appeared and opened the door, Agent Wong told him that he was calling for laundry and dry cleaning. Toy replied that he didn't open until 8 o'clock and told the agent to come back at that time. Toy started to close the door. Agent Wong thereupon took his badge from his pocket and said, "I am a federal narcotics agent." Toy immediately "slammed the door and started running" down the hallway through the laundry to his living quarters at the back where his wife and child were sleeping in a bedroom. Agent Wong and the other federal officers broke open the door and followed Toy down the hallway to the living quarters and into the bedroom. Toy reached into a nightstand drawer. Agent Wong thereupon drew his pistol, pulled Toy's hand out of the drawer, placed him under arrest and handcuffed him. There was nothing in the drawer and a search of the premises uncovered no narcotics.

One of the agents said to Toy ". . . [Hom Way] says he got narcotics from you." Toy responded, "No. I haven't been selling any narcotics at all. However, I do know somebody who has." When asked who that was, Toy said, "I only know him as Johnny. I don't know his last name." However, Toy described a house on Eleventh Avenue where he said Johnny lived; he also described a bedroom in the house where he said "Johnny kept about a piece" 2 of heroin and where he and Johnny had smoked some of the drug the night before.

The agents [371 U.S. 471, 475] left immediately for Eleventh Avenue and located the house. They entered and found one Johnny Yee in the bedroom. After a discussion with the agents, Yee took from a bureau drawer several tubes containing in all just less than one ounce of heroin, and surrendered them. Within the hour Yee and Toy were taken to the Office of the Bureau of Narcotics. Yee there stated that the heroin had been brought to him some four days earlier by petitioner Toy and another Chinese known to him only as "Sea Dog."

Toy was questioned as to the identity of "Sea Dog" and said that "Sea Dog" was Wong Sun. Some agents, including Agent Alton Wong, took Toy to Wong Sun's neighborhood where Toy pointed out a multifamily dwelling where he said Wong Sun lived. Agent Wong rang a downstairs door bell and a buzzer sounded, opening the door. The officer identified himself as a narcotics agent to a woman on the landing and asked "for Mr. Wong." The woman was the wife of petitioner Wong Sun. She said that Wong Sun was "in the back room sleeping." Alton Wong and some six other officers climbed the stairs and entered the apartment. One of the officers went into the back room and brought petitioner Wong

Sun from the bedroom in handcuffs. A thorough search of the apartment followed, but no narcotics were discovered.

Petitioner Toy and Johnny Yee were arraigned before a United States Commissioner on June 4 on a complaint charging a violation of 21 U.S.C. 174. Later that day, each was released on his own recognizance. Petitioner Wong Sun was arraigned on a similar complaint filed the next day and was also released on his own recognizance. 3 [371 U.S. 471, 476] Within a few days, both petitioners and Yee were interrogated at the office of the Narcotics Bureau by Agent William Wong, also of Chinese ancestry. 4 The agent advised each of the three of his right to withhold information which might be used against him, and stated to each that he was entitled to the advice of counsel, though it does not appear that any attorney was present during the questioning of any of the three. The officer also explained to each that no promises or offers of immunity or leniency were being or could be made.

The agent interrogated each of the three separately. After each had been interrogated the agent prepared a statement in English from rough notes. The agent read petitioner Toy's statement to him in English and interpreted certain portions of it for him in Chinese. Toy also read the statement in English aloud to the agent, said there were corrections to be made, and made the corrections in his own hand. Toy would not sign the statement, however; in the agent's words "he wanted to know first if the other persons involved in the case had signed theirs." Wong Sun had considerable difficulty understanding the [371 U.S. 471, 477]   statement in English and the agent restated its substance in Chinese. Wong Sun refused to sign the statement although he admitted the accuracy of its contents. 5

Hom Way did not testify at petitioners' trial. The Government offered Johnny Yee as its principal witness but excused him after he invoked the privilege against self-incrimination and flatly repudiated the statement he had given to Agent William Wong. That statement was not offered in evidence nor was any testimony elicited from him identifying either petitioner as the source of the heroin in his possession, or otherwise tending to support the charges against the petitioners.

The statute expressly provides that proof of the accused's possession of the drug will support a conviction under the statute unless the accused satisfactorily explains the possession. The Government's evidence tending to prove the petitioners' possession (the petitioners offered no exculpatory testimony) consisted of four items which the trial court admitted over timely objections that they were inadmissible as "fruits" of unlawful arrests or of attendant searches: (1) the statements made orally by petitioner Toy in his bedroom at the time of his arrest; (2) the heroin surrendered to the agents by Johnny Yee; (3) petitioner Toy's pretrial unsigned statement; and (4) petitioner Wong Sun's similar statement. The dispute below and here has centered around the correctness of the rulings of the trial judge allowing these items in evidence.

The Court of Appeals held that the arrests of both petitioners were illegal because not based on "'probable cause' within the meaning of the Fourth Amendment" nor "reasonable grounds" within the meaning of the Narcotic [371 U.S. 471, 478] Control Act of 1956. 6 The Court said as to Toy's arrest, "There is no showing in this case that the agent knew Hom Way to be reliable," and, furthermore, found "nothing in the circumstances occurring at Toy's premises that would provide sufficient justification for his arrest without a warrant." 288 F.2d, at 369, 370. As to Wong Sun's arrest, the Court said "there is no showing that Johnnie Yee was a reliable informer." The Court of Appeals nevertheless held that the four items of proof were not the "fruits" of the illegal arrests and that they were therefore properly admitted in evidence.

The Court of Appeals rejected two additional contentions of the petitioners. The first was that there was insufficient evidence to corroborate the petitioners' unsigned admissions of possession of narcotics. The court held that the narcotics in evidence surrendered by Johnny Yee, together with Toy's statements in his bedroom at the time of arrest corroborated petitioners' admissions. The second contention was that the confessions were [371 U.S. 471, 479]   inadmissible because they were not signed. The Court of Appeals held on this point that the petitioners were not prejudiced, since the agent might properly have testified to the substance of the conversations which produced the statements.

We believe that significant differences between the cases of the two petitioners require separate discussion of each. We shall first consider the case of petitioner Toy.

I.

The Court of Appeals found there was neither reasonable grounds nor probable cause for Toy's arrest. Giving due weight to that finding, we think it is amply justified by the facts clearly shown on this record. It is basic that an arrest with or without a warrant must stand upon firmer ground than mere suspicion, see Henry v. United States, 361 U.S. 98, 101 , though the arresting officer need not have in hand evidence which would suffice to convict. The quantum of information which constitutes probable cause - evidence which would "warrant a man of reasonable caution in the belief" that a felony has been committed, Carroll v. United States, 267 U.S. 132, 162 - must be measured by the facts of the particular case. The history of the use, and not infrequent abuse, of the power to arrest cautions that a relaxation of the fundamental requirements of probable cause would "leave law-abiding citizens at the mercy of the officers' whim or caprice." 7 Brinegar v. United States, 338 U.S. 160, 176 .

Whether or not the requirements of reliability and particularity of the information on which an officer may act are more stringent where an arrest warrant is absent, they surely cannot be less stringent than where an arrest warrant is obtained. Otherwise, a principal incentive now [371 U.S. 471, 480] existing for the procurement of arrest warrants would be destroyed. 8 The threshold question in this case, therefore, is whether the officers could, on the information which impelled them to act, have procured a warrant for the arrest of Toy. We think that no warrant would have issued on evidence then available.

The narcotics agents had no basis in experience for confidence in the reliability of Hom Way's information; he had never before given information. And yet they acted upon his imprecise suggestion that a person described only as "Blackie Toy," the proprietor of a laundry somewhere on Leavenworth Street, had sold one ounce of heroin. We have held that identification of the suspect by a reliable informant may constitute probable cause for arrest where the information given is sufficiently accurate to lead the officers directly to the suspect. Draper v. United States, 358 U.S. 307 . That rule does not, however, fit this case. For aught that the record discloses, Hom Way's accusation merely invited the officers to roam the length of Leavenworth Street (some 30 blocks) in search of one "Blackie Toy's" laundry - and whether by chance or other [371 U.S. 471, 481] means (the record does not say) they came upon petitioner Toy's laundry, which bore not his name over the door, but the unrevealing label "Oye's." Not the slightest intimation appears on the record, or was made on oral argument, to suggest that the agents had information giving them reason to equate

"Blackie" Toy and James Wah Toy - e. g., that they had the criminal record of a Toy, or that they had consulted some other kind of official record or list, or had some information of some kind which had narrowed the scope of their search to this particular Toy.

It is conceded that the officers made no attempt to obtain a warrant for Toy's arrest. The simple fact is that on the sparse information at the officers' command, no arrest warrant could have issued consistently with Rules 3 and 4 of the Federal Rules of Criminal Procedure. Giordenello v. United States, 357 U.S. 480, 486 . 9 The arrest warrant procedure serves to insure that the deliberate, impartial judgment of a judicial officer will be interposed [371 U.S. 471, 482] between the citizen and the police, to assess the weight and credibility of the information which the complaining officer adduces as probable cause. Cf. Jones v. United States, 362 U.S. 257, 270 . To hold that an officer may act in his own, unchecked discretion upon information too vague and from too untested a source to permit a judicial officer to accept it as probable cause for an arrest warrant, would subvert this fundamental policy.

The Government contends, however, that any defects in the information which somehow took the officers to petitioner Toy's laundry were remedied by events which occurred after they arrived. Specifically, it is urged that Toy's flight down the hall when the supposed customer at the door revealed that he was a narcotics agent adequately corroborates the suspicion generated by Hom Way's accusation. Our holding in Miller v. United States, 357 U.S. 301 , is relevant here, and exposes the fallacy of this contention. We noted in that case that the lawfulness of an officer's entry to arrest without a warrant "must be tested by criteria identical with those embodied in 18 U.S.C. 3109, which deals with entry to execute a search warrant." 357 U.S., at 306 . That statute requires that an officer must state his authority and his purpose at the threshold, and be refused admittance, before he may break open the door. We held that when an officer insufficiently or unclearly identifies his office or his mission, the occupant's flight from the door must be regarded as ambiguous conduct. We expressly reserved the question "whether the unqualified requirements of the rule admit of an exception justifying non-compliance in exigent circumstances." 357 U.S., at 309 . In the instant case, Toy's flight from the door afforded no surer an inference of guilty knowledge than did the suspect's conduct in the Miller case. Agent Wong did eventually disclose that he was a narcotics officer. However, he affirmatively misrepresented his mission at the [371 U.S. 471, 483]   outset, by stating that he had come for laundry and dry cleaning. And before Toy fled, the officer never adequately dispelled the misimpression engendered by his own ruse. Cf. Gouled v. United States, 255 U.S. 298 ; Gatewood v. United States, 209 F.2d 789.

Moreover, he made no effort at that time, nor indeed at any time thereafter, to ascertain whether the man at the door was the "Blackie Toy" named by Hom Way. Therefore, this is not the case we hypothesized in Miller where "without an express announcement of purpose, the facts known to officers would justify them in being virtually certain" that the person at the door knows their purpose. 357 U.S., at 310 . Toy's refusal to admit the officers and his flight down the hallway thus signified a guilty knowledge no more clearly than it did a natural desire to repel an apparently unauthorized intrusion. 10 Here, as in Miller, [371 U.S. 471, 484]   the Government claims no extraordinary circumstances - such as the imminent destruction of vital evidence, or the need to rescue a victim in peril -

see 357 U.S., at 309 - which excused the officer's failure truthfully to state his mission before he broke in.

A contrary holding here would mean that a vague suspicion could be transformed into probable cause for arrest by reason of ambiguous conduct which the arresting officers themselves have provoked. Cf. Henry v. United States, 361 U.S. 98, 104 . That result would have the same essential vice as a proposition we have consistently rejected - that a search unlawful at its inception may be validated by what it turns up. Byars v. United States, 273 U.S. 28 ; United States v. Di Re, 332 U.S. 581, 595 . Thus we conclude that the Court of Appeals' finding that the officers' uninvited entry into Toy's living quarters was unlawful and that the bedroom arrest which followed was likewise unlawful, was fully justified on the evidence. It remains to be seen what consequences flow from this conclusion.

II.

It is conceded that Toy's declarations in his bedroom are to be excluded if they are held to be "fruits" of the agents' unlawful action.

In order to make effective the fundamental constitutional guarantees of sanctity of the home and inviolability of the person, Boyd v. United States, 116 U.S. 616 , this Court held nearly half a century ago that evidence seized during an unlawful search could not constitute proof against the victim of the search. Weeks v. United States, 232 U.S. 383 . The exclusionary prohibition extends as well to the indirect as the direct products of such invasions. Silverthorne Lumber Co. v. United States, [371 U.S. 471, 485] 251 U.S. 385 . Mr. Justice Holmes, speaking for the Court in that case, in holding that the Government might not make use of information obtained during an unlawful search to subpoena from the victims the very documents illegally viewed, expressed succinctly the policy of the broad exclusionary rule:

"The essence of a provision forbidding the acquisition of evidence in a certain way is that not merely evidence so acquired shall not be used before the Court but that it shall not be used at all. Of course this does not mean that the facts thus obtained become sacred and inaccessible. If knowledge of them is gained from an independent source they may be proved like any others, but the knowledge gained by the Government's own wrong cannot be used by it in the way proposed." 251 U.S., at 392 .

The exclusionary rule has traditionally barred from trial physical, tangible materials obtained either during or as a direct result of an unlawful invasion. It follows from our holding in Silverman v. United States, 365 U.S. 505 , that the Fourth Amendment may protect against the overhearing of verbal statements as well as against the more traditional seizure of "papers and effects." Similarly, testimony as to matters observed during an unlawful invasion has been excluded in order to enforce the basic constitutional policies. McGinnis v. United States, 227 F.2d 598. Thus, verbal evidence which derives so immediately from an unlawful entry and an unauthorized arrest as the officers' action in the present case is no less the "fruit" of official illegality than the more common tangible fruits of the unwarranted intrusion. 11 See [371 U.S. 471, 486]   Nueslein v. District of Columbia, 115 F.2d 690. Nor do the policies underlying the exclusionary rule invite any logical distinction between physical and verbal evidence. Either in terms of deterring lawless conduct by federal officers, Rea v. United States, 350 U.S. 214 , or of closing the doors of the federal courts to any use of evidence unconstitutionally obtained, Elkins v. United States, 364 U.S. 206 , the danger in relaxing the exclusionary rules in the case of verbal evidence would seem too great to warrant introducing such a distinction.

The Government argues that Toy's statements to the officers in his bedroom, although closely consequent upon the invasion which we hold unlawful, were nevertheless admissible because they resulted from "an intervening independent act of a free will." This contention, however, takes insufficient account of the circumstances. Six or seven officers had broken the door and followed on Toy's heels into the bedroom where his wife and child were sleeping. He had been almost immediately handcuffed and arrested. Under such circumstances it is unreasonable to infer that Toy's response was sufficiently an act of free will to purge the primary taint of the unlawful invasion. 12   [371 U.S. 471, 487]

The Government also contends that Toy's declarations should be admissible because they were ostensibly exculpatory rather than incriminating. There are two answers to this argument. First, the statements soon turned out to be incriminating, for they led directly to the evidence which implicated Toy. Second, when circumstances are shown such as those which induced these declarations, it is immaterial whether the declarations be termed "exculpatory." 13 Thus we find no substantial reason to omit Toy's declarations from the protection of the exclusionary rule.

III.

We now consider whether the exclusion of Toy's declarations requires also the exclusion of the narcotics taken from Yee, to which those declarations led the police. The prosecutor candidly told the trial court that "we wouldn't have found those drugs except that Mr. Toy helped us to." Hence this is not the case envisioned by this Court where the exclusionary rule has no application because the Government learned of the evidence "from an independent source," Silverthorne Lumber Co. v. United States, 251 U.S. 385, 392 ; nor is this a case in which the connection between the lawless conduct of the police and the discovery of the challenged evidence has "become so attenuated as to dissipate the taint." Nardone v. United States, 308 U.S. 338, 341 . We need not hold that all evidence [371 U.S. 471, 488] is "fruit of the poisonous tree" simply because it would not have come to light but for the illegal actions of the police. Rather, the more apt question in such a case is "whether, granting establishment of the primary illegality, the evidence to which instant objection is made has been come at by exploitation of that illegality or instead by means sufficiently distinguishable to be purged of the primary taint." Maguire, Evidence of Guilt, 221 (1959). We think it clear that the narcotics were "come at by the exploitation of that illegality" and hence that they may not be used against Toy.

IV.

It remains only to consider Toy's unsigned statement. We need not decide whether, in light of the fact that Toy was free on his own recognizance when he made the statement, that statement was a fruit of the illegal arrest. Cf. United States v. Bayer, 331 U.S. 532. Since we have concluded that his declarations in the bedroom and the narcotics surrendered by Yee should not have been admitted in evidence against him, the only proofs remaining to sustain his conviction are his and Wong Sun's unsigned statements. Without scrutinizing the contents of Toy's ambiguous recitals, we conclude that no reference to Toy in Wong Sun's statement constitutes admissible evidence corroborating any admission by Toy. We arrive at this conclusion upon two clear lines of decisions which converge to require it. One line of our decisions establishes that criminal confessions and admissions of guilt require extrinsic corroboration; the other line of precedents holds that an out-of-court declaration made after arrest may not be used at trial against one of the declarant's partners in crime.

It is a settled principle of the administration of criminal justice in the federal courts that a conviction must rest upon firmer ground than the uncorroborated admission or [371 U.S. 471, 489] confession of the accused. 14 We observed in Smith v. United States, 348 U.S. 147, 153 , that the requirement of corroboration is rooted in "a long history of judicial experience with confessions and in the realization that sound law enforcement requires police investigations which extend beyond the words of the accused." In Opper v. United States, 348 U.S. 84, 89 -90, we elaborated the reasons for the requirement:

"In our country the doubt persists that the zeal of the agencies of prosecution to protect the peace, the self-interest of the accomplice, the maliciousness of an enemy or the aberration or weakness of the accused under the strain of suspicion may tinge or warp the facts of the confession. Admissions, retold at a trial, are much like hearsay, that is, statements not made at the pending trial. They had neither the compulsion of the oath nor the test of cross-examination."

It is true that in Smith v. United States, supra, we held that although "corroboration is necessary for all elements of the offense established by admissions alone," extrinsic proof was sufficient which "merely fortifies the truth of the confession, without independently establishing the crime charged . . . ." 348 U.S., at 156 . 15 [371 U.S. 471, 490] However, Wong Sun's unsigned confession does not furnish competent corroborative evidence. The second governing principle, likewise well settled in our decisions, is that an out-of-court declaration made after arrest may not be used at trial against one of the declarant's partners in crime. While such a statement is "admissible against the others where it is in furtherance of the criminal undertaking . . . all such responsibility is at an end when the conspiracy ends." Fiswick v. United States, 329 U.S. 211, 217 . We have consistently refused to broaden that very narrow exception to the traditional hearsay rule which admits statements of a codefendant made in furtherance of a conspiracy or joint undertaking. 16 See Krulewitch v. United States, 336 U.S. 440, 443 -445. And where post-conspiracy declarations have been admitted, we have carefully ascertained that limiting instructions kept the jury from considering the contents with respect to the guilt of anyone but the declarant. Lutwak v. United States, 344 U.S. 604, 618 -

619; Delli Paoli v. United States, 352 U.S. 232, 236 -237. We have never ruled squarely on the question presented here, whether a codefendant's statement might serve to corroborate even where it will not suffice to convict. 17 We see [371 U.S. 471, 491] no warrant for a different result so long as the rule which regulates the use of out-of-court statements is one of admissibility, rather than simply of weight, of the evidence. The import of our previous holdings is that a co-conspirator's hearsay statements may be admitted against the accused for no purpose whatever, unless made during and in furtherance of the conspiracy. Thus as to Toy the only possible source of corroboration is removed and his conviction must be set aside for lack of competent evidence to support it.

V.

We turn now to the case of the other petitioner, Wong Sun. We have no occasion to disagree with the finding of the Court of Appeals that his arrest, also, was without probable cause or reasonable grounds. At all events no evidentiary consequences turn upon that question. For Wong Sun's unsigned confession was not the fruit of that arrest, and was therefore properly admitted at trial. On the evidence that

Wong Sun had been released on his own recognizance after a lawful arraignment, and had returned voluntarily several days later to make the statement, we hold that the connection between the arrest and the statement had "become so attenuated as to dissipate the taint." Nardone v. United States, 308 U.S. 338, 341 . The fact that the statement was unsigned, whatever bearing this may have upon its weight and credibility. does not render it inadmissible; Wong Sun understood and adopted its substance, though he could not comprehend the English words. The petitioner has never suggested any impropriety in the interrogation itself which would require the exclusion of this statement.

We must then consider the admissibility of the narcotics surrendered by Yee. Our holding, supra, that this [371 U.S. 471, 492]   ounce of heroin was inadmissible against Toy does not compel a like result with respect to Wong Sun. The exclusion of the narcotics as to Toy was required solely by their tainted relationship to information unlawfully obtained from Toy, and not by any official impropriety connected with their surrender by Yee. The seizure of this heroin invaded no right of privacy of person or premises which would entitle Wong

Sun to object to its use at his trial. Cf. Goldstein v. United States, 316 U.S. 114 . 18

However, for the reasons that Wong Sun's statement was incompetent to corroborate Toy's admissions contained in Toy's own statement, any references to Wong Sun in Toy's statement were incompetent to corroborate Wong Sun's admissions. Thus, the only competent source of corroboration for Wong Sun's statement was the heroin itself. We cannot be certain, however, on this state of the record, that the trial judge may not also have considered the contents of Toy's statement as a source of corroboration. Petitioners raised as one ground of objection to the introduction of the statements the claim that each statement, "even if it were a purported admission or confession or declaration against interest of a defendant . . . would not be binding upon the other defendant." The trial judge, in allowing the statements in, apparently overruled all of petitioners' objections, including this one. Thus we presume that he considered all portions of both statements as bearing upon the guilt of both petitioners.

We intimate no view one way or the other as to whether the trial judge might have found in the narcotics alone sufficient evidence to corroborate Wong Sun's admissions [371 U.S.

471, 493] that he delivered heroin to Yee and smoked heroin at Yee's house around the date in question. But because he might, as the factfinder, have found insufficient corroboration from the narcotics alone, we cannot be sure that the scales were not tipped in favor of conviction by reliance upon the inadmissible Toy statement. This is particularly important because of the nature of the offense involved here.

Surely, under the narcotics statute, the discovery of heroin raises a presumption that someone - generally the possessor - violated the law. As to him, once possession alone is proved, the other elements of the offense - transportation and concealment with knowledge of the illegal importation of the drug - need not be separately demonstrated, much less corroborated. 21 U.S.C. 174. Thus particular care ought to be taken in this area, when the crucial element of the accused's possession is proved solely by his own admissions, that the requisite corroboration be found among the evidence which is properly before the trier of facts. We therefore hold that petitioner Wong Sun is also entitled to a new trial.

The judgment of the Court of Appeals is reversed and the case is remanded to the District Court for further proceedings consistent with this opinion.

It is so ordered.

[For concurring opinion of MR. JUSTICE DOUGLAS, see post, p. 497.]

[For dissenting opinion of MR. JUSTICE CLARK, see post, p. 498.]

APPENDIX TO OPINION OF THE COURT.

Statement of JAMES WAH TOY taken on June 5, 1959, concerning his knowledge of WONG SUN's narcotic trafficking

I have know WONG SUN for about 3 months. I know him as SEA DOG which is what everyone calls him. [371 U.S. 471, 494]   I first met him in Marysville, California, during a Chinese holiday. I drove him back to San Francisco on that occasion. Sometimes he asks me to drive him home and to different places in San Francisco.

Sometime during April or May of this year, he asked me to drive him out to JOHNNY YEE's house, at 11th and Balboa Streets. He asked me to call JOHNNY and tell him we were coming. When we got there we went into the house and WONG SUN took a paper package out of his pocket and put it on the table. Then both WONG SUN and JOHNNY YEE opened the package. I don't know how much heroin was in it, but I know it was more than 10 spoons. I asked them if I could have some for myself and they said yes. I took a little bit and went across the room and smoked it in a cigarette.

WONG SUN and JOHNNY YEE talked for about 10 or 15 minutes, but they were talking in low tones so that I could not hear what they were saying. I didn't see any money change hands, because I wasn't paying too much attention. WONG SUN and I then left the house and drove. I drove WONG SUN to his home and he gave me $15.00. He said the money was for driving him out there.

I have driven WONG SUN out to JOHNNY YEE's house about 5 times altogether. Each time WONG SUN gave me $10 or $15 for doing it and also, Johnny gave me a little heroin - enough to put in 3 or 4 cigarettes. The last time I drove WONG SUN out to YEE's house was last Tuesday, May 26, 1959. On Wednesday night June 3, 1959, at about 10:00 p. m., I called JOHNNY YEE and told him that "I'm coming out pretty soon - I don't have anything." He said okay, so I drove out there. When I got there I went in the house and Johnny gave me a paper of heroin. The bindle had about enough for 5 or 6 cigarettes. I didn't give him any money and he didn't ask for any. He gives it to me just out of friendship. He has given me heroin like this quite a few times. I don't remember how many times. I have known HOM WEI [371 U.S. 471, 495] about 2 or 3 years but I have never dealt in narcotics with him. I have known ED FONG about 1 year and I have never dealt in narcotics with him, either. I have heard people that I know in the Hop Sing Tong Club talk about HOM WEI dealing in narcotics but nothing about ED FONG. I do not know JOHN MOW LIM or BILL FONG. The only connection I have now is JOHNNY YEE.

I have carefully read the foregoing statement, which was made of my own free will, without promise of reward or immunity and not under duress. I have been given ample opportunity to make corrections have initialed or signed each page as evidence thereof and hereby state that this statement is true to the best of my knowledge and belief.

_____

JAMES WAH TOY

. . . . .

JAMES WAH TOY did not wish to sign this statement at this time. He stated he may change his mind at a later date. However, I read this statement to him and in addition he read it also and stated that the contents thereof were true to the best of his knowledge. Corrections made were by JAMES WAH TOY without his initials.

/s/ WILLIAM WONG William Wong. Narcotic Agent

STATEMENT OF WONG SUN

I met JAMES TOY approximately the middle of March, this year, at Marysville, California, during a Chinese celebration. We returned to San Francisco together and we discussed the possible sale of heroin. I told JAMES that I could get a piece of heroin for $450 from a person known as BILL.

Shortly after returning to San Francisco, JAMES told me he wanted me to get a piece. I asked him who it was [371 U.S. 471, 496]   for and he told me it was for JOHNNY. He gave me $450 and I obtained a piece of heroin from BILL. I did this on approximately 8 occasions, however, at least one of these times the heroin was not for JOHNNY - for another friend of JAMES TOY. JOHNNY would pay JAMES $600 for each piece.

On several occasions after I had obtained the piece for JAMES I would drive with him to JOHNNY's house, 606 11th Avenue, and we would go upstairs to the bedroom. There, all three of us would smoke some of the heroin and JAMES would give the piece to JOHNNY. I also went with JAMES on approximately 3 other occasions when he did not take any heroin and then we smoked at JOHNNY's and we would also get some for our own use.

About 4 days before I was arrested (arrested on June 4, 1959) JAMES called me at home about 7 o'clock in the evening and told me to come by. I went to the laundry and JAMES told me to get a piece. I called BILL and arranged to meet him. JAMES gave me $450 which I gave to BILL when I met him. BILL called me about one hour later at the laundry and I met him. He gave me one piece, which I gave to JAMES, and JAMES immediately thereafter called JOHNNY. We drove to 606 - 11th Ave. at approximately midnight and JAMES gave the piece to JOHNNY. It was contained in a rubber contraceptive in a small brown paper bag.

Again on June 3rd, the night before I was arrested, I met JAMES at the laundry, prior to 11 o'clock in the evening, and JAMES telephoned JOHNNY at EV - 6-9336. Then we went out to JOHNNY's and smoked heroin and also had one paper for our own use later. We were there approximately 1/2 hour and then left.

The laundry mentioned is OYE's LAUNDRY, 1733 Leaven-worth Street, which is run by JAMES TOY. I do not know JOHNNY's last name and know him only [371 U.S. 471, 497] through JAMES TOY. As well as the few times at JOHNNY's home, I have seen JOHNNY on a number of oc-casions at the laundry.

I have carefully read the foregoing statement, consisting of 2 pages which was made of my own free will, without prom-ise of reward or immunity and not under duress. I have been given ample opportunity to make corrections, have initialed or signed each page as evidence thereof and hereby state that this statement is true to the best of my knowledge and belief.

_____

WONG SUN

. . . . .

WONG SUN, being unable to read English, did not sign this statement. However, I read this statement to him and he stated that the contents thereof were true to the best of his knowledge.

/s/ WILLIAM WONG William Wong, Narcotic Agent

Anlage 5:

U.S. Supreme Court

UNITED STATES v. CECCOLINI, 435 U.S. 268 (1978)

435 U.S. 268

UNITED STATES v. CECCOLINI
CERTIORARI TO THE UNITED STATES COURT OF APPEALS FOR THE SECOND CIR-
CUIT

No. 76-1151.

Argued December 5, 1977
Decided March 21, 1978

A police officer (Biro), while taking a break in respondent's flower shop and conversing with an employee of the shop (Hennessey), noticed an envelope with money protruding therefrom lying on the cash register. Upon examination, he found it contained not only money but policy slips. Biro then placed the envelope back on the register and without telling Hennessey what he had found asked her to whom the envelope belonged. She told him it belonged to respondent. Biro's finding was reported to local detectives and to the FBI, who interviewed Hennessey some four months later without referring to the incident involving Biro. About six months after that incident respondent was summoned before a federal grand jury where he testified that he had never taken policy bets at his shop, but Hennessey testified to the contrary, and

203

shortly thereafter respondent was indicted for perjury. Hennessey testified against respondent at his trial, but after a finding of guilt the District Court granted respondent's motion to suppress Hennessey's testimony and set aside that finding. The Court of Appeals affirmed, noting that the "road" to that testimony from the concededly unconstitutional search was "both straight and uninterrupted." Held: The Court of Appeals erred in concluding that the degree of attenuation between Biro's search of the envelope and Hennessey's testimony at the trial was not sufficient to dissipate the connection between the illegality of the search and challenged testimony. Pp. 273-280.

(a) In determining whether the exclusionary rule with its deterrent purpose should be applied, its benefits should be balanced against its costs, and, in evaluating the standards for application of the rule to live-witness testimony in light of this balance, material factors to be considered are the length of the "road" between the Fourth Amendment violation and the witness' testimony; the degree of free will exercised by the witness; and the fact that exclusion of the witness' testimony would perpetually disable the witness from testifying about relevant and material facts regardless of how unrelated such testimony might be to the purpose of the originally illegal search or the evidence discovered thereby. Pp. 273-279.

(b) Here, where the evidence indicates overwhelmingly that Hennesey's [435 U.S. 268, 269] testimony was an act of her own free will in no way coerced or induced by official authority as a result of Biro's discovery of the policy slips, where substantial time elapsed between the illegal search and the initial contact with the witness and between the latter and her trial testimony, and where both Hennessey's identity and her relationship with respondent were well known to the investigating officers, and there is no evidence that Biro entered the shop or picked up the envelope with the intent of finding evidence of an illicit gambling operation, application of the exclusionary rule could not have the slightest deterrent effect on the behavior of an officer such as Biro, and the cost of permanently silencing Hennessey is too great for an evenhanded system of law enforcement to bear in order to secure such a speculative and very likely negligible deterrent effect. Pp. 279-280.

(c) The exclusionary rule should be invoked with much greater reluctance where the claim is based on a causal relationship between a constitutional violation and the discovery of a live witness than when a similar claim is advanced to support suppression of an inanimate object. P. 280.

542 F.2d 136, reversed.

REHNQUIST, J., delivered the opinion of the Court, in which STEWART, WHITE, POWELL, and STEVENS, JJ., joined. BURGER, C. J., filed an opinion concurring in the judgment, post, p. 280. MARSHALL, J., filed a dissenting opinion, in which BRENNAN, J., joined, post, p. 285. BLACKMUN, J., took no part in the consideration or decision of the case.

Richard A. Allen argued the cause for the United States. With him on the brief were Solicitor General McCree, Assistant Attorney General Civiletti, Deputy Solicitor General Frey, and Sidney M. Glazer.

Leon J. Greenspan argued the cause and filed a brief for respondent.

MR. JUSTICE REHNQUIST delivered the opinion of the Court.

In December 1974, Ronald Biro, a uniformed police officer on assignment to patrol school crossings, entered respondent's place of business, the Sleepy Hollow Flower Shop, in

North Tarrytown, N. Y. He went behind the customer counter and, in the words of Ichabod Crane, one of Tarrytown's more [435 U.S. 268, 270]   illustrious inhabitants of days gone past, "tarried," spending his short break engaged in conversation with his friend Lois Hennessey, an employee of the shop. During the course of the conversation he noticed an envelope with money sticking out of it lying on the drawer of the cash register behind the counter. Biro picked up the envelope and, upon examining its contents, discovered that it contained not only money but policy slips. He placed the envelope back on the register and, without telling Hennessey what he had seen, asked her to whom the envelope belonged. She replied that the envelope belonged to respondent Ceccolini, and that he had instructed her to give it to someone.

The next day, Officer Biro mentioned his discovery to North Tarrytown detectives who in turn told Lance Emory, an FBI agent. This very ordinary incident in the lives of Biro and Hennessey requires us, over three years later, to decide whether Hennessey's testimony against respondent Ceccolini should have been suppressed in his trial for perjury. Respondent was charged with that offense because he denied that he knew anything of, or was in any way involved with, gambling operations. Respondent was found guilty after a bench trial in the United States District Court for the Southern District of New York, but immediately after the finding of guilt the District Court granted respondent's motion to "suppress" the testimony of Hennessey because the court concluded that the testimony was a "fruit of the poisonous tree"; assuming respondent's motion for a directed verdict included a motion to set aside the verdict of guilty, the District Court granted the motion because it concluded that without Hennessey's testimony there was insufficient evidence of respondent's guilt. The Government appealed these rulings to the Court of Appeals for the Second Circuit.

That court rightly concluded that the Government was entitled to appeal both the order granting the motion to suppress and the order setting aside the verdict of guilty, since [435 U.S. 268, 271] further proceedings if the Government were successful on the appeal would not be barred by the Double Jeopardy Clause. 1 542 F.2d 136, 139-140 (1976). The District Court had sensibly first made its finding on the factual question of guilt or innocence, and then ruled on the motion to suppress; a reversal of these rulings would require no fur-

ther proceedings in the District Court, but merely a reinstate-
ment of the finding of guilt. United States v. Morrison, 429 U.S.
1 (1976); United States v. Wilson, 420 U.S. 332, 352 -353
(1975).

The Government, however, was not successful on the merits
of its appeal; the Court of Appeals by a divided vote affirmed
the District Court's suppression ruling. 542 F.2d, at 140-142.
We granted certiorari to consider the correctness of this ruling of the Court of Appeals. 431 U.S. 903 (1977).

I

During the latter part of 1973, the Federal Bureau of Investigation was exploring suspected gambling operations in
North Tarrytown. Among the establishments under surveillance was respondent's place of business, which was a fre-
quent and regular stop of one Francis Millow, himself a suspect in the investigation. While the investigation continued
on a reduced scale after December 1973, 2 surveillance of
the flower [435 U.S. 268, 272]   shop was curtailed at that
time. It was thus a full year after this discontinuance of FBI
surveillance that Biro spent his patrol break behind the counter with Hennessey. When Biro's discovery of the policy slips
was reported the following day to Emory, Emory was not fully

informed of the manner in which Biro had obtained the information. Four months later, Emory interviewed Hennessey at her home for about half an hour in the presence of her mother and two sisters. He identified himself, indicated that he had learned through the local police department that she worked for respondent, and told her that the Government would appreciate any information regarding respondent's activities that she had acquired in the shop. Emory did not specifically refer to the incident involving Officer Biro. Hennessey told Emory that she was studying police science in college and would be willing to help. She then related the events which had occurred during her visit with Officer Biro.

In May 1975, respondent was summoned before a federal grand jury where he testified that he had never taken policy bets for Francis Millow at the flower shop. The next week Hennessey testified to the contrary, and shortly thereafter respondent was indicted for perjury. 3 Respondent waived a jury, and with the consent of all parties the District Court considered simultaneously with the trial on the merits respondent's motion to suppress both the policy slips and the testimony of Hennessey. At the conclusion of the evidence, the District Court excluded from its consideration "the envelope

and the contents of the envelope," but nonetheless found respondent guilty of the offense charged. The court then, as
previously [435 U.S. 268, 273] described, granted respondent's motion to suppress the testimony of Hennessey, because she "first came directly to the attention of the government as a result of an illegal search" and the Government
had not "sustained its burden of showing that Lois Hen-
ness[e]y's testimony definitely would have been obtained
without the illegal search." App. to Pet. for Cert. 28a-29a.

The Court of Appeals affirmed this ruling on the Government's appeal, reasoning that "the road to Miss Hen-
ness[e]y's testimony from Officer Biro's concededly unconstitutional search is both straight and uninterrupted." 542
F.2d, at 142. The Court of Appeals also concluded that there
was support in the record for the District Court's finding that
the ongoing investigation would not have inevitably led to the
evidence in question without Biro's discovery of the two policy slips. Id., at 141. Because of our traditional deference to
the "two court rule," Graver Mfg. Co. v. Linde Co., 336 U.S.
271, 275 (1949), and the fact that the Government has not
sought review of this latter ruling, we leave undisturbed this
part of the Court of Appeals' decision. Because we decide

that the Court of Appeals was wrong in concluding that there was insufficient attenuation between Officer Biro's search and Hennessey's testimony at the trial, we also do not reach the Government's contention that the exclusionary rule should not be applied when the evidence derived from the search is being used to prove a subsequent crime such as perjury.

II

The "road" to which the Court of Appeals analogized the train of events from Biro's discovery of the policy slips to Hennessey's testimony at respondent's trial for perjury is one of literally thousands of such roads traveled periodically between an original investigative discovery and the ultimate trial of the accused. The constitutional question under the Fourth Amendment was phrased in Wong Sun v. United States, 371 U.S. 471 (1963), as whether "the connection [435 U.S. 268, 274] between the lawless conduct of the police and the discovery of the challenged evidence has `become so attenuated as to dissipate the taint.'" Id., at 487, 491. The question was in turn derived from the Court's earlier decision in Nardone v. United States, 308 U.S. 338, 341 (1939), where Mr. Justice Frankfurter stated for the Court:

"Here, as in the Silverthorne case [Silverthorne Lumber Co. v. United States], the facts improperly obtained do not `become sacred and inaccessible. If knowledge of them is gained from an independent source they may be proved like any others, but the knowledge gained by the Government's own wrong cannot be used by it' simply because it is used derivatively. 251 U.S. 385, 392 .

"In practice this generalized statement may conceal concrete complexities. Sophisticated argument may prove a causal connection between information obtained through illicit wire-tapping and the Government's proof. As a matter of good sense, however, such connection may have become so attenuated as to dissipate the taint."

This, of course, makes it perfectly clear, if indeed ever there was any doubt about the matter, that the question of causal connection in this setting, as in so many other questions with which the law concerns itself, is not to be determined solely through the sort of analysis which would be applicable in the physical sciences. The issue cannot be decided on the basis of causation in the logical sense alone, but necessarily includes other elements as well. And our cases subsequent to Nardone, supra, have laid out the fundamental tenets of the exclusionary rule, from which the elements that are relevant to the causal inquiry can be divined.

An examination of these cases leads us to reject the Government's suggestion that we adopt what would in practice amount to a per se rule that the testimony of a live witness should not be excluded at trial no matter how close and proximate [435 U.S. 268, 275]   the connection between it and a violation of the Fourth Amendment. We also reaffirm the holding of Wong Sun, supra, at 485, that "verbal evidence which derives so immediately from an unlawful entry and an unauthorized arrest as the officers' action in the present case is no less the `fruit' of official illegality than the more common tangible fruits of the unwarranted intrusion." We are of the view, however, that cases decided since Wong Sun significantly qualify its further observation that "the policies underlying the exclusionary rule [do not] invite any logical distinction between physical and verbal evidence." 371 U.S., at 486 . Rather, at least in a case such as this, where not only was the alleged "fruit of the poisonous tree" the testimony of a live witness, but unlike Wong Sun the witness was not a putative defendant, an examination of our cases persuades us that the Court of Appeals was simply wrong in concluding that if the road were uninterrupted, its length was immaterial.

Its length, we hold, is material, as are certain other factors enumerated below to which the court gave insufficient weight.

In Stone v. Powell, 428 U.S. 465, 486 (1976), we observed that "despite the broad deterrent purpose of the exclusionary rule, it has never been interpreted to proscribe the introduction of illegally seized evidence in all proceedings or against all persons." Recognizing not only the benefits but the costs, which are often substantial, of the exclusionary rule, we have said that "application of the rule has been restricted to those areas where its remedial objectives are thought most efficaciously served," United States v. Calandra, 414 U.S. 338, 348 (1974). In that case, we refused to require that illegally seized evidence be excluded from presentation to a grand jury. We have likewise declined to prohibit the use of such evidence for the purpose of impeaching a defendant who testifies in his own behalf. Walder v. United States, 347 U.S. 62 (1954).

We have limited the standing requirement in the exclusionary rule context because the "additional benefits of extending [435 U.S. 268, 276] the . . . rule" to persons other than the ones subject to the illegal search are outweighed by the "further encroachment upon the public interest in prosecuting those accused of crime and having them acquitted or convicted on the basis of all the evidence which exposes the truth." Alderman v. United States, 394 U.S. 165, 174 -175 (1969). Even in situations where the exclusionary rule is plainly applicable, we have declined to adopt a "per se or `but for' rule" that would make inadmissible any evidence, whether tangible or live-witness testimony, which somehow came to light through a chain of causation that began with an illegal arrest. Brown v. Illinois, 422 U.S. 590, 603 (1975).

Evaluating the standards for application of the exclusionary rule to live-witness testimony in light of this balance, we are first impelled to conclude that the degree of free will exercised by the witness is not irrelevant in determining the extent to which the basic purpose of the exclusionary rule will be advanced by its application. This is certainly true when the challenged statements are made by a putative defendant after arrest, Wong Sun, supra, at 491; Brown v. Illinois, supra, and a fortiori is true of testimony given by nondefendants.

The greater the willingness of the witness to freely testify, the greater the likelihood that he or she will be discovered by legal means and, concomitantly, the smaller the incentive to conduct an illegal search to discover the witness. 4 Witnesses are not like guns or documents which remain hidden from view until one turns over a sofa or opens a filing cabinet. Witnesses can, and often do, come forward and offer evidence entirely of their own volition. And evaluated properly, the degree of free will necessary to dissipate the taint will very likely be found more often in the case of live-witness testimony [435 U.S. 268, 277] than other kinds of evidence. the time, place and manner of the initial questioning of the witness may be such that any statements are truly the product of detached reflection and a desire to be cooperative on the part of the witness. And the illegality which led to the discovery of the witness very often will not play any meaningful part in the witness' willingness to testify.

"The proffer of a living witness is not to be mechanically equated with the proffer of inanimate evidentiary objects illegally seized. The fact that the name of a potential witness is disclosed to police is of no evidentiary significance, per se, since the living witness is an individual human personality whose attributes of will, perception, memory and volition interact to determine what testimony he will give. The uniqueness of this human process distinguishes the evidentiary character of a witness from the relative immutability of inanimate evidence." Smith v. United States, 117 U.S. App. D.C. 1, 3-4, 324 F.2d 879, 881-882 (1963) (Burger, J.) (footnotes omitted), cert. denied, 377 U.S. 954 (1964).

Another factor which not only is relevant in determining the usefulness of the exclusionary rule in a particular context, but also seems to us to differentiate the testimony of all live witnesses - even putative defendants - from the exclusion of the typical documentary evidence, is that such exclusion would perpetually disable a witness from testifying about relevant and material facts, regardless of how unrelated such testimony might be to the purpose of the originally illegal search or the evidence discovered thereby. Rules which disqualify knowledgeable witnesses from testifying at trial are, in the words of Professor McCormick, "serious obstructions to the ascertainment of truth"; accordingly, "[f]or a century the course of legal evolution has been in the direction of sweeping away these obstructions." C. McCormick, Law of Evidence 71 (1954). Alluding to the enormous cost engendered by [435 U.S. 268, 278]   such a permanent disability in an analogous context, we have specifically refused to hold that "making a confession under circumstances which preclude its use, perpetually disables the confessor from making a usable one after those conditions have been removed." United States v. Bayer, 331 U.S. 532, 541 (1947). For many of these same reasons, the Court has also held admissible at trial testimony of a witness whose identity was disclosed by the defendant's statement given after inadequate Miranda warnings. Michigan v. Tucker, 417 U.S. 433, 450 -451 (1974).

"For, when balancing the interests involved, we must weigh the strong interest under any system of justice of making available to the trier of fact all concededly relevant and trustworthy evidence which either party seeks to adduce. . . . Here respondent's own statement, which might have helped the prosecution show respondent's guilty conscience at trial, had already been excised from the prosecution's case pursuant to this Court's Johnson [v. New Jersey, 384 U.S. 719 (1966)] decision. To extend the excision further under the circumstances of this case and exclude relevant testimony of a third-party witness would require far more persuasive arguments than those advanced by respondent."

In short, since the cost of excluding live-witness testimony often will be greater, a closer, more direct link between the illegality and that kind of testimony is required.

This is not to say, of course, that live-witness testimony is always or even usually more reliable or dependable than inanimate evidence. Indeed, just the opposite may be true. But a determination that the discovery of certain evidence is sufficiently unrelated to or independent of the constitutional violation to permit its introduction at trial is not a determination which rests on the comparative reliability of that evidence. Attenuation analysis, appropriately concerned with the differences between live-witness testimony and inanimate evidence, [435 U.S. 268, 279]   can consistently focus on the factors enumerated above with respect to the former, but on different factors with respect to the latter.

In holding that considerations relating to the exclusionary rule and the constitutional principles which it is designed to protect must play a factor in the attenuation analysis, we do no more than reaffirm an observation made by this Court half a century ago:

"A criminal prosecution is more than a game in which the Government may be checkmated and the game lost merely because its officers have not played according to rule." McGuire v. United States, 273 U.S. 95, 99 (1927).

The penalties visited upon the Government, and in turn upon the public, because its officers have violated the law must bear some relation to the purposes which the law is to serve.

III

Viewing this case in the light of the principles just discussed, we hold that the Court of Appeals erred in holding that the degree of attenuation was not sufficient to dissipate the connection between the illegality and the testimony. The evidence indicates overwhelmingly that the testimony given by the witness was an act of her own free will in no way coerced or even induced by official authority as a result of Biro's discovery of the policy slips. Nor were the slips themselves used in questioning Hennessey. Substantial periods of time elapsed between the time of the illegal search and the initial contact with the witness, on the one hand, and between the latter and the testimony at trial on the other. While the particular knowledge to which Hennessey testified at trial can be logically traced back to Biro's discovery of the policy slips, both the identity of Hennessey and her relationship with the respondent were well known to those investigating the case. There is, in addition, not the slightest evidence to suggest [435 U.S. 268, 280]   that Biro entered the shop or picked up the envelope with the intent of finding tangible evidence bearing on an illicit gambling operation, much less any suggestion that he entered the shop and searched with the intent of finding a willing and knowledgeable witness to testify against respondent. Application of the exclusionary rule in this situation could not have the slightest deterrent effect on the behavior of an officer such as Biro. The cost of permanently silencing Hennessey is too great for an evenhanded system of law enforcement to bear in order to secure such a speculative and very likely negligible deterrent effect.

Obviously no mathematical weight can be assigned to any of the factors which we have discussed, but just as obviously they all point to the conclusion that the exclusionary rule should be invoked with much greater reluctance where the claim is based on a causal relationship between a constitutional violation and the discovery of a live witness than when a similar claim is advanced to support suppression of an inanimate object. The judgment of the Court of Appeals is accordingly

Reversed.

MR. JUSTICE BLACKMUN took no part in the consideration or decision of this case.

Anlage 6:

U.S. Supreme Court

MIRANDA v. ARIZONA, 384 U.S. 436 (1966)

384 U.S. 436

MIRANDA v. ARIZONA.
CERTIORARI TO THE SUPREME COURT OF ARIZONA.
No. 759.
Argued February 28 - March 1, 1966.
Decided June 13, 1966.*

[Footnote *] Together with No. 760, Vignera v. New York, on certiorari to the Court of Appeals of New York and No. 761, Westover v. United States, on certiorari to the United States Court of Appeals for the Ninth Circuit, both argued February 28 - March 1, 1966; and No. 584, California v. Stewart, on certiorari to the Supreme Court of California, argued February 28 - March 2, 1966.

In each of these cases the defendant while in police custody was questioned by police officers, detectives, or a prosecuting attorney in a room in which he was cut off from the outside world. None of the defendants was given a full and effective warning of his rights at the outset of the interrogation process. In all four cases the questioning elicited oral admissions, and in three of them signed statements as well, which were admitted at their trials. All defendants were convicted and all convictions, except in No. 584, were affirmed on appeal. Held:

1. The prosecution may not use statements, whether exculpatory or inculpatory, stemming from questioning initiated by law enforcement officers after a person has been taken into custody or otherwise deprived of his freedom of action in any significant way, unless it demonstrates the use of procedural safeguards effective to secure the Fifth Amendment's privilege against self-incrimination. Pp. 444-491.

(a) The atmosphere and environment of incommunicado interrogation as it exists today is inherently intimidating and works to undermine the privilege against self-incrimination. Unless adequate preventive measures are taken to dispel the compulsion inherent in custodial surroundings, no statement obtained from the defendant can truly be the product of his free choice. Pp. 445-458.

(b) The privilege against self-incrimination, which has had a long and expansive historical development, is the essential mainstay of our adversary system and guarantees to the individual the "right to remain silent unless he chooses to speak in the unfettered exercise of his own will," during a period of custodial interrogation [384 U.S. 436, 437]   as well as in the courts or during the course of other official investigations. Pp. 458-465.

(c) The decision in Escobedo v. Illinois, 378 U.S. 478, stressed the need for protective devices to make the process of police interrogation conform to the dictates of the privilege. Pp. 465-466.

(d) In the absence of other effective measures the following procedures to safeguard the Fifth Amendment privilege must be observed: The person in custody must, prior to interrogation, be clearly informed that he has the right to remain silent, and that anything he says will be used against him in court; he must be clearly informed that he has the right to consult with a lawyer and to have the lawyer with him during interrogation, and that, if he is indigent, a lawyer will be appointed to represent him. Pp. 467-473.

(e) If the individual indicates, prior to or during questioning, that he wishes to remain silent, the interrogation must cease; if he states that he wants an attorney, the questioning must cease until an attorney is present. Pp. 473-474.

(f) Where an interrogation is conducted without the presence of an attorney and a statement is taken, a heavy burden rests on the Government to demonstrate that the defendant knowingly and intelligently waived his right to counsel. P. 475.

(g) Where the individual answers some questions during in-custody interrogation he has not waived his privilege and may invoke his right to remain silent thereafter. Pp. 475-476.

(h) The warnings required and the waiver needed are, in the absence of a fully effective equivalent, prerequisites to the admissibility of any statement, inculpatory or exculpatory, made by a defendant. Pp. 476-477.

2. The limitations on the interrogation process required for the protection of the individual's constitutional rights should not cause an undue interference with a proper system of law enforcement, as demonstrated by the procedures of the FBI and the safeguards afforded in other jurisdictions. Pp. 479-491.

3. In each of these cases the statements were obtained under circumstances that did not meet constitutional standards for protection of the privilege against self-incrimination. Pp. 491-499.

98 Ariz. 18, 401 P.2d 721; 15 N. Y. 2d 970, 207 N. E. 2d 527; 16 N. Y. 2d 614, 209 N. E. 2d 110; 342 F.2d 684, reversed; 62 Cal. 2d 571, 400 P.2d 97, affirmed. [384 U.S. 436, 438]

John J. Flynn argued the cause for petitioner in No. 759. With him on the brief was John P. Frank. Victor M. Earle III argued the cause and filed a brief for petitioner in No. 760. F. Conger Fawcett argued the cause and filed a brief for petitioner in No. 761. Gordon Ringer, Deputy Attorney General of California, argued the cause for petitioner in No. 584. With him on the briefs were Thomas C. Lynch, Attorney General, and William E. James, Assistant Attorney General.

Gary K. Nelson, Assistant Attorney General of Arizona, argued the cause for respondent in No. 759. With him on the brief was Darrell F. Smith, Attorney General. William I. Siegel argued the cause for respondent in No. 760. With him on the brief was Aaron E. Koota. Solicitor General Marshall argued the cause for the United States in No. 761. With him on the brief were Assistant Attorney General Vinson, Ralph S. Spritzer, Nathan Lewin, Beatrice Rosenberg and Ronald L. Gainer. William A. Norris, by appointment of the Court, 382 U.S. 952 , argued the cause and filed a brief for respondent in No. 584.

Telford Taylor, by special leave of Court, argued the cause for the State of New York, as amicus curiae, in all cases. With him on the brief were Louis J. Lefkowitz, Attorney General of New York, Samuel A. Hirshowitz, First Assistant Attorney General, and Barry Mahoney and George D. Zuckerman, Assistant Attorneys General, joined by the Attorneys General for their respective States and jurisdictions as follows: Richmond M. Flowers of Alabama, Darrell F. Smith of Arizona, Bruce Bennett of Arkansas, Duke W. Dunbar of Colorado, David P. Buckson of Delaware, Earl Faircloth of Florida, Arthur K. Bolton of Georgia, Allan G. Shepard of Idaho, William G. Clark of Illinois, Robert C. Londerholm of Kansas, Robert Matthews of Kentucky, Jack P. F. [384 U.S. 436, 439]   Gremillion of Louisiana, Richard J. Dubord of Maine, Thomas B. Finan of Maryland, Norman H. Anderson of Missouri, Forrest H. Anderson of Montana, Clarence A. H. Meyer of Nebraska, T. Wade Bruton of North Carolina, Helgi Johanneson of North Dakota, Robert Y. Thornton of Oregon, Walter E. Alessandroni of Pennsylvania, J. Joseph Nugent of Rhode Island, Daniel R. McLeod of South Carolina, Waggoner Carr of Texas, Robert Y. Button of Virginia, John J.

O'Connell of Washington, C. Donald Robertson of West Virginia, John F. Raper of Wyoming, Rafael Hernandez Colon of Puerto Rico and Francisco Corneiro of the Virgin Islands.

Duane R. Nedrud, by special leave of Court, argued the cause for the National District Attorneys Association, as amicus curiae, urging affirmance in Nos. 759 and 760, and reversal in No. 584. With him on the brief was Marguerite D. Oberto.

Anthony G. Amsterdam, Paul J. Mishkin, Raymond L. Bradley, Peter Hearn and Melvin L. Wulf filed a brief for the American Civil Liberties Union, as amicus curiae, in all cases.

MR. CHIEF JUSTICE WARREN delivered the opinion of the Court.

The cases before us raise questions which go to the roots of our concepts of American criminal jurisprudence: the restraints society must observe consistent with the Federal Constitution in prosecuting individuals for crime. More specifically, we deal with the admissibility of statements obtained from an individual who is subjected to custodial police interrogation and the necessity for procedures which assure that the individual is accorded his privilege under the Fifth

Amendment to the Constitution not to be compelled to incriminate himself. [384 U.S. 436, 440]

We dealt with certain phases of this problem recently in Escobedo v. Illinois, 378 U.S. 478 (1964). There, as in the four cases before us, law enforcement officials took the defendant into custody and interrogated him in a police station for the purpose of obtaining a confession. The police did not effectively advise him of his right to remain silent or of his right to consult with his attorney. Rather, they confronted him with an alleged accomplice who accused him of having perpetrated a murder. When the defendant denied the accusation and said "I didn't shoot Manuel, you did it," they handcuffed him and took him to an interrogation room. There, while handcuffed and standing, he was questioned for four hours until he confessed. During this interrogation, the police denied his request to speak to his attorney, and they prevented his retained attorney, who had come to the police station, from consulting with him. At his trial, the State, over his objection, introduced the confession against him. We held that the statements thus made were constitutionally inadmissible.

This case has been the subject of judicial interpretation and spirited legal debate since it was decided two years ago. Both state and federal courts, in assessing its implications, have arrived at varying conclusions. 1 A wealth of scholarly material has been written tracing its ramifications and under-pinnings. 2 Police and prosecutor [384 U.S. 436, 441] have speculated on its range and desirability. 3 We granted certi-orari in these cases, 382 U.S. 924, 925 , 937, in order further to explore some facets of the problems, thus exposed, of ap-plying the privilege against self-incrimination to in-custody interrogation, and to give [384 U.S. 436, 442] concrete con-stitutional guidelines for law enforcement agencies and courts to follow.

We start here, as we did in Escobedo, with the premise that our holding is not an innovation in our jurisprudence, but is an application of principles long recognized and applied in other settings. We have undertaken a thorough re-examina-tion of the Escobedo decision and the principles it an-nounced, and we reaffirm it. That case was but an explica-tion of basic rights that are enshrined in our Constitution - that "No person . . . shall be compelled in any criminal case to be a witness against himself," and that "the accused shall

. . . have the Assistance of Counsel" - rights which were put in jeopardy in that case through official overbearing. These precious rights were fixed in our Constitution only after centuries of persecution and struggle. And in the words of Chief Justice Marshall, they were secured "for ages to come, and . . . designed to approach immortality as nearly as human institutions can approach it," Cohens v. Virginia, 6 Wheat. 264, 387 (1821).

Over 70 years ago, our predecessors on this Court eloquently stated:

"The maxim nemo tenetur seipsum accusare had its origin in a protest against the inquisitorial and manifestly unjust methods of interrogating accused persons, which [have] long obtained in the continental system, and, until the expulsion of the Stuarts from the British throne in 1688, and the erection of additional barriers for the protection of the people against the exercise of arbitrary power, [were] not uncommon even in England. While the admissions or confessions of the prisoner, when voluntarily and freely made, have always ranked high in the scale of incriminating evidence, if an accused person be asked to explain his apparent connection with a crime under investigation, the ease with which the

[384 U.S. 436, 443] questions put to him may assume an inquisitorial character, the temptation to press the witness unduly, to browbeat him if he be timid or reluctant, to push him into a corner, and to entrap him into fatal contradictions, which is so painfully evident in many of the earlier state trials, notably in those of Sir Nicholas Throckmorton, and Udal, the Puritan minister, made the system so odious as to give rise to a demand for its total abolition. The change in the English criminal procedure in that particular seems to be founded upon no statute and no judicial opinion, but upon a general and silent acquiescence of the courts in a popular demand. But, however adopted, it has become firmly embedded in English, as well as in American jurisprudence. So deeply did the iniquities of the ancient system impress themselves upon the minds of the American colonists that the States, with one accord, made a denial of the right to question an accused person a part of their fundamental law, so that a maxim, which in England was a mere rule of evidence, became clothed in this country with the impregnability of a constitutional enactment." Brown v. Walker, 161 U.S. 591, 596 -597 (1896).

In stating the obligation of the judiciary to apply these constitutional rights, this Court declared in Weems v. United States, 217 U.S. 349, 373 (1910):

". . . our contemplation cannot be only of what has been but of what may be. Under any other rule a constitution would indeed be as easy of application as it would be deficient in efficacy and power. Its general principles would have little value and be converted by precedent into impotent and lifeless formulas. Rights declared in words might be lost in reality. And this has been recognized. The [384 U.S. 436, 444] meaning and vitality of the Constitution have developed against narrow and restrictive construction."

This was the spirit in which we delineated, in meaningful language, the manner in which the constitutional rights of the individual could be enforced against overzealous police practices. It was necessary in Escobedo, as here, to insure that what was proclaimed in the Constitution had not become but a "form of words," Silverthorne Lumber Co. v. United States, 251 U.S. 385, 392 (1920), in the hands of government officials. And it is in this spirit, consistent with our role as judges, that we adhere to the principles of Escobedo today.

Our holding will be spelled out with some specificity in the pages which follow but briefly stated it is this: the prosecution may not use statements, whether exculpatory or inculpatory, stemming from custodial interrogation of the defendant unless it demonstrates the use of procedural safeguards effective to secure the privilege against self-incrimination. By custodial interrogation, we mean questioning initiated by law enforcement officers after a person has been taken into custody or otherwise deprived of his freedom of action in any significant way. 4 As for the procedural safeguards to be employed, unless other fully effective means are devised to inform accused persons of their right of silence and to assure a continuous opportunity to exercise it, the following measures are required. Prior to any questioning, the person must be warned that he has a right to remain silent, that any statement he does make may be used as evidence against him, and that he has a right to the presence of an attorney, either retained or appointed. The defendant may waive effectuation of these rights, provided the waiver is made voluntarily, knowingly and intelligently. If, however, he indicates in any manner and at any stage of the [384 U.S. 436, 445] process that he wishes to consult with an attorney before speaking there can be no questioning. Likewise, if the individual is alone and indicates in any manner that he does not wish to be interrogated, the police may not question him. The mere fact that he may have answered some questions or volunteered some statements on his own does not deprive him of the right to refrain from answering any further inquiries until he has consulted with an attorney and thereafter consents to be questioned.

I.

The constitutional issue we decide in each of these cases is the admissibility of statements obtained from a defendant questioned while in custody or otherwise deprived of his freedom of action in any significant way. In each, the defendant was questioned by police officers, detectives, or a prosecuting attorney in a room in which he was cut off from the outside world. In none of these cases was the defendant given a full and effective warning of his rights at the outset of the interrogation process. In all the cases, the questioning elicited oral admissions, and in three of them, signed statements as well which were admitted at their trials. They all thus share salient features - incommunicado interrogation of individuals in a police-dominated atmosphere, resulting in self-incriminating statements without full warnings of constitutional rights.

An understanding of the nature and setting of this in-custody interrogation is essential to our decisions today. The difficulty in depicting what transpires at such interrogations stems from the fact that in this country they have largely taken place incommunicado. From extensive factual studies undertaken in the early 1930's, including the famous Wickersham Report to Congress by a Presidential Commission, it is clear that police violence and the "third degree" flourished at that time. 5 [384 U.S. 436, 446] In a series of cases decided by this Court long after these studies, the police resorted to physical brutality - beating, hanging, whipping - and to sustained and protracted questioning incommunicado in order to extort confessions. 6 The Commission on Civil Rights in 1961 found much evidence to indicate that "some policemen still resort to physical force to obtain confessions," 1961 Comm'n on Civil Rights Rep., Justice, pt. 5, 17. The use of physical brutality and violence is not, unfortunately, relegated to the past or to any part of the country. Only recently in Kings County, New York, the police brutally beat, kicked and placed lighted cigarette butts on the back of a potential witness under interrogation for the purpose of securing a statement incriminating a third party. People v. Portelli, 15 N. Y. 2d 235, 205 N. E. 2d 857, 257 N. Y. S. 2d 931 (1965). 7 [384 U.S. 436, 447]

The examples given above are undoubtedly the exception now, but they are sufficiently widespread to be the object of concern. Unless a proper limitation upon custodial interrogation is achieved - such as these decisions will advance - there can be no assurance that practices of this nature will be eradicated in the foreseeable future. The conclusion of the Wickersham Commission Report, made over 30 years ago, is still pertinent:

"To the contention that the third degree is necessary to get the facts, the reporters aptly reply in the language of the present Lord Chancellor of England (Lord Sankey): `It is not admissible to do a great right by doing a little wrong. . . . It is not sufficient to do justice by obtaining a proper result by irregular or improper means.' Not only does the use of the third degree involve a flagrant violation of law by the officers of the law, but it involves also the dangers of false confessions, and it tends to make police and prosecutors less zealous in the search for objective evidence. As the New York prosecutor quoted in the report said, 'It is a short cut and makes the police lazy and unenterprising.' Or, as another official quoted remarked: 'If you use your fists, you [384 U.S. 436, 448]   are not so likely to use your wits.' We agree with the conclusion expressed in the report, that 'The third degree brutalizes the police, hardens the prisoner against society, and lowers the esteem in which the administration of justice is held by the public.'" IV National Commission on Law Observance and Enforcement, Report on Lawlessness in Law Enforcement 5 (1931).

Again we stress that the modern practice of in-custody interrogation is psychologically rather than physically oriented. As we have stated before, "Since Chambers v. Florida, 309 U.S. 227 , this Court has recognized that coercion can be mental as well as physical, and that the blood of the accused is not the only hallmark of an unconstitutional inquisition." Blackburn v. Alabama, 361 U.S. 199, 206 (1960). Interrogation still takes place in privacy. Privacy results in secrecy and this in turn results in a gap in our knowledge as to what in fact goes on in the interrogation rooms. A valuable source of information about present police practices, however, may be found in various police manuals and texts which document procedures employed with success in the past, and which recommend various other effective tactics. 8 These [384 U.S. 436, 449] texts are used by law enforcement agencies themselves as guides. 9 It should be noted that these texts professedly present the most enlightened and effective means presently used to obtain statements through custodial interrogation. By considering these texts and other data, it is possible to describe procedures observed and noted around the country.

The officers are told by the manuals that the "principal psychological factor contributing to a successful interrogation is privacy - being alone with the person under interrogation." 10 The efficacy of this tactic has been explained as follows:

"If at all practicable, the interrogation should take place in the investigator's office or at least in a room of his own choice. The subject should be deprived of every psychological advantage. In his own home he may be confident, indignant, or recalcitrant. He is more keenly aware of his rights and [384 U.S. 436, 450] more reluctant to tell of his indiscretions or criminal behavior within the walls of his home. Moreover his family and other friends are nearby, their presence lending moral support. In his own office, the investigator possesses all the advantages. The atmosphere suggests the invincibility of the forces of the law." 11

To highlight the isolation and unfamiliar surroundings, the manuals instruct the police to display an air of confidence in the suspect's guilt and from outward appearance to maintain only an interest in confirming certain details. The guilt of the subject is to be posited as a fact. The interrogator should direct his comments toward the reasons why the subject committed the act, rather than court failure by asking the subject whether he did it. Like other men, perhaps the subject has had a bad family life, had an unhappy childhood, had too much to drink, had an unrequited desire for women. The officers are instructed to minimize the moral seriousness of the offense, 12 to cast blame on the victim or on society. 13 These tactics are designed to put the subject in a psychological state where his story is but an elaboration of what the police purport to know already - that he is guilty. Explanations to the contrary are dismissed and discouraged.

The texts thus stress that the major qualities an interrogator should possess are patience and perseverance. [384 U.S. 436, 451] One writer describes the efficacy of these characteristics in this manner:

"In the preceding paragraphs emphasis has been placed on kindness and stratagems. The investigator will, however, encounter many situations where the sheer weight of his personality will be the deciding factor. Where emotional appeals and tricks are employed to no avail, he must rely on an oppressive atmosphere of dogged persistence. He must interrogate steadily and without relent, leaving the subject no prospect of surcease. He must dominate his subject and overwhelm him with his inexorable will to obtain the truth. He should interrogate for a spell of several hours pausing only for the subject's necessities in acknowledgment of the need to avoid a charge of duress that can be technically substantiated. In a serious case, the interrogation may continue for days, with the required intervals for food and sleep, but with no respite from the atmosphere of domination. It is possible in this way to induce the subject to talk without resorting to duress or coercion. The method should be used only when the guilt of the subject appears highly probable." 14

The manuals suggest that the suspect be offered legal excuses for his actions in order to obtain an initial admission of guilt. Where there is a suspected revenge-killing, for example, the interrogator may say:

"Joe, you probably didn't go out looking for this fellow with the purpose of shooting him. My guess is, however, that you expected something from him and that's why you carried a gun - for your own protection. You knew him for what he was, no good. Then when you met him he probably started using foul, abusive language and he gave some indication [384 U.S. 436, 452]   that he was about to pull a gun on you, and that's when you had to act to save your own life. That's about it, isn't it, Joe?" 15

Having then obtained the admission of shooting, the interrogator is advised to refer to circumstantial evidence which negates the self-defense explanation. This should enable him to secure the entire story. One text notes that "Even if he fails to do so, the inconsistency between the subject's original denial of the shooting and his present admission of at least doing the shooting will serve to deprive him of a self-defense `out' at the time of trial." 16

When the techniques described above prove unavailing, the texts recommend they be alternated with a show of some hostility. One ploy often used has been termed the "friendly-unfriendly" or the "Mutt and Jeff" act:

". . . In this technique, two agents are employed. Mutt, the relentless investigator, who knows the subject is guilty and is not going to waste any time. He's sent a dozen men away for this crime and he's going to send the subject away for the full term. Jeff, on the other hand, is obviously a kindhearted man. He has a family himself. He has a brother who was involved in a little scrape like this. He disapproves of Mutt and his tactics and will arrange to get him off the case if the subject will cooperate. He can't hold Mutt off for very long. The subject would be wise to make a quick decision. The technique is applied by having both investigators present while Mutt acts out his role. Jeff may stand by quietly and demur at some of Mutt's tactics. When Jeff makes his plea for cooperation, Mutt is not present in the room." 17 [384 U.S. 436, 453]

The interrogators sometimes are instructed to induce a con-fession out of trickery. The technique here is quite effective in crimes which require identification or which run in series. In the identification situation, the interrogator may take a break in his questioning to place the subject among a group of men in a line-up. "The witness or complainant (previously coached, if necessary) studies the line-up and confidently points out the subject as the guilty party." 18 Then the questioning resumes "as though there were now no doubt about the guilt of the subject." A variation on this technique is called the "reverse line-up":

"The accused is placed in a line-up, but this time he is identified by several fictitious witnesses or victims who associated him with different offenses. It is expected that the subject will become desperate and confess to the offense under investigation in order to escape from the false accusations." 19

The manuals also contain instructions for police on how to handle the individual who refuses to discuss the matter entirely, or who asks for an attorney or relatives. The examiner is to concede him the right to remain silent. "This usually has a very undermining effect. First of all, he is disappointed in his expectation of an unfavorable reaction on the part of the interrogator. Secondly, a concession of this right to remain silent impresses [384 U.S. 436, 454]   the subject with the apparent fairness of his interrogator." 20 After this psychological conditioning, however, the officer is told to point out the incriminating significance of the suspect's refusal to talk:

"Joe, you have a right to remain silent. That's your privilege and I'm the last person in the world who'll try to take it away from you. If that's the way you want to leave this, O. K. But let me ask you this. Suppose you were in my shoes and I were in yours and you called me in to ask me about this and I told you, `I don't want to answer any of your questions.' You'd think I had something to hide, and you'd probably be right in thinking that. That's exactly what I'll have to think about you, and so will everybody else. So let's sit here and talk this whole thing over." 21

Few will persist in their initial refusal to talk, it is said, if this monologue is employed correctly.

In the event that the subject wishes to speak to a relative or an attorney, the following advice is tendered:

"[T]he interrogator should respond by suggesting that the subject first tell the truth to the interrogator himself rather than get anyone else involved in the matter. If the request is for an attorney, the interrogator may suggest that the subject save himself or his family the expense of any such professional service, particularly if he is innocent of the offense under investigation. The interrogator may also add, `Joe, I'm only looking for the truth, and if you're telling the truth, that's it. You can handle this by yourself.'" 22 [384 U.S. 436, 455]

From these representative samples of interrogation techniques, the setting prescribed by the manuals and observed in practice becomes clear. In essence, it is this: To be alone with the subject is essential to prevent distraction and to deprive him of any outside support. The aura of confidence in his guilt undermines his will to resist. He merely confirms the preconceived story the police seek to have him describe. Patience and persistence, at times relentless questioning, are employed. To obtain a confession, the interrogator must "patiently maneuver himself or his quarry into a position from which the desired objective may be attained." 23 When normal procedures fail to produce the needed result, the police may resort to deceptive stratagems such as giving false legal advice. It is important to keep the subject off balance, for example, by trading on his insecurity about himself or his surroundings. The police then persuade, trick, or cajole him out of exercising his constitutional rights.

Even without employing brutality, the "third degree" or the specific stratagems described above, the very fact of custodial interrogation exacts a heavy toll on individual liberty and trades on the weakness of individuals. 24 [384 U.S. 436, 456] This fact may be illustrated simply by referring to three confession cases decided by this Court in the Term immediately preceding our Escobedo decision. In Townsend v. Sain, 372 U.S. 293 (1963), the defendant was a 19-year-old heroin addict, described as a "near mental defective," id., at 307-310. The defendant in Lynumn v. Illinois, 372 U.S. 528 (1963), was a woman who confessed to the arresting officer after being importuned to "cooperate" in order to prevent her children from being taken by relief authorities. This Court as in those cases reversed the conviction of a defendant in Haynes v. Washington, 373 U.S. 503 (1963), whose persistent request during his interrogation was to phone his wife or attorney. 25 In other settings, these individuals might have exercised their constitutional rights. In the incommunicado police-dominated atmosphere, they succumbed.

In the cases before us today, given this background, we concern ourselves primarily with this interrogation atmosphere and the evils it can bring. In No. 759, Miranda v. Arizona, the police arrested the defendant and took him to a special interrogation room where they secured a confession. In No.

760, Vignera v. New York, the defendant made oral admissions to the police after interrogation in the afternoon, and then signed an inculpatory statement upon being questioned by an assistant district attorney later the same evening. In No. 761, Westover v. United States, the defendant was handed over to the Federal Bureau of Investigation by [384 U.S. 436, 457] local authorities after they had detained and interrogated him for a lengthy period, both at night and the following morning. After some two hours of questioning, the federal officers had obtained signed statements from the defendant. Lastly, in No. 584, California v. Stewart, the local police held the defendant five days in the station and interrogated him on nine separate occasions before they secured his inculpatory statement.

In these cases, we might not find the defendants' statements to have been involuntary in traditional terms. Our concern for adequate safeguards to protect precious Fifth Amendment rights is, of course, not lessened in the slightest. In each of the cases, the defendant was thrust into an unfamiliar atmosphere and run through menacing police interrogation procedures. The potentiality for compulsion is forcefully apparent, for example, in Miranda, where the indigent Mexican defendant was a seriously disturbed individual with pronounced sexual fantasies, and in Stewart, in which the defendant was an indigent Los Angeles Negro who had dropped out of school in the sixth grade. To be sure, the records do not evince overt physical coercion or patent psychological ploys. The fact remains that in none of these cases did the officers undertake to afford appropriate safeguards at the outset of the interrogation to insure that the statements were truly the product of free choice.

It is obvious that such an interrogation environment is created for no purpose other than to subjugate the individual to the will of his examiner. This atmosphere carries its own badge of intimidation. To be sure, this is not physical intimidation, but it is equally destructive of human dignity. 26 The current practice of incommunicado interrogation is at odds with one of our [384 U.S. 436, 458] Nation's most cherished principles - that the individual may not be compelled to incriminate himself. Unless adequate protective devices are employed to dispel the compulsion inherent in custodial surroundings, no statement obtained from the defendant can truly be the product of his free choice.

From the foregoing, we can readily perceive an intimate connection between the privilege against self-incrimination and police custodial questioning. It is fitting to turn to history and precedent underlying the Self-Incrimination Clause to determine its applicability in this situation.

II.

We sometimes forget how long it has taken to establish the privilege against self-incrimination, the sources from which it came and the fervor with which it was defended. Its roots go back into ancient times. 27 Perhaps [384 U.S. 436, 459] the critical historical event shedding light on its origins and evolution was the trial of one John Lilburn, a vocal anti-Stuart Leveller, who was made to take the Star Chamber Oath in 1637. The oath would have bound him to answer to all questions posed to him on any subject. The Trial of John Lilburn and John Wharton, 3 How. St. Tr. 1315 (1637). He resisted the oath and declaimed the proceedings, stating:

"Another fundamental right I then contended for, was, that no man's conscience ought to be racked by oaths imposed, to answer to questions concerning himself in matters criminal, or pretended to be so." Haller & Davies, The Leveller Tracts 1647-1653, p. 454 (1944).

On account of the Lilburn Trial, Parliament abolished the inquisitorial Court of Star Chamber and went further in giving him generous reparation. The lofty principles to which Lilburn had appealed during his trial gained popular acceptance in England. 28 These sentiments worked their way over to the Colonies and were implanted after great struggle into the Bill of Rights. 29 Those who framed our Constitution and the Bill of Rights were ever aware of subtle encroachments on individual liberty. They knew that "illegitimate and unconstitutional practices get their first footing . . . by silent approaches and slight deviations from legal modes of procedure." Boyd v. United States, 116 U.S. 616, 635 (1886). The privilege was elevated to constitutional status and has always been "as broad as the mischief [384 U.S. 436, 460] against which it seeks to guard." Counselman v. Hitchcock, 142 U.S. 547, 562 (1892). We cannot depart from this noble heritage.

Thus we may view the historical development of the privilege as one which groped for the proper scope of governmental power over the citizen. As a "noble principle often transcends its origins," the privilege has come rightfully to be recognized in part as an individual's substantive right, a "right to a private enclave where he may lead a private life. That right is the hallmark of our democracy." United States v.

Grunewald, 233 F.2d 556, 579, 581-582 (Frank, J., dissenting), rev'd, 353 U.S. 391 (1957). We have recently noted that the privilege against self-incrimination - the essential mainstay of our adversary system - is founded on a complex of values, Murphy v. Waterfront Comm'n, 378 U.S. 52, 55 -57, n. 5 (1964); Tehan v. Shott, 382 U.S. 406, 414 -415, n. 12 (1966). All these policies point to one overriding thought: the constitutional foundation underlying the privilege is the respect a government - state or federal - must accord to the dignity and integrity of its citizens. To maintain a "fair state-individual balance," to require the government "to shoulder the entire load," 8 Wigmore, Evidence 317 (McNaughton rev. 1961), to respect the inviolability of the human personality, our accusatory system of criminal justice demands that the government seeking to punish an individual produce the evidence against him by its own independent labors, rather than by the cruel, simple expedient of compelling it from his own mouth. Chambers v. Florida, 309 U.S. 227, 235 -238 (1940). In sum, the privilege is fulfilled only when the person is guaranteed the right "to remain silent unless he chooses to speak in the unfettered exercise of his own will." Malloy v. Hogan, 378 U.S. 1, 8 (1964).

The question in these cases is whether the privilege is fully applicable during a period of custodial interrogation. [384 U.S. 436, 461] In this Court, the privilege has consistently been accorded a liberal construction. Albertson v. SACB, 382 U.S. 70, 81 (1965); Hoffman v. United States, 341 U.S. 479, 486 (1951); Arndstein v. McCarthy, 254 U.S. 71, 72 -73 (1920); Counselman v. Hitchock, 142 U.S. 547, 562 (1892). We are satisfied that all the principles embodied in the privilege apply to informal compulsion exerted by law-enforcement officers during in-custody questioning. An individual swept from familiar surroundings into police custody, surrounded by antagonistic forces, and subjected to the techniques of persuasion described above cannot be otherwise than under compulsion to speak. As a practical matter, the compulsion to speak in the isolated setting of the police station may well be greater than in courts or other official investigations, where there are often impartial observers to guard against intimidation or trickery. 30

This question, in fact, could have been taken as settled in federal courts almost 70 years ago, when, in Bram v. United States, 168 U.S. 532, 542 (1897), this Court held:

"In criminal trials, in the courts of the United States, wherever a question arises whether a confession is incompetent because not voluntary, the issue is controlled by that portion of the Fifth Amendment . . . commanding that no person `shall be compelled in any criminal case to be a witness against himself.'"

In Bram, the Court reviewed the British and American history and case law and set down the Fifth Amendment standard for compulsion which we implement today:

"Much of the confusion which has resulted from the effort to deduce from the adjudged cases what [384 U.S. 436, 462] would be a sufficient quantum of proof to show that a confession was or was not voluntary, has arisen from a misconception of the subject to which the proof must address itself. The rule is not that in order to render a statement admissible the proof must be adequate to establish that the particular communications contained in a statement were voluntarily made, but it must be sufficient to establish that the making of the statement was voluntary; that is to say, that from the causes, which the law treats as legally sufficient to engender in the mind of the accused hope or fear in respect to the crime charged, the accused was not involuntarily impelled to make a statement, when but for the improper influences he would have remained silent. . . ." 168 U.S., at 549 . And see, id., at 542.

The Court has adhered to this reasoning. In 1924, Mr. Justice Brandeis wrote for a unanimous Court in reversing a conviction resting on a compelled confession, Wan v. United States, 266 U.S. 1 . He stated:

"In the federal courts, the requisite of voluntariness is not satisfied by establishing merely that the confession was not induced by a promise or a threat. A confession is voluntary in law if, and only if, it was, in fact, voluntarily made. A confession may have been given voluntarily, although it was made to police officers, while in custody, and in answer to an examination conducted by them. But a confession obtained by compulsion must be excluded whatever may have been the character of the compulsion, and whether the compulsion was applied in a judicial proceeding or otherwise. Bram v. United States, 168 U.S. 532 ." 266 U.S., at 14 -15.

In addition to the expansive historical development of the privilege and the sound policies which have nurtured [384 U.S. 436, 463] its evolution, judicial precedent thus clearly establishes its application to incommunicado interrogation. In fact, the Government concedes this point as well established in No. 761, Westover v. United States, stating: "We have no doubt . . . that it is possible for a suspect's Fifth Amendment right to be violated during in-custody questioning by a law-enforcement officer." 31

Because of the adoption by Congress of Rule 5 (a) of the Federal Rules of Criminal Procedure, and this Court's effectuation of that Rule in McNabb v. United States, 318 U.S. 332 (1943), and Mallory v. United States, 354 U.S. 449 (1957), we have had little occasion in the past quarter century to reach the constitutional issues in dealing with federal interrogations. These supervisory rules, requiring production of an arrested person before a commissioner "without unnecessary delay" and excluding evidence obtained in default of that statutory obligation, were nonetheless responsive to the same considerations of Fifth Amendment policy that unavoidably face us now as to the States. In McNabb, 318 U.S., at 343 -344, and in Mallory, 354 U.S., at 455 -456, we recognized both the dangers of interrogation and the appropriateness of prophylaxis stemming from the very fact of interrogation itself. 32

Our decision in Malloy v. Hogan, 378 U.S. 1 (1964), necessitates an examination of the scope of the privilege in state cases as well. In Malloy, we squarely held the [384 U.S. 436, 464] privilege applicable to the States, and held that the substantive standards underlying the privilege applied with full force to state court proceedings. There, as in Murphy v. Waterfront Comm'n, 378 U.S. 52 (1964), and Griffin v. California, 380 U.S. 609 (1965), we applied the existing Fifth Amendment standards to the case before us. Aside from the holding itself, the reasoning in Malloy made clear what had already become apparent - that the substantive and procedural safeguards surrounding admissibility of confessions in state cases had become exceedingly exacting, reflecting all the policies embedded in the privilege, 378 U.S., at 7 -8. 33 The voluntariness doctrine in the state cases, as Malloy indicates, encompasses all interrogation practices which are likely to exert such pressure upon an individual as to disable him from [384 U.S. 436, 465] making a free and rational choice. 34 The implications of this proposition were elaborated in our decision in Escobedo v. Illinois, 378 U.S. 478 , decided one week after Malloy applied the privilege to the States.

Our holding there stressed the fact that the police had not advised the defendant of his constitutional privilege to remain silent at the outset of the interrogation, and we drew attention to that fact at several points in the decision, 378 U.S., at 483 , 485, 491. This was no isolated factor, but an essential ingredient in our decision. The entire thrust of police interrogation there, as in all the cases today, was to put the defendant in such an emotional state as to impair his capacity for rational judgment. The abdication of the constitutional privilege - the choice on his part to speak to the police - was not made knowingly or competently because of the failure to apprise him of his rights; the compelling atmosphere of the in-custody interrogation, and not an independent decision on his part, caused the defendant to speak.

A different phase of the Escobedo decision was significant in its attention to the absence of counsel during the questioning. There, as in the cases today, we sought a protective device to dispel the compelling atmosphere of the interrogation. In Escobedo, however, the police did not relieve the defendant of the anxieties which they had created in the interrogation rooms. Rather, they denied his request for the assistance of counsel, 378 U.S., at 481 , 488, 491. 35 This heightened his dilemma, and [384 U.S. 436, 466] made his later statements the product of this compulsion. Cf. Haynes v. Washington, 373 U.S. 503, 514 (1963). The denial of the defendant's request for his attorney thus undermined his ability to exercise the privilege - to remain silent if he chose or to speak without any intimidation, blatant or subtle. The presence of counsel, in all the cases before us today, would be the adequate protective device necessary to make the process of police interrogation conform to the dictates of the privilege. His presence would insure that statements made in the government-established atmosphere are not the product of compulsion.

It was in this manner that Escobedo explicated another facet of the pre-trial privilege, noted in many of the Court's prior decisions: the protection of rights at trial. 36 That counsel is present when statements are taken from an individual during interrogation obviously enhances the integrity of the fact-finding processes in court. The presence of an attorney, and the warnings delivered to the individual, enable the defendant under otherwise compelling circumstances to tell his story without fear, effectively, and in a way that eliminates the evils in the interrogation process. Without the protections flowing from adequate warnings and the rights of counsel, "all the careful safeguards erected around the giving of testimony, whether by an accused or any other witness, would become empty formalities in a procedure where the most compelling possible evidence of guilt, a confession, would have already been obtained at the unsupervised pleasure of the police." Mapp v. Ohio, 367 U.S. 643, 685 (1961) (HARLAN, J., dissenting). Cf. Pointer v. Texas, 380 U.S. 400 (1965). [384 U.S. 436, 467]

III.

Today, then, there can be no doubt that the Fifth Amendment privilege is available outside of criminal court proceedings and serves to protect persons in all settings in which their freedom of action is curtailed in any significant way from being compelled to incriminate themselves. We have concluded that without proper safeguards the process of in-custody interrogation of persons suspected or accused of crime contains inherently compelling pressures which work to undermine the individual's will to resist and to compel him to speak where he would not otherwise do so freely. In order to combat these pressures and to permit a full opportunity to exercise the privilege against self-incrimination, the accused must be adequately and effectively apprised of his rights and the exercise of those rights must be fully honored.

It is impossible for us to foresee the potential alternatives for protecting the privilege which might be devised by Congress or the States in the exercise of their creative rule-making capacities. Therefore we cannot say that the Constitution necessarily requires adherence to any particular solution for the inherent compulsions of the interrogation process as it is presently conducted. Our decision in no way creates a constitutional straitjacket which will handicap sound efforts at reform, nor is it intended to have this effect. We encourage Congress and the States to continue their laudable search for increasingly effective ways of protecting the rights of the individual while promoting efficient enforcement of our criminal laws. However, unless we are shown other procedures which are at least as effective in apprising accused persons of their right of silence and in assuring a continuous opportunity to exercise it, the following safeguards must be observed.

At the outset, if a person in custody is to be subjected to interrogation, he must first be informed in clear and [384 U.S.

436, 468] unequivocal terms that he has the right to remain silent. For those unaware of the privilege, the warning is needed simply to make them aware of it - the threshold requirement for an intelligent decision as to its exercise. More important, such a warning is an absolute prerequisite in overcoming the inherent pressures of the interrogation atmosphere. It is not just the subnormal or woefully ignorant who succumb to an interrogator's imprecations, whether implied or expressly stated, that the interrogation will continue until a confession is obtained or that silence in the face of accusation is itself damning and will bode ill when presented to a jury. 37 Further, the warning will show the individual that his interrogators are prepared to recognize his privilege should he choose to exercise it.

The Fifth Amendment privilege is so fundamental to our system of constitutional rule and the expedient of giving an adequate warning as to the availability of the privilege so simple, we will not pause to inquire in individual cases whether the defendant was aware of his rights without a warning being given. Assessments of the knowledge the defendant possessed, based on information [384 U.S. 436, 469] as to his age, education, intelligence, or prior contact with authorities, can never be more than speculation; 38 a warning is a clearcut fact. More important, whatever the background of the person interrogated, a warning at the time of the interrogation is indispensable to overcome its pressures and to insure that the individual knows he is free to exercise the privilege at that point in time.

The warning of the right to remain silent must be accompanied by the explanation that anything said can and will be used against the individual in court. This warning is needed in order to make him aware not only of the privilege, but also of the consequences of forgoing it. It is only through an awareness of these consequences that there can be any assurance of real understanding and intelligent exercise of the privilege. Moreover, this warning may serve to make the individual more acutely aware that he is faced with a phase of the adversary system - that he is not in the presence of persons acting solely in his interest.

The circumstances surrounding in-custody interrogation can operate very quickly to overbear the will of one merely made aware of his privilege by his interrogators. Therefore, the right to have counsel present at the interrogation is indispensable to the protection of the Fifth Amendment privilege under the system we delineate today. Our aim is to assure that the individual's right to choose between silence and speech remains unfettered throughout the interrogation process. A once-stated warning, delivered by those who will conduct the interrogation, cannot itself suffice to that end among those who most require knowledge of their rights. A mere [384 U.S. 436, 470] warning given by the interrogators is not alone sufficient to accomplish that end. Prosecutors themselves claim that the admonishment of the right to remain silent without more "will benefit only the recidivist and the professional." Brief for the National District Attorneys Association as amicus curiae, p. 14. Even preliminary advice given to the accused by his own attorney can be swiftly overcome by the secret interrogation process. Cf. Escobedo v. Illinois, 378 U.S. 478, 485 , n. 5. Thus, the need for counsel to protect the Fifth Amendment privilege comprehends not merely a right to consult with counsel prior to questioning, but also to have counsel present during any questioning if the defendant so desires.

The presence of counsel at the interrogation may serve several significant subsidiary functions as well. If the accused decides to talk to his interrogators, the assistance of counsel can mitigate the dangers of untrustworthiness. With a lawyer present the likelihood that the police will practice coercion is reduced, and if coercion is nevertheless exercised the lawyer can testify to it in court. The presence of a lawyer can also help to guarantee that the accused gives a fully accurate statement to the police and that the statement is rightly reported by the prosecution at trial. See Crooker v. California, 357 U.S. 433, 443 -448 (1958) (DOUGLAS, J., dissenting).

An individual need not make a pre-interrogation request for a lawyer. While such request affirmatively secures his right to have one, his failure to ask for a lawyer does not constitute a waiver. No effective waiver of the right to counsel during interrogation can be recognized unless specifically made after the warnings we here delineate have been given. The accused who does not know his rights and therefore does not make a request [384 U.S. 436, 471]   may be the person who most needs counsel. As the California Supreme Court has aptly put it:

"Finally, we must recognize that the imposition of the requirement for the request would discriminate against the defendant who does not know his rights. The defendant who does not ask for counsel is the very defendant who most needs counsel. We cannot penalize a defendant who, not understanding his constitutional rights, does not make the formal request and by such failure demonstrates his helplessness. To require the request would be to favor the defendant whose sophistication or status had fortuitously prompted him to make it." People v. Dorado, 62 Cal. 2d 338, 351, 398 P.2d 361, 369-370, 42 Cal. Rptr. 169, 177-178 (1965) (Tobriner, J.).

In Carnley v. Cochran, 369 U.S. 506, 513 (1962), we stated: "[I]t is settled that where the assistance of counsel is a constitutional requisite, the right to be furnished counsel does not depend on a request." This proposition applies with equal force in the context of providing counsel to protect an accused's Fifth Amendment privilege in the face of interrogation. 39 Although the role of counsel at trial differs from the role during interrogation, the differences are not relevant to the question whether a request is a prerequisite.

Accordingly we hold that an individual held for interrogation must be clearly informed that he has the right to consult with a lawyer and to have the lawyer with him during interrogation under the system for protecting the privilege we delineate today. As with the warnings of the right to remain silent and that anything stated can be used in evidence against him, this warning is an absolute prerequisite to interrogation. No amount of [384 U.S. 436, 472]   circumstantial evidence that the person may have been aware of this right will suffice to stand in its stead: Only through such a warning is there as-certainable assurance that the accused was aware of this right.

If an individual indicates that he wishes the assistance of counsel before any interrogation occurs, the authorities can-not rationally ignore or deny his request on the basis that the individual does not have or cannot afford a retained attorney. The financial ability of the individual has no relationship to the scope of the rights involved here. The privilege against self-incrimination secured by the Constitution applies to all individuals. The need for counsel in order to protect the priv-ilege exists for the indigent as well as the affluent. In fact, were we to limit these constitutional rights to those who can retain an attorney, our decisions today would be of little significance. The cases before us as well as the vast majority of confession cases with which we have dealt in the past involve those unable to retain counsel. 40 While authorities are not required to relieve the accused of his poverty, they have the obligation not to take advantage of indigence in the administration of justice. 41 Denial [384 U.S. 436, 473]   of counsel to the indigent at the time of interrogation while allowing an attorney to those who can afford one would be no more supportable by reason or logic than the similar situation at trial and on appeal struck down in Gideon v. Wainwright, 372 U.S. 335 (1963), and Douglas v. California, 372 U.S. 353 (1963).

In order fully to apprise a person interrogated of the extent of his rights under this system then, it is necessary to warn him not only that he has the right to consult with an attorney, but also that if he is indigent a lawyer will be appointed to represent him. Without this additional warning, the admonition of the right to consult with counsel would often be understood as meaning only that he can consult with a lawyer if he has one or has the funds to obtain one. The warning of a right to counsel would be hollow if not couched in terms that would convey to the indigent - the person most often subjected to interrogation - the knowledge that he too has a right to have counsel present. 42 As with the warnings of the right to remain silent and of the general right to counsel, only by effective and express explanation to the indigent of this right can there be assurance that he was truly in a position to exercise it. 43

Once warnings have been given, the subsequent procedure is clear. If the individual indicates in any manner, [384 U.S. 436, 474]   at any time prior to or during questioning, that he wishes to remain silent, the interrogation must cease. 44 At this point he has shown that he intends to exercise his Fifth Amendment privilege; any statement taken after the person invokes his privilege cannot be other than the product of compulsion, subtle or otherwise. Without the right to cut off questioning, the setting of in-custody interrogation operates on the individual to overcome free choice in producing a statement after the privilege has been once invoked. If the individual states that he wants an attorney, the interrogation must cease until an attorney is present. At that time, the individual must have an opportunity to confer with the attorney and to have him present during any subsequent questioning.

If the individual cannot obtain an attorney and he indicates that he wants one before speaking to police, they must respect his decision to remain silent.

This does not mean, as some have suggested, that each police station must have a "station house lawyer" present at all times to advise prisoners. It does mean, however, that if police propose to interrogate a person they must make known to him that he is entitled to a lawyer and that if he cannot afford one, a lawyer will be provided for him prior to any interrogation. If authorities conclude that they will not provide counsel during a reasonable period of time in which investigation in the field is carried out, they may refrain from doing so without violating the person's Fifth Amendment privilege so long as they do not question him during that time. [384 U.S. 436, 475]

If the interrogation continues without the presence of an attorney and a statement is taken, a heavy burden rests on the government to demonstrate that the defendant knowingly and intelligently waived his privilege against self-incrimination and his right to retained or appointed counsel. Escobedo v. Illinois, 378 U.S. 478, 490 , n. 14. This Court has always set high standards of proof for the waiver of constitutional rights,

Johnson v. Zerbst, 304 U.S. 458 (1938), and we re-assert these standards as applied to in-custody interrogation. Since the State is responsible for establishing the isolated circumstances under which the interrogation takes place and has the only means of making available corroborated evidence of warnings given during incommunicado interrogation, the burden is rightly on its shoulders.

An express statement that the individual is willing to make a statement and does not want an attorney followed closely by a statement could constitute a waiver. But a valid waiver will not be presumed simply from the silence of the accused after warnings are given or simply from the fact that a confession was in fact eventually obtained. A statement we made in Carnley v. Cochran, 369 U.S. 506, 516 (1962), is applicable here:

"Presuming waiver from a silent record is impermissible. The record must show, or there must be an allegation and evidence which show, that an accused was offered counsel but intelligently and understandingly rejected the offer. Anything less is not waiver."

See also Glasser v. United States, 315 U.S. 60 (1942). Moreover, where in-custody interrogation is involved, there is no room for the contention that the privilege is waived if the individual answers some questions or gives [384 U.S. 436, 476] some information on his own prior to invoking his right to remain silent when interrogated. 45

Whatever the testimony of the authorities as to waiver of rights by an accused, the fact of lengthy interrogation or incommunicado incarceration before a statement is made is strong evidence that the accused did not validly waive his rights. In these circumstances the fact that the individual eventually made a statement is consistent with the conclusion that the compelling influence of the interrogation finally forced him to do so. It is inconsistent with any notion of a voluntary relinquishment of the privilege. Moreover, any evidence that the accused was threatened, tricked, or cajoled into a waiver will, of course, show that the defendant did not voluntarily waive his privilege. The requirement of warnings and waiver of rights is a fundamental with respect to the Fifth Amendment privilege and not simply a preliminary ritual to existing methods of interrogation.

The warnings required and the waiver necessary in accordance with our opinion today are, in the absence of a fully effective equivalent, prerequisites to the admissibility of any statement made by a defendant. No distinction can be drawn between statements which are direct confessions and statements which amount to "admissions" of part or all of an offense. The privilege against self-incrimination protects the individual from being compelled to incriminate himself in any manner; it does not distinguish degrees of incrimination. Similarly, [384 U.S. 436, 477]   for precisely the same reason, no distinction may be drawn between inculpatory statements and statements alleged to be merely "exculpatory." If a statement made were in fact truly exculpatory it would, of course, never be used by the prosecution. In fact, statements merely intended to be exculpatory by the defendant are often used to impeach his testimony at trial or to demonstrate untruths in the statement given under interrogation and thus to prove guilt by implication. These statements are incriminating in any meaningful sense of the word and may not be used without the full warnings and effective waiver required for any other statement. In Escobedo itself, the defendant fully intended his accusation of another as the slayer to be exculpatory as to himself.

The principles announced today deal with the protection which must be given to the privilege against self-incrimination when the individual is first subjected to police interrogation while in custody at the station or otherwise deprived of his freedom of action in any significant way. It is at this point that our adversary system of criminal proceedings commences, distinguishing itself at the outset from the inquisitorial system recognized in some countries. Under the system of warnings we delineate today or under any other system which may be devised and found effective, the safeguards to be erected about the privilege must come into play at this point.

Our decision is not intended to hamper the traditional function of police officers in investigating crime. See Escobedo v. Illinois, 378 U.S. 478, 492 . When an individual is in custody on probable cause, the police may, of course, seek out evidence in the field to be used at trial against him. Such investigation may include inquiry of persons not under restraint. General on-the-scene questioning as to facts surrounding a crime or other general questioning of citizens in the fact-finding process is not affected by our holding. It is an act of [384 U.S. 436, 478] responsible citizenship for individuals to give whatever information they may have to aid in law enforcement. In such situations the compelling atmosphere inherent in the process of in-custody interrogation is not necessarily present. 46

In dealing with statements obtained through interrogation, we do not purport to find all confessions inadmissible. Confessions remain a proper element in law enforcement. Any statement given freely and voluntarily without any compelling influences is, of course, admissible in evidence. The fundamental import of the privilege while an individual is in custody is not whether he is allowed to talk to the police without the benefit of warnings and counsel, but whether he can be interrogated. There is no requirement that police stop a person who enters a police station and states that he wishes to confess to a crime, 47 or a person who calls the police to offer a confession or any other statement he desires to make. Volunteered statements of any kind are not barred by the Fifth Amendment and their admissibility is not affected by our holding today.

To summarize, we hold that when an individual is taken into custody or otherwise deprived of his freedom by the authorities in any significant way and is subjected to questioning, the privilege against self-incrimination is jeopardized. Procedural safeguards must be employed to [384 U.S. 436,

479] protect the privilege, and unless other fully effective means are adopted to notify the person of his right of silence and to assure that the exercise of the right will be scrupulously honored, the following measures are required. He must be warned prior to any questioning that he has the right to remain silent, that anything he says can be used against him in a court of law, that he has the right to the presence of an attorney, and that if he cannot afford an attorney one will be appointed for him prior to any questioning if he so desires. Opportunity to exercise these rights must be afforded to him throughout the interrogation. After such warnings have been given, and such opportunity afforded him, the individual may knowingly and intelligently waive these rights and agree to answer questions or make a statement. But unless and until such warnings and waiver are demonstrated by the prosecution at trial, no evidence obtained as a result of interrogation can be used against him. 48

IV.

A recurrent argument made in these cases is that society's need for interrogation outweighs the privilege. This argument is not unfamiliar to this Court. See, e. g., Chambers v. Florida, 309 U.S. 227, 240 -241 (1940). The whole thrust of our foregoing discussion demonstrates that the Constitution has prescribed the rights of the individual when confronted with the power of government when it provided in the Fifth Amendment that an individual cannot be compelled to be a witness against himself. That right cannot be abridged. As Mr. Justice Brandeis once observed:

"Decency, security and liberty alike demand that government officials shall be subjected to the same [384 U.S. 436, 480] rules of conduct that are commands to the citizen. In a government of laws, existence of the government will be imperilled if it fails to observe the law scrupulously. Our Government is the potent, the omnipresent teacher. For good or for ill, it teaches the whole people by its example. Crime is contagious. If the Government becomes a lawbreaker, it breeds contempt for law; it invites every man to become a law unto himself; it invites anarchy. To declare that in the administration of the criminal law the end justifies the means . . . would bring terrible retribution. Against that pernicious doctrine this Court should resolutely set its face." Olmstead v. United States, 277 U.S. 438, 485 (1928) (dissenting opinion). 49

In this connection, one of our country's distinguished jurists has pointed out: "The quality of a nation's civilization can be largely measured by the methods it uses in the enforcement of its criminal law." 50

If the individual desires to exercise his privilege, he has the right to do so. This is not for the authorities to decide. An attorney may advise his client not to talk to police until he has had an opportunity to investigate the case, or he may wish to be present with his client during any police questioning. In doing so an attorney is merely exercising the good professional judgment he has been taught. This is not cause for considering the attorney a menace to law enforcement. He is merely carrying out what he is sworn to do under his oath - to protect to the extent of his ability the rights of his [384 U.S. 436, 481] client. In fulfilling this responsibility the attorney plays a vital role in the administration of criminal justice under our Constitution.

In announcing these principles, we are not unmindful of the burdens which law enforcement officials must bear, often under trying circumstances. We also fully recognize the obligation of all citizens to aid in enforcing the criminal laws. This Court, while protecting individual rights, has always given ample latitude to law enforcement agencies in the legitimate exercise of their duties. The limits we have placed on the interrogation process should not constitute an undue interference with a proper system of law enforcement. As we have noted, our decision does not in any way preclude police from carrying out their traditional investigatory functions. Although confessions may play an important role in some convictions, the cases before us present graphic examples of the overstatement of the "need" for confessions. In each case authorities conducted interrogations ranging up to five days in duration despite the presence, through standard investigating practices, of considerable evidence against each defendant. 51 Further examples are chronicled in our prior cases. See, e. g., Haynes v. Washington, 373 U.S. 503, 518 - 519 (1963); Rogers v. Richmond, 365 U.S. 534, 541 (1961); Malinski v. New York, 324 U.S. 401, 402 (1945). 52   [384 U.S. 436, 482]

It is also urged that an unfettered right to detention for interrogation should be allowed because it will often redound to the benefit of the person questioned. When police inquiry determines that there is no reason to believe that the person has committed any crime, it is said, he will be released without need for further formal procedures. The person who has committed no offense, however, will be better able to clear himself after warnings with counsel present than without. It can be assumed that in such circumstances a lawyer would advise his client to talk freely to police in order to clear himself.

Custodial interrogation, by contrast, does not necessarily afford the innocent an opportunity to clear themselves. A serious consequence of the present practice of the interrogation alleged to be beneficial for the innocent is that many arrests "for investigation" subject large numbers of innocent persons to detention and interrogation. In one of the cases before us, No. 584, California v. Stewart, police held four persons, who were in the defendant's house at the time of the arrest, in jail for five days until defendant confessed. At that time they were finally released. Police stated that there was "no evidence to connect them with any crime." Available statistics on the extent of this practice where it is condoned indicate that these four are far from alone in being subjected to arrest, prolonged detention, and interrogation without the requisite probable cause. 53   [384 U.S. 436, 483]

Over the years the Federal Bureau of Investigation has compiled an exemplary record of effective law enforcement while advising any suspect or arrested person, at the outset of an interview, that he is not required to make a statement, that any statement may be used against him in court, that the individual may obtain the services of an attorney of his own choice and, more recently, that he has a right to free counsel if he is unable to pay. 54 A letter received from the Solicitor General in response to a question from the Bench makes it clear that the present pattern of warnings and respect for the [384 U.S. 436, 484]   rights of the individual followed as a practice by the FBI is consistent with the procedure which we delineate today. It states:

"At the oral argument of the above cause, Mr. Justice Fortas asked whether I could provide certain information as to the practices followed by the Federal Bureau of Investigation. I have directed these questions to the attention of the Director of the Federal Bureau of Investigation and am submitting herewith a statement of the questions and of the answers which we have received.

"`(1) When an individual is interviewed by agents of the Bureau, what warning is given to him?

"'The standard warning long given by Special Agents of the FBI to both suspects and persons under arrest is that the person has a right to say nothing and a right to counsel, and that any statement he does make may be used against him in court. Examples of this warning are to be found in the Westover case at 342 F.2d 684 (1965), and Jackson v. U.S., 337 F.2d 136 (1964), cert. den. 380 U.S. 935 .

"'After passage of the Criminal Justice Act of 1964, which provides free counsel for Federal defendants unable to pay, we added to our instructions to Special Agents the requirement that any person who is under arrest for an offense under FBI jurisdiction, or whose arrest is contemplated following the interview, must also be advised of his right to free counsel if he is unable to pay, and the fact that such counsel will be assigned by the Judge. At the same time, we broadened the right to counsel warning [384 U.S. 436, 485] to read counsel of his own choice, or anyone else with whom he might wish to speak.

"'(2) When is the warning given?

"'The FBI warning is given to a suspect at the very outset of the interview, as shown in the Westover case, cited above. The warning may be given to a person arrested as soon as practicable after the arrest, as shown in the Jackson case, also cited above, and in U.S. v. Konigsberg, 336 F.2d 844 (1964), cert. den. 379 U.S. 933 , but in any event it must precede the interview with the person for a confession or admission of his own guilt.

"'(3) What is the Bureau's practice in the event that (a) the individual requests counsel and (b) counsel appears?

"'When the person who has been warned of his right to counsel decides that he wishes to consult with counsel before making a statement, the interview is terminated at that point, Shultz v. U.S., 351 F.2d 287 (1965). It may be continued, however, as to all matters other than the person's own guilt or innocence. If he is indecisive in his request for counsel, there may be some question on whether he did or did not waive counsel. Situations of this kind must necessarily be left to the judgment of the interviewing Agent. For example, in Hiram v. U.S., 354 F.2d 4 (1965), the Agent's conclusion that the person arrested had waived his right to counsel was upheld by the courts.

"'A person being interviewed and desiring to consult counsel by telephone must be permitted to do so, as shown in Caldwell v. U.S., 351 F.2d 459 (1965). When counsel appears in person, he is permitted to confer with his client in private. [384 U.S. 436, 486]

"'(4) What is the Bureau's practice if the individual requests counsel, but cannot afford to retain an attorney?

"'If any person being interviewed after warning of counsel decides that he wishes to consult with counsel before proceeding further the interview is terminated, as shown above. FBI Agents do not pass judgment on the ability of the person to pay for counsel. They do, however, advise those who have been arrested for an offense under FBI jurisdiction, or whose arrest is contemplated following the interview, of a right to free counsel if they are unable to pay, and the availability of such counsel from the Judge.'" 55

The practice of the FBI can readily be emulated by state and local enforcement agencies. The argument that the FBI deals with different crimes than are dealt with by state authorities does not mitigate the significance of the FBI experience. 56

The experience in some other countries also suggests that the danger to law enforcement in curbs on interrogation is overplayed. The English procedure since 1912 under the Judges' Rules is significant. As recently [384 U.S. 436,

487]   strengthened, the Rules require that a cautionary warning be given an accused by a police officer as soon as he has evidence that affords reasonable grounds for suspicion; they also require that any statement made be given by the accused without questioning by police. 57   [384 U.S. 436, 488]   The right of the individual to consult with an attorney during this period is expressly recognized. 58

The safeguards present under Scottish law may be even greater than in England. Scottish judicial decisions bar use in evidence of most confessions obtained through police interrogation. 59 In India, confessions made to police not in the presence of a magistrate have been excluded [384 U.S. 436, 489]   by rule of evidence since 1872, at a time when it operated under British law. 60 Identical provisions appear in the Evidence Ordinance of Ceylon, enacted in 1895. 61 Similarly, in our country the Uniform Code of Military Justice has long provided that no suspect may be interrogated without first being warned of his right not to make a statement and that any statement he makes may be used against him. 62 Denial of the right to consult counsel during interrogation has also been proscribed by military tribunals. 63 There appears to have been no marked detrimental effect on criminal law enforcement in these jurisdictions as a result of these rules. Conditions of law enforcement in our country are sufficiently similar to permit reference to this experience as assurance that lawlessness will not result from warning an individual of his rights or allowing him to exercise them. Moreover, it is consistent with our legal system that we give at least as much protection to these rights as is given in the jurisdictions described. We deal in our country with rights grounded in a specific requirement of the Fifth Amendment of the Constitution, [384 U.S. 436, 490]   whereas other jurisdictions arrived at their conclusions on the basis of principles of justice not so specifically defined. 64

It is also urged upon us that we withhold decision on this issue until state legislative bodies and advisory groups have had an opportunity to deal with these problems by rule making. 65 We have already pointed out that the Constitution does not require any specific code of procedures for protecting the privilege against self-incrimination during custodial interrogation. Congress and the States are free to develop their own safeguards for the privilege, so long as they are fully as effective as those described above in informing accused persons of their right of silence and in affording a continuous opportunity to exercise it. In any event, however, the issues presented are of constitutional dimensions and must be determined by the courts. The admissibility of a statement in the face of a claim that it was obtained in violation of the defendant's constitutional rights is an issue the resolution of which has long since been undertaken by this Court. See Hopt v. Utah, 110 U.S. 574 (1884). Judicial solutions to problems of constitutional dimension have evolved decade by decade. As courts have been presented with the need to enforce constitutional rights, they have found means of doing so. That was our responsibility when Escobedo was before us and it is our [384 U.S. 436, 491] responsibility today. Where rights secured by the Constitution are involved, there can be no rule making or legislation which would abrogate them.

V.

Because of the nature of the problem and because of its recurrent significance in numerous cases, we have to this point discussed the relationship of the Fifth Amendment privilege to police interrogation without specific concentration on the facts of the cases before us. We turn now to these facts to consider the application to these cases of the constitutional principles discussed above. In each instance, we have concluded that statements were obtained from the defendant under circumstances that did not meet constitutional standards for protection of the privilege.

No. 759. Miranda v. Arizona.

On March 13, 1963, petitioner, Ernesto Miranda, was arrested at his home and taken in custody to a Phoenix police station. He was there identified by the complaining witness. The police then took him to "Interrogation Room No. 2" of the detective bureau. There he was questioned by two police officers. The officers admitted at trial that Miranda was not advised that he had a right to have an attorney present. 66 Two hours later, the [384 U.S. 436, 492]   officers emerged from the interrogation room with a written confession signed by Miranda. At the top of the statement was a typed paragraph stating that the confession was made voluntarily, without threats or promises of immunity and "with full knowledge of my legal rights, understanding any statement I make may be used against me." 67

At his trial before a jury, the written confession was admitted into evidence over the objection of defense counsel, and the officers testified to the prior oral confession made by Miranda during the interrogation. Miranda was found guilty of kidnapping and rape. He was sentenced to 20 to 30 years' imprisonment on each count, the sentences to run concurrently. On appeal, the Supreme Court of Arizona held that Miranda's constitutional rights were not violated in obtaining the confession and affirmed the conviction. 98 Ariz. 18, 401 P.2d 721. In reaching its decision, the court emphasized heavily the fact that Miranda did not specifically request counsel.

We reverse. From the testimony of the officers and by the admission of respondent, it is clear that Miranda was not in any way apprised of his right to consult with an attorney and to have one present during the interrogation, nor was his right not to be compelled to incriminate himself effectively protected in any other manner. Without these warnings the statements were inadmissible. The mere fact that he signed a statement which contained a typed-in clause stating that he had "full knowledge" of his "legal rights" does not approach the knowing and intelligent waiver required to relinquish constitutional rights. Cf. Haynes v. Washington, 373

U.S. 503 , [384 U.S. 436, 493] 512-513 (1963); Haley v. Ohio, 332 U.S. 596, 601 (1948) (opinion of MR. JUSTICE DOUG-LAS).

No. 760. Vignera v. New York.

Petitioner, Michael Vignera, was picked up by New York police on October 14, 1960, in connection with the robbery three days earlier of a Brooklyn dress shop. They took him to the 17th Detective Squad headquarters in Manhattan. Sometime thereafter he was taken to the 66th Detective Squad. There a detective questioned Vignera with respect to the robbery. Vignera orally admitted the robbery to the detective. The detective was asked on cross-examination at trial by defense counsel whether Vignera was warned of his right to counsel before being interrogated. The prosecution objected to the question and the trial judge sustained the objection. Thus, the defense was precluded from making any showing that warnings had not been given. While at the 66th Detective Squad, Vignera was identified by the store owner and a saleslady as the man who robbed the dress shop. At about 3 p. m. he was formally arrested. The police then transported him to still another station, the 70th Precinct in

Brooklyn, "for detention." At 11 p. m. Vignera was questioned by an assistant district attorney in the presence of a hearing reporter who transcribed the questions and Vignera's answers. This verbatim account of these proceedings contains no statement of any warnings given by the assistant district attorney. At Vignera's trial on a charge of first degree robbery, the detective testified as to the oral confession. The transcription of the statement taken was also introduced in evidence. At the conclusion of the testimony, the trial judge charged the jury in part as follows:

"The law doesn't say that the confession is void or invalidated because the police officer didn't advise the defendant as to his rights. Did you hear what [384 U.S. 436, 494] I said? I am telling you what the law of the State of New York is."

Vignera was found guilty of first degree robbery. He was subsequently adjudged a third-felony offender and sentenced to 30 to 60 years' imprisonment. 68 The conviction was affirmed without opinion by the Appellate Division, Second Department, 21 App. Div. 2d 752, 252 N. Y. S. 2d 19, and by the Court of Appeals, also without opinion, 15 N. Y. 2d 970, 207 N. E. 2d 527, 259 N. Y. S. 2d 857, remittitur amended, 16 N.

Y. 2d 614, 209 N. E. 2d 110, 261 N. Y. S. 2d 65. In argument to the Court of Appeals, the State contended that Vignera had no constitutional right to be advised of his right to counsel or his privilege against self-incrimination.

We reverse. The foregoing indicates that Vignera was not warned of any of his rights before the questioning by the detective and by the assistant district attorney. No other steps were taken to protect these rights. Thus he was not effectively apprised of his Fifth Amendment privilege or of his right to have counsel present and his statements are inadmissible.

No. 761. Westover v. United States.

At approximately 9:45 p. m. on March 20, 1963, petitioner, Carl Calvin Westover, was arrested by local police in Kansas City as a suspect in two Kansas City robberies. A report was also received from the FBI that he was wanted on a felony charge in California. The local authorities took him to a police station and placed him in a line-up on the local charges, and at about 11:45 p. m. he was booked. Kansas City police interrogated Westover [384 U.S. 436, 495] on the night of his arrest. He denied any knowledge of criminal activities. The next day local officers interrogated him again throughout the morning. Shortly before noon they informed the FBI that they were through interrogating Westover and that the FBI could proceed to interrogate him. There is nothing in the record to indicate that Westover was ever given any warning as to his rights by local police. At noon, three special agents of the FBI continued the interrogation in a private interview room of the Kansas City Police Department, this time with respect to the robbery of a savings and loan association and a bank in Sacramento, California. After two or two and one-half hours, Westover signed separate confessions to each of these two robberies which had been prepared by one of the agents during the interrogation. At trial one of the agents testified, and a paragraph on each of the statements states, that the agents advised Westover that he did not have to make a statement, that any statement he made could be used against him, and that he had the right to see an attorney.

Westover was tried by a jury in federal court and convicted of the California robberies. His statements were introduced at trial. He was sentenced to 15 years' imprisonment on each count, the sentences to run consecutively. On appeal, the conviction was affirmed by the Court of Appeals for the Ninth Circuit. 342 F.2d 684.

We reverse. On the facts of this case we cannot find that Westover knowingly and intelligently waived his right to remain silent and his right to consult with counsel prior to the time he made the statement. 69 At the [384 U.S. 436, 496] time the FBI agents began questioning Westover, he had been in custody for over 14 hours and had been interrogated at length during that period. The FBI interrogation began immediately upon the conclusion of the interrogation by Kansas City police and was conducted in local police headquarters. Although the two law enforcement authorities are legally distinct and the crimes for which they interrogated Westover were different, the impact on him was that of a continuous period of questioning. There is no evidence of any warning given prior to the FBI interrogation nor is there any evidence of an articulated waiver of rights after the FBI commenced its interrogation. The record simply shows that the defendant did in fact confess a short time after being turned over to the FBI following interrogation by local police. Despite the fact that the FBI agents gave warnings at the outset of their interview, from Westover's point of view the warnings came at the end of the interrogation process. In these circumstances an intelligent waiver of constitutional rights cannot be assumed.

We do not suggest that law enforcement authorities are precluded from questioning any individual who has been held for a period of time by other authorities and interrogated by them without appropriate warnings. A different case would be presented if an accused were taken into custody by the second authority, removed both in time and place from his original surroundings, and then adequately advised of his rights and given an opportunity to exercise them. But here the FBI interrogation was conducted immediately following the state interrogation in the same police station - in the same compelling surroundings. Thus, in obtaining a confession from Westover [384 U.S. 436, 497] the federal authorities were the beneficiaries of the pressure applied by the local in-custody interrogation. In these circumstances the giving of warnings alone was not sufficient to protect the privilege.

No. 584. California v. Stewart.

In the course of investigating a series of purse-snatch robberies in which one of the victims had died of injuries inflicted by her assailant, respondent, Roy Allen Stewart, was pointed out to Los Angeles police as the endorser of dividend checks taken in one of the robberies. At about 7:15 p. m.,

January 31, 1963, police officers went to Stewart's house and arrested him. One of the officers asked Stewart if they could search the house, to which he replied, "Go ahead." The search turned up various items taken from the five robbery victims. At the time of Stewart's arrest, police also arrested Stewart's wife and three other persons who were visiting him. These four were jailed along with Stewart and were interrogated. Stewart was taken to the University Station of the Los Angeles Police Department where he was placed in a cell. During the next five days, police interrogated Stewart on nine different occasions. Except during the first interrogation session, when he was confronted with an accusing witness, Stewart was isolated with his interrogators.

During the ninth interrogation session, Stewart admitted that he had robbed the deceased and stated that he had not meant to hurt her. Police then brought Stewart before a magistrate for the first time. Since there was no evidence to connect them with any crime, the police then released the other four persons arrested with him.

Nothing in the record specifically indicates whether Stewart was or was not advised of his right to remain silent or his right to counsel. In a number of instances, [384 U.S. 436,

498] however, the interrogating officers were asked to re-count everything that was said during the interrogations. None indicated that Stewart was ever advised of his rights.

Stewart was charged with kidnapping to commit robbery, rape, and murder. At his trial, transcripts of the first interrogation and the confession at the last interrogation were introduced in evidence. The jury found Stewart guilty of robbery and first degree murder and fixed the penalty as death. On appeal, the Supreme Court of California reversed. 62 Cal. 2d 571, 400 P.2d 97, 43 Cal. Rptr. 201. It held that under this Court's decision in Escobedo, Stewart should have been advised of his right to remain silent and of his right to counsel and that it would not presume in the face of a silent record that the police advised Stewart of his rights. 70

We affirm. 71 In dealing with custodial interrogation, we will not presume that a defendant has been effectively apprised of his rights and that his privilege against self-incrimination has been adequately safeguarded on a record that does not show that any warnings have been given or that any effective alternative has been employed. Nor can a knowing and intelligent waiver of [384 U.S. 436, 499] these rights be assumed on a silent record. Furthermore, Stewart's steadfast denial of the alleged offenses through eight of the nine inter-rogations over a period of five days is subject to no other construction than that he was compelled by persistent inter-rogation to forgo his Fifth Amendment privilege.

Therefore, in accordance with the foregoing, the judgments of the Supreme Court of Arizona in No. 759, of the New York Court of Appeals in No. 760, and of the Court of Appeals for the Ninth Circuit in No. 761 are reversed. The judgment of the Supreme Court of California in No. 584 is affirmed.

It is so ordered.

Footnotes

[Footnote 1] Compare United States v. Childress, 347 F.2d 448 (C. A. 7th Cir. 1965), with Collins v. Beto, 348 F.2d 823 (C. A. 5th Cir. 1965). Compare People v. Dorado, 62 Cal. 2d 338, 398 P.2d 361, 42 Cal. Rptr. 169 (1964) with People v. Hartgraves, 31 Ill. 2d 375, 202 N. E. 2d 33 (1964).

[Footnote 2] See, e. g., Enker & Elsen, Counsel for the Sus-pect: Massiah v. United States and Escobedo v. Illinois, 49 Minn. L. Rev. 47 (1964); Herman, The Supreme Court and Restrictions on Police Interrogation, 25 Ohio St. L. J. 449

(1964); Kamisar, Equal Justice in the Gatehouses and Mansions of American Criminal Procedure, in Criminal Justice in Our Time 1 (1965); Dowling, Escobedo and [384 U.S. 436, 441] Beyond: The Need for a Fourteenth Amendment Code of Criminal Procedure, 56 J. Crim. L., C. & P. S. 143, 156 (1965).

The complex problems also prompted discussions by jurists. Compare Bazelon, Law, Morality, and Civil Liberties, 12 U. C. L. A. L. Rev. 13 (1964), with Friendly, The Bill of Rights as a Code of Criminal Procedure, 53 Calif. L. Rev. 929 (1965).

[Footnote 3] For example, the Los Angeles Police Chief stated that "If the police are required . . . to . . . establish that the defendant was apprised of his constitutional guarantees of silence and legal counsel prior to the uttering of any admission or confession, and that he intelligently waived these guarantees . . . a whole Pandora's box is opened as to under what circumstances . . . can a defendant intelligently waive these rights. . . . Allegations that modern criminal investigation can compensate for the lack of a confession or admission in every criminal case is totally absurd!" Parker, 40 L. A.

Bar Bull. 603, 607, 642 (1965). His prosecutorial counterpart, District Attorney Younger, stated that "[I]t begins to appear that many of these seemingly restrictive decisions are going to contribute directly to a more effective, efficient and professional level of law enforcement." L. A. Times, Oct. 2, 1965, p. 1. The former Police Commissioner of New York, Michael J. Murphy, stated of Escobedo: "What the Court is doing is akin to requiring one boxer to fight by Marquis of Queensbury rules while permitting the other to butt, gouge and bite." N. Y. Times, May 14, 1965, p. 39. The former United States Attorney for the District of Columbia, David C. Acheson, who is presently Special Assistant to the Secretary of the Treasury (for Enforcement), and directly in charge of the Secret Service and the Bureau of Narcotics, observed that "Prosecution procedure has, at most, only the most remote causal connection with crime. Changes in court decisions and prosecution procedure would have about the same effect on the crime rate as an aspirin would have on a tumor of the brain." Quoted in Herman, supra, n. 2, at 500, n. 270. Other views on the subject in general are collected in Weisberg, Police Interrogation of Arrested Persons: A Skeptical View, 52 J. Crim. L., C. & P. S. 21 (1961).

[Footnote 4] This is what we meant in Escobedo when we spoke of an investigation which had focused on an accused.

[Footnote 5] See, for example, IV National Commission on Law Observance and Enforcement, Report on Lawlessness in Law Enforcement (1931) [384 U.S. 436, 446] [Wickersham Report]; Booth, Confessions, and Methods Employed in Procuring Them, 4 So. Calif. L. Rev. 83 (1930); Kauper, Judicial Examination of the Accused - A Remedy for the Third Degree, 30 Mich. L. Rev. 1224 (1932). It is significant that instances of third-degree treatment of prisoners almost invariably took place during the period between arrest and preliminary examination. Wickersham Report, at 169; Hall, The Law of Arrest in Relation to Contemporary Social Problems, 3 U. Chi. L. Rev. 345, 357 (1936). See also Foote, Law and Police Practice: Safeguards in the Law of Arrest, 52 Nw. U. L. Rev. 16 (1957).

[Footnote 6] Brown v. Mississippi, 297 U.S. 278 (1936); Chambers v. Florida, 309 U.S. 227 (1940); Canty v. Alabama, 309 U.S. 629 (1940); White v. Texas, 310 U.S. 530 (1940); Vernon v. Alabama, 313 U.S. 547 (1941); Ward v. Texas, 316 U.S. 547 (1942); Ashcraft v. Tennessee, 322 U.S. 143 (1944); Malinski

v. New York, 324 U.S. 401 (1945); Leyra v. Denno, 347 U.S. 556 (1954). See also Williams v. United States, 341 U.S. 97 (1951).

[Footnote 7] In addition, see People v. Wakat, 415 Ill. 610, 114 N. E. 2d 706 (1953); Wakat v. Harlib, 253 F.2d 59 (C. A. 7th Cir. 1958) (defendant suffering from broken bones, multiple bruises and injuries sufficiently serious to require eight months' medical treatment after being manhandled by five policemen); Kier v. State, 213 Md. 556, 132 A. 2d 494 (1957) (police doctor told accused, who was [384 U.S. 436, 447] strapped to a chair completely nude, that he proposed to take hair and skin scrapings from anything that looked like blood or sperm from various parts of his body); Bruner v. People, 113 Colo. 194, 156 P.2d 111 (1945) (defendant held in custody over two months, deprived of food for 15 hours, forced to submit to a lie detector test when he wanted to go to the toilet); People v. Matlock, 51 Cal. 2d 682, 336 P.2d 505 (1959) (defendant questioned incessantly over an evening's time, made to lie on cold board and to answer questions whenever it appeared he was getting sleepy). Other cases are documented in American Civil Liberties Union, Illinois Division, Secret Detention by the Chicago Police (1959); Potts, The Preliminary Examination and "The Third

Degree," 2 Baylor L. Rev. 131 (1950); Sterling, Police Inter-rogation and the Psychology of Confession, 14 J. Pub. L. 25 (1965).

[Footnote 8] The manuals quoted in the text following are the most recent and representative of the texts currently availa-ble. Material of the same nature appears in Kidd, Police In-terrogation (1940); Mulbar, Interrogation (1951); Dienstein, Technics for the Crime Investigator 97-115 (1952). Studies concerning the observed practices of the police appear in LaFave, Arrest: The Decision To Take a Suspect Into Cus-tody 244-437, 490-521 (1965); LaFave, Detention for Inves-tigation by the Police: An Analysis of Current Practices, 1962 Wash. U. L. Q. 331; Barrett, Police Practices and the Law - From Arrest to Release or Charge, 50 Calif. L. Rev. 11 (1962); Sterling, supra, n. 7, at 47-65.

[Footnote 9] The methods described in Inbau & Reid, Crimi-nal Interrogation and Confessions (1962), are a revision and enlargement of material presented in three prior editions of a predecessor text, Lie Detection and Criminal Interrogation (3d ed. 1953). The authors and their associates are officers of the Chicago Police Scientific Crime Detection Laboratory and have had extensive experience in writing, lecturing and speaking to law enforcement authorities over a 20-year period. They say that the techniques portrayed in their manuals reflect their experiences and are the most effective psychological stratagems to employ during interrogations. Similarly, the techniques described in O'Hara, Fundamentals of Criminal Investigation (1956), were gleaned from long service as observer, lecturer in police science, and work as a federal criminal investigator. All these texts have had rather extensive use among law enforcement agencies and among students of police science, with total sales and circulation of over 44,000.

[Footnote 10] Inbau & Reid, Criminal Interrogation and Confessions (1962), at 1.

[Footnote 11] O'Hara, supra, at 99.

[Footnote 12] Inbau & Reid, supra, at 34-43, 87. For example, in Leyra v. Denno, 347 U.S. 556 (1954), the interrogator-psychiatrist told the accused, "We do sometimes things that are not right, but in a fit of temper or anger we sometimes do things we aren't really responsible for," id., at 562, and again, "We know that morally you were just in anger. Morally, you are not to be condemned," id., at 582.

[Footnote 13] Inbau & Reid, supra, at 43-55.

[Footnote 14] O'Hara, supra, at 112.

[Footnote 15] Inbau & Reid, supra, at 40.

[Footnote 16] Ibid.

[Footnote 17] O'Hara, supra, at 104, Inbau & Reid, supra, at 58-59. See Spano v. New York, 360 U.S. 315 (1959). A variant on the technique [384 U.S. 436, 453] of creating hostility is one of engendering fear. This is perhaps best described by the prosecuting attorney in Malinski v. New York, 324 U.S. 401, 407 (1945): "Why this talk about being undressed? Of course, they had a right to undress him to look for bullet scars, and keep the clothes off him. That was quite proper police procedure. That is some more psychology - let him sit around with a blanket on him, humiliate him there for a while; let him sit in the corner, let him think he is going to get a shellacking."

[Footnote 18] O'Hara, supra, at 105-106.

[Footnote 19] Id., at 106.

[Footnote 20] Inbau & Reid, supra, at 111.

[Footnote 21] Ibid.

[Footnote 22] Inbau & Reid, supra, at 112.

[Footnote 23] Inbau & Reid, Lie Detection and Criminal Interrogation 185 (3d ed. 1953).

[Footnote 24] Interrogation procedures may even give rise to a false confession. The most recent conspicuous example occurred in New York, in 1964, when a Negro of limited intelligence confessed to two brutal murders and a rape which he had not committed. When this was discovered, the prosecutor was reported as saying: "Call it what you want - brainwashing, hypnosis, fright. They made him give an untrue confession. The only thing I don't believe is that Whitmore was beaten." N. Y. Times, Jan. 28, 1965, p. 1, col. 5. In two other instances, similar events had occurred. N. Y. Times, Oct. 20, 1964, p. 22, col. 1; N. Y. Times, Aug. 25, 1965, p. 1, col. 1. In general, see Borchard, Convicting the Innocent (1932); Frank & Frank, Not Guilty (1957).

[Footnote 25] In the fourth confession case decided by the Court in the 1962 Term, Fay v. Noia, 372 U.S. 391 (1963), our disposition made it unnecessary to delve at length into the facts. The facts of the defendant's case there, however, paralleled those of his co-defendants, whose confessions were found to have resulted from continuous and coercive interrogation for 27 hours, with denial of requests for friends or attorney. See United States v. Murphy, 222 F.2d 698 (C. A. 2d Cir. 1955) (Frank, J.); People v. Bonino, 1 N. Y. 2d 752, 135 N. E. 2d 51 (1956).

[Footnote 26] The absurdity of denying that a confession obtained under these circumstances is compelled is aptly portrayed by an example in Professor [384 U.S. 436, 458] Sutherland's recent article, Crime and Confession, 79 Harv. L. Rev. 21, 37 (1965):

"Suppose a well-to-do testatrix says she intends to will her property to Elizabeth. John and James want her to bequeath it to them instead. They capture the testatrix, put her in a carefully designed room, out of touch with everyone but themselves and their convenient 'witnesses,' keep her secluded there for hours while they make insistent demands, weary her with contradictions of her assertions that she wants to leave her money to Elizabeth, and finally induce her to execute the will in their favor. Assume that John and James are deeply and correctly convinced that Elizabeth is unworthy and will make base use of the property if she gets her hands on it, whereas John and James have the noblest and most righteous intentions. Would any judge of probate accept the will so procured as the `voluntary' act of the testatrix?"

[Footnote 27] Thirteenth century commentators found an analogue to the privilege grounded in the Bible. "To sum up the matter, the principle that no man is to be declared guilty on his own admission is a divine decree." Maimonides, Mishneh Torah (Code of Jewish Law), Book of Judges, Laws of the Sanhedrin, c. 18, 6, III Yale Judaica Series 52-53. See also Lamm, The Fifth Amendment and Its Equivalent in the Halakhah, 5 Judaism 53 (Winter 1956).

[Footnote 28] See Morgan, The Privilege Against Self-Incrimination, 34 Minn. L. Rev. 1, 9-11 (1949); 8 Wigmore, Evidence 289-295 (McNaughton rev. 1961). See also Lowell, The Judicial Use of Torture, Parts I and II, 11 Harv. L. Rev. 220, 290 (1897).

[Footnote 29] See Pittman, The Colonial and Constitutional History of the Privilege Against Self-Incrimination in America, 21 Va. L. Rev. 763 (1935); Ullmann v. United States, 350 U.S. 422, 445 -449 (1956) (DOUGLAS, J., dissenting).

[Footnote 30] Compare Brown v. Walker, 161 U.S. 591 (1896); Quinn v. United States, 349 U.S. 155 (1955).

[Footnote 31] Brief for the United States, p. 28. To the same effect, see Brief for the United States, pp. 40-49, n. 44, Anderson v. United States, 318 U.S. 350 (1943); Brief for the United States, pp. 17-18, McNabb v. United States, 318 U.S. 332 (1943).

[Footnote 32] Our decision today does not indicate in any manner, of course, that these rules can be disregarded. When federal officials arrest an individual, they must as always comply with the dictates of the congressional legislation and cases thereunder. See generally, Hogan & Snee, The McNabb-Mallory Rule: Its Rise, Rationale and Rescue, 47 Geo. L. J. 1 (1958).

[Footnote 33] The decisions of this Court have guaranteed the same procedural protection for the defendant whether his confession was used in a federal or state court. It is now axiomatic that the defendant's constitutional rights have been violated if his conviction is based, in whole or in part, on an involuntary confession, regardless of its truth or falsity. Rogers v. Richmond, 365 U.S. 534, 544 (1961); Wan v. United States, 266 U.S. 1 (1924). This is so even if there is ample evidence aside from the confession to support the conviction, e. g., Malinski v. New York, 324 U.S. 401, 404 (1945);

Bram v. United States, 168 U.S. 532, 540 -542 (1897). Both state and federal courts now adhere to trial procedures which seek to assure a reliable and clear-cut determination of the voluntariness of the confession offered at trial, Jackson v. Denno, 378 U.S. 368 (1964); United States v. Carignan, 342 U.S. 36, 38 (1951); see also Wilson v. United States, 162 U.S. 613, 624 (1896). Appellate review is exacting, see Haynes v. Washington, 373 U.S. 503 (1963); Blackburn v. Alabama, 361 U.S. 199 (1960). Whether his conviction was in a federal or state court, the defendant may secure a post-conviction hearing based on the alleged involuntary character of his confession, provided he meets the procedural requirements, Fay v. Noia, 372 U.S. 391 (1963); Townsend v. Sain, 372 U.S. 293 (1963). In addition, see Murphy v. Waterfront Comm'n, 378 U.S. 52 (1964).

[Footnote 34] See Lisenba v. California, 314 U.S. 219, 241 (1941); Ashcraft v. Tennessee, 322 U.S. 143 (1944); Malinski v. New York, 324 U.S. 401 (1945); Spano v. New York, 360 U.S. 315 (1959); Lynumn v. Illinois, 372 U.S. 528 (1963); Haynes v. Washington, 373 U.S. 503 (1963).

[Footnote 35] The police also prevented the attorney from consulting with his client. Independent of any other constitutional proscription, this action constitutes a violation of the Sixth Amendment right to the assistance of counsel and excludes any statement obtained in its [384 U.S. 436, 466] wake. See People v. Donovan, 13 N. Y. 2d 148, 193 N. E. 2d 628, 243 N. Y. S. 2d 841 (1963) (Fuld, J.).

[Footnote 36] In re Groban, 352 U.S. 330, 340 -352 (1957) (BLACK, J., dissenting); Note, 73 Yale L. J. 1000, 1048-1051 (1964); Comment, 31 U. Chi. L. Rev. 313, 320 (1964) and authorities cited.

[Footnote 37] See p. 454, supra. Lord Devlin has commented:

"It is probable that even today, when there is much less ignorance about these matters than formerly, there is still a general belief that you must answer all questions put to you by a policeman, or at least that it will be the worse for you if you do not." Devlin, The Criminal Prosecution in England 32 (1958).

In accord with our decision today, it is impermissible to penalize an individual for exercising his Fifth Amendment privilege when he is under police custodial interrogation. The prosecution may not, therefore, use at trial the fact that he stood mute or claimed his privilege in the face of accusation. Cf. Griffin v. California, 380 U.S. 609 (1965); Malloy v. Hogan, 378 U.S. 1, 8 (1964); Comment, 31 U. Chi. L. Rev. 556 (1964); Developments in the Law - Confessions, 79 Harv. L. Rev. 935, 1041-1044 (1966). See also Bram v. United States, 168 U.S. 532, 562 (1897).

[Footnote 38] Cf. Betts v. Brady, 316 U.S. 455 (1942), and the recurrent inquiry into special circumstances it necessitated. See generally, Kamisar, Betts v. Brady Twenty Years Later: The Right to Counsel and Due Process Values, 61 Mich. L. Rev. 219 (1962).

[Footnote 39] See Herman, The Supreme Court and Restrictions on Police Interrogation, 25 Ohio St. L. J. 449, 480 (1964).

[Footnote 40] Estimates of 50-90% indigency among felony defendants have been reported. Pollock, Equal Justice in Practice, 45 Minn. L. Rev. 737, 738-739 (1961); Birzon, Kasanof & Forma, The Right to Counsel and the Indigent Accused in Courts of Criminal Jurisdiction in New York State, 14 Buffalo L. Rev. 428, 433 (1965).

[Footnote 41] See Kamisar, Equal Justice in the Gatehouses and Mansions of American Criminal Procedure, in Criminal Justice in Our Time 1, 64-81 (1965). As was stated in the Report of the Attorney General's Committee on Poverty and the Administration of Federal Criminal Justice 9 (1963):

"When government chooses to exert its powers in the criminal area, its obligation is surely no less than that of taking reasonable measures to eliminate those factors that are irrelevant to just administration of the law but which, nevertheless, may occasionally affect determinations of the accused's liability or penalty. While government [384 U.S. 436, 473] may not be required to relieve the accused of his poverty, it may properly be required to minimize the influence of poverty on its administration of justice."

[Footnote 42] Cf. United States ex rel. Brown v. Fay, 242 F. Supp. 273, 277 (D.C. S. D. N. Y. 1965); People v. Witenski, 15 N. Y. 2d 392, 207 N. E. 2d 358, 259 N. Y. S. 2d 413 (1965).

[Footnote 43] While a warning that the indigent may have counsel appointed need not be given to the person who is known to have an attorney or is known to have ample funds to secure one, the expedient of giving a warning is too simple and the rights involved too important to engage in ex post facto inquiries into financial ability when there is any doubt at all on that score.

[Footnote 44] If an individual indicates his desire to remain silent, but has an attorney present, there may be some circumstances in which further questioning would be permissible. In the absence of evidence of overbearing, statements then made in the presence of counsel might be free of the compelling influence of the interrogation process and might fairly be construed as a waiver of the privilege for purposes of these statements.

[Footnote 45] Although this Court held in Rogers v. United States, 340 U.S. 367 (1951), over strong dissent, that a witness before a grand jury may not in certain circumstances decide to answer some questions and then refuse to answer others, that decision has no application to the interrogation situation we deal with today. No legislative or judicial fact-finding authority is involved here, nor is there a possibility that the individual might make self-serving statements of which he could make use at trial while refusing to answer incriminating statements.

[Footnote 46] The distinction and its significance has been aptly described in the opinion of a Scottish court:

"In former times such questioning, if undertaken, would be conducted by police officers visiting the house or place of business of the suspect and there questioning him, probably in the presence of a relation or friend. However convenient the modern practice may be, it must normally create a situation very unfavorable to the suspect." Chalmers v. H. M. Advocate, 1954. Sess. Cas. 66, 78 (J. C.).

[Footnote 47] See People v. Dorado, 62 Cal. 2d 338, 354, 398 P.2d 361, 371, 42 Cal. Rptr. 169, 179 (1965).

[Footnote 48] In accordance with our holdings today and in Escobedo v. Illinois, 378 U.S. 478, 492 , Crooker v. California, 357 U.S. 433 (1958) and Cicenia v. Lagay, 357 U.S. 504 (1958) are not to be followed.

[Footnote 49] In quoting the above from the dissenting opinion of Mr. Justice Brandeis we, of course, do not intend to pass on the constitutional questions involved in the Olmstead case.

[Footnote 50] Schaefer, Federalism and State Criminal Procedure, 70 Harv. L. Rev. 1, 26 (1956).

[Footnote 51] Miranda, Vignera, and Westover were identified by eyewitnesses. Marked bills from the bank robbed were found in Westover's car. Articles stolen from the victim as well as from several other robbery victims were found in Stewart's home at the outset of the investigation.

[Footnote 52] Dealing as we do here with constitutional standards in relation to statements made, the existence of independent corroborating evidence produced at trial is, of course, irrelevant to our decisions. Haynes v. Washington, 373 U.S. 503, 518 -519 (1963); Lynumn v. [384 U.S. 436, 482] Illinois, 372 U.S. 528, 537 -538 (1963); Rogers v. Richmond, 365 U.S. 534, 541 (1961); Blackburn v. Alabama, 361 U.S. 199, 206 (1960).

[Footnote 53] See, e. g., Report and Recommendations of the [District of Columbia] Commissioners' Committee on Police Arrests for Investigation (1962); American Civil Liberties Union, Secret Detention by the Chicago Police (1959). An extreme example of this practice occurred in the District of Columbia in 1958. Seeking three "stocky" young Negroes who had robbed a restaurant, police rounded up 90 persons of that general description. Sixty-three were held overnight

[384 U.S. 436, 483]   before being released for lack of evidence. A man not among the 90 arrested was ultimately charged with the crime. Washington Daily News, January 21, 1958, p. 5, col. 1; Hearings before a Subcommittee of the Senate Judiciary Committee on H. R. 11477, S. 2970, S. 3325, and S. 3355, 85th Cong., 2d Sess. (July 1958), pp. 40, 78.

[Footnote 54] In 1952, J. Edgar Hoover, Director of the Federal Bureau of Investigation, stated:

"Law enforcement, however, in defeating the criminal, must maintain inviolate the historic liberties of the individual. To turn back the criminal, yet, by so doing, destroy the dignity of the individual, would be a hollow victory.

. . . . .

"We can have the Constitution, the best laws in the land, and the most honest reviews by courts - but unless the law enforcement profession is steeped in the democratic tradition, maintains the highest in ethics, and makes its work a career of honor, civil liberties will continually - and without end - be violated. . . . The best protection of civil liberties is an alert, intelligent and honest law enforcement agency. There can be no alternative.

318

. . . . .

". . . Special Agents are taught that any suspect or arrested person, at the outset of an interview, must be advised that he is not required to make a statement and that any statement given can be used against him in court. Moreover, the individual must be informed that, if he desires, he may obtain the services of an attorney of his own choice."

Hoover, Civil Liberties and Law Enforcement: The Role of the FBI, 37 Iowa L. Rev. 175, 177-182 (1952).

[Footnote 55] We agree that the interviewing agent must exercise his judgment in determining whether the individual waives his right to counsel. Because of the constitutional basis of the right, however, the standard for waiver is necessarily high. And, of course, the ultimate responsibility for resolving this constitutional question lies with the courts.

[Footnote 56] Among the crimes within the enforcement jurisdiction of the FBI are kidnapping, 18 U.S.C. 1201 (1964 ed.), white slavery, 18 U.S.C. 2421-2423 (1964 ed.), bank robbery, 18 U.S.C. 2113 (1964 ed.), interstate transportation and sale of stolen property, 18 U.S.C. 2311-2317 (1964 ed.), all manner of conspiracies, 18 U.S.C. 371 (1964 ed.), and violations of civil rights, 18 U.S.C. 241-242 (1964 ed.). See also 18 U.S.C. 1114 (1964 ed.) (murder of officer or employee of the United States).

[Footnote 57] 1964. Crim. L. Rev., at 166-170. These Rules provide in part:

"II. As soon as a police officer has evidence which would afford reasonable grounds for suspecting that a person has committed an offence, he shall caution that person or cause him to be cautioned before putting to him any questions, or further questions, relating to that offence.

"The caution shall be in the following terms:

"'You are not obliged to say anything unless you wish to do so but what you say may be put into writing and given in evidence.'

"When after being cautioned a person is being questioned, or elects to make a statement, a record shall be kept of the time and place at which any such questioning or statement began and ended and of the persons present.

. . . . .

"III. . . .

. . . . .

320

"(b) It is only in exceptional cases that questions relating to the offence should be put to the accused person after he has been charged or informed that he may be prosecuted.

. . . . .

"IV. All written statements made after caution shall be taken in the following manner:

"(a) If a person says that he wants to make a statement he shall be told that it is intended to make a written record of what he says.

"He shall always be asked whether he wishes to write down himself what he wants to say; if he says that he cannot write or that he would like someone to write it for him, a police officer may offer to write the statement for him. . . .

"(b) Any person writing his own statement shall be allowed to do so without any prompting as distinct from indicating to him what matters are material.

. . . . .

"(d) Whenever a police officer writes the statement, he shall take down the exact words spoken by the person making the statement, without putting any questions other than such as may be needed to [384 U.S. 436, 488]   make the statement coherent, intelligible and relevant to the material matters: he shall not prompt him."

The prior Rules appear in Devlin, The Criminal Prosecution in England 137-141 (1958).

Despite suggestions of some laxity in enforcement of the Rules and despite the fact some discretion as to admissibility is invested in the trial judge, the Rules are a significant influence in the English criminal law enforcement system. See, e. g., 1964. Crim. L. Rev., at 182; and articles collected in 1960. Crim. L. Rev., at 298-356.

[Footnote 58] The introduction to the Judges' Rules states in part:

"These Rules do not affect the principles

. . . . .

"(c) That every person at any stage of an investigation should be able to communicate and to consult privately with a solicitor. This is so even if he is in custody provided that in such a case no unreasonable delay or hindrance is caused to the processes of investigation or the administration of justice by his doing so . . . ." 1964. Crim. L. Rev., at 166-167.

[Footnote 59] As stated by the Lord Justice General in Chalmers v. H. M. Advocate, 1954. Sess. Cas. 66, 78 (J. C.):

"The theory of our law is that at the stage of initial investigation the police may question anyone with a view to acquiring information which may lead to the detection of the criminal; but that, when the stage has been reached at which suspicion, or more than suspicion, has in their view centred upon some person as the likely perpetrator of the crime, further interrogation of that person becomes very dangerous, and, if carried too far, e. g., to the point of extracting a confession by what amounts to cross-examination, the evidence of that confession will almost certainly be excluded. Once the accused has been apprehended and charged he has the statutory right to a private interview with a solicitor and to be brought before a magistrate with all convenient speed so that he may, if so advised, emit a declaration in presence of his solicitor under conditions which safeguard him against prejudice."

[Footnote 60] "No confession made to a police officer shall be proved as against a person accused of any offence." Indian Evidence Act 25.

"No confession made by any person whilst he is in the custody of a police officer unless it be made in the immediate presence of a Magistrate, shall be proved as against such person." Indian Evidence Act 26. See 1 Ramaswami & Rajagopalan, Law of Evidence in India 553-569 (1962). To avoid any continuing effect of police pressure or inducement, the Indian Supreme Court has invalidated a confession made shortly after police brought a suspect before a magistrate, suggesting: "[I]t would, we think, be reasonable to insist upon giving an accused person at least 24 hours to decide whether or not he should make a confession." Sarwan Singh v. State of Punjab, 44 All India Rep. 1957, Sup. Ct. 637, 644.

[Footnote 61] I Legislative Enactments of Ceylon 211 (1958).

[Footnote 62] 10 U.S.C. 831 (b) (1964 ed.).

[Footnote 63] United States v. Rose, 24 CMR 251 (1957); United States v. Gunnels, 23 CMR 354 (1957).

[Footnote 64] Although no constitution existed at the time confessions were excluded by rule of evidence in 1872, India now has a written constitution which includes the provision that "No person accused of any offence shall be compelled to be a witness against himself." Constitution of India, Article 20 (3). See Tope, The Constitution of India 63-67 (1960).

[Footnote 65] Brief for United States in No. 761, Westover v. United States, pp. 44-47; Brief for the State of New York as amicus curiae, pp. 35-39. See also Brief for the National District Attorneys Association as amicus curiae, pp. 23-26.

[Footnote 66] Miranda was also convicted in a separate trial on an unrelated robbery charge not presented here for review. A statement introduced at that trial was obtained from Miranda during the same interrogation which resulted in the confession involved here. At the robbery trial, one officer testified that during the interrogation he did not tell Miranda that anything he said would be held against him or that he could consult with an attorney. The other officer stated that they had both told Miranda that anything he said would be used against him and that he was not required by law to tell them anything.

[Footnote 67] One of the officers testified that he read this paragraph to Miranda. Apparently, however, he did not do so until after Miranda had confessed orally.

[Footnote 68] Vignera thereafter successfully attacked the validity of one of the prior convictions, Vignera v. Wilkins,

Civ. 9901 (D.C. W. D. N. Y. Dec. 31, 1961) (unreported), but was then resentenced as a second-felony offender to the same term of imprisonment as the original sentence. R. 31-33.

[Footnote 69] The failure of defense counsel to object to the introduction of the confession at trial, noted by the Court of Appeals and emphasized by the Solicitor General, does not preclude our consideration of the issue. Since the trial was held prior to our decision in Escobedo and, of course, prior to our decision today making the [384 U.S. 436, 496] objection available, the failure to object at trial does not constitute a waiver of the claim. See, e. g., United States ex rel. Angelet v. Fay, 333 F.2d 12, 16 (C. A. 2d Cir. 1964), aff'd, 381 U.S. 654 (1965). Cf. Ziffrin, Inc. v. United States, 318 U.S. 73, 78 (1943).

[Footnote 70] Because of this disposition of the case, the California Supreme Court did not reach the claims that the confession was coerced by police threats to hold his ailing wife in custody until he confessed, that there was no hearing as required by Jackson v. Denno, 378 U.S. 368 (1964), and that the trial judge gave an instruction condemned by the

California Supreme Court's decision in People v. Morse, 60 Cal. 2d 631, 388 P.2d 33, 36 Cal. Rptr. 201 (1964).

[Footnote 71] After certiorari was granted in this case, respondent moved to dismiss on the ground that there was no final judgment from which the State could appeal since the judgment below directed that he be retried. In the event respondent was successful in obtaining an acquittal on retrial, however, under California law the State would have no appeal. Satisfied that in these circumstances the decision below constituted a final judgment under 28 U.S.C. 1257 (3) (1964 ed.), we denied the motion. 383 U.S. 903 .

MR. JUSTICE CLARK, dissenting in Nos. 759, 760, and 761, and concurring in the result in No. 584.

It is with regret that I find it necessary to write in these cases. However, I am unable to join the majority because its opinion goes too far on too little, while my dissenting brethren do not go quite far enough. Nor can I join in the Court's criticism of the present practices of police and investigatory agencies as to custodial interrogation. The materials it refers to as "police manuals" 1 are, as I read them, merely writings in this field by professors and some police officers. Not one is shown by

the record here to be the official manual of any police department, much less in universal use in crime detection. Moreover, the examples of police brutality mentioned by the Court
2 are rare exceptions to the thousands of cases [384 U.S.
436, 500]   that appear every year in the law reports. The
police agencies - all the way from municipal and state forces
to the federal bureaus - are responsible for law enforcement
and public safety in this country. I am proud of their efforts,
which in my view are not fairly characterized by the Court's
opinion.

I.

The ipse dixit of the majority has no support in our cases.
Indeed, the Court admits that "we might not find the defendants' statements [here] to have been involuntary in traditional
terms." Ante, p. 457. In short, the Court has added more to
the requirements that the accused is entitled to consult with
his lawyer and that he must be given the traditional warning
that he may remain silent and that anything that he says may
be used against him. Escobedo v. Illinois, 378 U.S. 478, 490 -
491 (1964). Now, the Court fashions a constitutional rule that
the police may engage in no custodial interrogation without
additionally advising the accused that he has a right under

the Fifth Amendment to the presence of counsel during interrogation and that, if he is without funds, counsel will be furnished him. When at any point during an interrogation the accused seeks affirmatively or impliedly to invoke his rights to silence or counsel, interrogation must be forgone or postponed. The Court further holds that failure to follow the new procedures requires inexorably the exclusion of any statement by the accused, as well as the fruits thereof. Such a strict constitutional specific inserted at the nerve center of crime detection may well kill the patient. 3 [384 U.S. 436, 501] Since there is at this time a paucity of information and an almost total lack of empirical knowledge on the practical operation of requirements truly comparable to those announced by the majority, I would be more restrained lest we go too far too fast.

II.

Custodial interrogation has long been recognized as "undoubtedly an essential tool in effective law enforcement." Haynes v. Washington, 373 U.S. 503, 515 (1963). Recognition of this fact should put us on guard against the promulgation of doctrinaire rules. Especially is this true where the Court finds that "the Constitution has prescribed" its holding and where the light of our past cases, from Hopt v. Utah, 110 U.S. 574 , (1884), down to Haynes v. Washington, supra, is to [384 U.S. 436, 502] the contrary. Indeed, even in Escobedo the Court never hinted that an affirmative "waiver" was a prerequisite to questioning; that the burden of proof as to waiver was on the prosecution; that the presence of counsel - absent a waiver - during interrogation was required; that a waiver can be withdrawn at the will of the accused; that counsel must be furnished during an accusatory stage to those unable to pay; nor that admissions and exculpatory statements are "confessions." To require all those things at one gulp should cause the Court to choke over more cases than Crooker v. California, 357 U.S. 433 (1958), and Cicenia v. Lagay, 357 U.S. 504 (1958), which it expressly overrules today.

The rule prior to today - as Mr. Justice Goldberg, the author of the Court's opinion in Escobedo, stated it in Haynes v. Washington - depended upon "a totality of circumstances evidencing an involuntary . . . admission of guilt." 373 U.S., at 514 . And he concluded:

"Of course, detection and solution of crime is, at best, a difficult and arduous task requiring determination and persistence on the part of all responsible officers charged with the duty of law enforcement. And, certainly, we do not mean to suggest that all interrogation of witnesses and suspects is impermissible. Such questioning is undoubtedly an essential tool in effective law enforcement. The line between proper and permissible police conduct and techniques and methods offensive to due process is, at best, a difficult one to draw, particularly in cases such as this where it is necessary to make fine judgments as to the effect of psychologically coercive pressures and inducements on the mind and will of an accused. . . . We are here impelled to the conclusion, from all of the facts presented, that the bounds of due process have been exceeded." Id., at 514-515. [384 U.S. 436, 503]

III.

I would continue to follow that rule. Under the "totality of circumstances" rule of which my Brother Goldberg spoke in Haynes, I would consider in each case whether the police officer prior to custodial interrogation added the warning that the suspect might have counsel present at the interrogation and, further, that a court would appoint one at his request if he was too poor to employ counsel. In the absence of warnings, the burden would be on the State to prove that counsel was knowingly and intelligently waived or that in the totality of the circumstances, including the failure to give the necessary warnings, the confession was clearly voluntary.

Rather than employing the arbitrary Fifth Amendment rule 4 which the Court lays down I would follow the more pliable dictates of the Due Process Clauses of the Fifth and Fourteenth Amendments which we are accustomed to administering and which we know from our cases are effective instruments in protecting persons in police custody. In this way we would not be acting in the dark nor in one full sweep changing the traditional rules of custodial interrogation which this Court has for so long recognized as a justifiable and proper tool in balancing individual rights against the rights of society. It will be soon enough to go further when we are able to appraise with somewhat better accuracy the effect of such a holding.

I would affirm the convictions in Miranda v. Arizona, No. 759; Vignera v. New York, No. 760; and Westover v. United States, No. 761. In each of those cases I find from the circumstances no warrant for reversal. In [384 U.S. 436,

504] California v. Stewart, No. 584, I would dismiss the writ of certiorari for want of a final judgment, 28 U.S.C. 1257 (3) (1964 ed.); but if the merits are to be reached I would affirm on the ground that the State failed to fulfill its burden, in the absence of a showing that appropriate warnings were given, of proving a waiver or a totality of circumstances showing voluntariness. Should there be a retrial, I would leave the State free to attempt to prove these elements.

[Footnote 1] E. g., Inbau & Reid, Criminal Interrogation and Confessions (1962); O'Hara, Fundamentals of Criminal Investigation (1956); Dienstein, Technics for the Crime Investigator (1952); Mulbar, Interrogation (1951); Kidd, Police Interrogation (1940).

[Footnote 2] As developed by my Brother HARLAN, post, pp. 506-514, such cases, with the exception of the long-discredited decision in Bram v. United States, 168 U.S. 532 (1897), were adequately treated in terms of due process.

[Footnote 3] The Court points to England, Scotland, Ceylon and India as having equally rigid rules. As my Brother HARLAN points out, post, pp. 521-523, the Court is mistaken in this regard, for it overlooks counterbalancing prosecutorial advantages. Moreover, the requirements of the Federal Bureau of Investigation do not appear from the Solicitor General's letter, ante, pp. 484-486, to be as strict as [384 U.S. 436, 501] those imposed today in at least two respects: (1) The offer of counsel is articulated only as "a right to counsel"; nothing is said about a right to have counsel present at the custodial interrogation. (See also the examples cited by the Solicitor General, Westover v. United States, 342 F.2d 684, 685 (1965) ("right to consult counsel"); Jackson v. United States, 337 F.2d 136, 138 (1964) (accused "entitled to an attorney").) Indeed, the practice is that whenever the suspect "decides that he wishes to consult with counsel before making a statement, the interview is terminated at that point . . . . When counsel appears in person, he is permitted to confer with his client in private." This clearly indicates that the FBI does not warn that counsel may be present during custodial interrogation. (2) The Solicitor General's letter states: "[T]hose who have been arrested for an offense under FBI jurisdiction, or whose arrest is contemplated following the interview, [are advised] of a right to free counsel if they are unable to pay, and the availability of such counsel from the Judge." So phrased, this warning does not indicate that the agent will secure counsel. Rather, the statement may well be interpreted by the suspect to mean that the burden is placed upon himself and that he may have counsel appointed only when brought before the judge or at trial - but not at custodial interrogation. As I view the FBI practice, it is not as broad as the one laid down today by the Court.

[Footnote 4] In my view there is "no significant support" in our cases for the holding of the Court today that the Fifth Amendment privilege, in effect, forbids custodial interrogation. For a discussion of this point see the dissenting opinion of my Brother WHITE, post, pp. 526-531.

MR. JUSTICE HARLAN, whom MR. JUSTICE STEWART and MR. JUSTICE WHITE join, dissenting.

I believe the decision of the Court represents poor constitutional law and entails harmful consequences for the country at large. How serious these consequences may prove to be only time can tell. But the basic flaws in the Court's justification seem to me readily apparent now once all sides of the problem are considered.

I. INTRODUCTION.

At the outset, it is well to note exactly what is required by the Court's new constitutional code of rules for confessions. The foremost requirement, upon which later admissibility of a confession depends, is that a fourfold warning be given to a person in custody before he is questioned, namely, that he has a right to remain silent, that anything he says may be used against him, that he has a right to have present an attorney during the questioning, and that if indigent he has a right to a lawyer without charge. To forgo these rights, some affirmative statement of rejection is seemingly required, and threats, tricks, or cajolings to obtain this waiver are forbidden. If before or during questioning the suspect seeks to invoke his right to remain silent, interrogation must be forgone or cease; a request for counsel [384 U.S. 436, 505]   brings about the same result until a lawyer is procured. Finally, there are a miscellany of minor directives, for example, the burden of proof of waiver is on the State, admissions and exculpatory statements are treated just like confessions, withdrawal of a waiver is always permitted, and so forth. 1

While the fine points of this scheme are far less clear than the Court admits, the tenor is quite apparent. The new rules are not designed to guard against police brutality or other unmistakably banned forms of coercion. Those who use third-degree tactics and deny them in court are equally able and destined to lie as skillfully about warnings and waivers.

Rather, the thrust of the new rules is to negate all pressures, to reinforce the nervous or ignorant suspect, and ultimately to discourage any confession at all. The aim in short is toward "voluntariness" in a utopian sense, or to view it from a different angle, voluntariness with a vengeance.

To incorporate this notion into the Constitution requires a strained reading of history and precedent and a disregard of the very pragmatic concerns that alone may on occasion justify such strains. I believe that reasoned examination will show that the Due Process Clauses provide an adequate tool for coping with confessions and that, even if the Fifth Amendment privilege against self-incrimination be invoked, its precedents taken as a whole do not sustain the present rules. Viewed as a choice based on pure policy, these new rules prove to be a highly debatable, if not one-sided, appraisal of the competing interests, imposed over widespread objection, at the very time when judicial restraint is most called for by the circumstances. [384 U.S. 436, 506]

II. CONSTITUTIONAL PREMISES.

It is most fitting to begin an inquiry into the constitutional precedents by surveying the limits on confessions the Court has evolved under the Due Process Clause of the Four-teenth Amendment. This is so because these cases show that there exists a workable and effective means of dealing with confessions in a judicial manner; because the cases are the baseline from which the Court now departs and so serve to measure the actual as opposed to the professed distance it travels; and because examination of them helps reveal how the Court has coasted into its present position.

The earliest confession cases in this Court emerged from federal prosecutions and were settled on a nonconstitutional basis, the Court adopting the common-law rule that the absence of inducements, promises, and threats made a confession voluntary and admissible. Hopt v. Utah, 110 U.S. 574 ; Pierce v. United States, 160 U.S. 355 . While a later case said the Fifth Amendment privilege controlled admissibility, this proposition was not itself developed in subsequent decisions. 2 The Court did, however, heighten the test of admissibility in federal trials to one of voluntariness "in fact," Wan v. [384 U.S. 436, 507] United States, 266 U.S. 1, 14 (quoted, ante, p. 462), and then by and large left federal judges to apply the same standards the Court began to derive in a string of state court cases.

This new line of decisions, testing admissibility by the Due Process Clause, began in 1936 with Brown v. Mississippi, 297 U.S. 278 , and must now embrace somewhat more than 30 full opinions of the Court. 3 While the voluntariness rubric was repeated in many instances, e. g., Lyons v. Oklahoma, 322 U.S. 596 , the Court never pinned it down to a single meaning but on the contrary infused it with a number of different values. To travel quickly over the main themes, there was an initial emphasis on reliability, e. g., Ward v. Texas, 316 U.S. 547 , supplemented by concern over the legality and fairness of the police practices, e. g., Ashcraft v. Tennessee, 322 U.S. 143 , in an "accusatorial" system of law enforcement, Watts v. Indiana, 338 U.S. 49, 54 , and eventually by close attention to the individual's state of mind and capacity for effective choice, e. g., Gallegos v. Colorado, 370 U.S. 49 . The outcome was a continuing re-evaluation on the facts of each case of how much pressure on the suspect was permissible. 4 [384 U.S. 436, 508]

Among the criteria often taken into account were threats or imminent danger, e. g., Payne v. Arkansas, 356 U.S. 560 , physical deprivations such as lack of sleep or food, e. g.,

Reck v. Pate, 367 U.S. 433 , repeated or extended interrogation, e. g., Chambers v. Florida, 309 U.S. 227 , limits on access to counsel or friends, Crooker v. California, 357 U.S. 433 ; Cicenia v. Lagay, 357 U.S. 504 , length and illegality of detention under state law, e. g., Haynes v. Washington, 373 U.S. 503 , and individual weakness or incapacities, Lynumn v. Illinois, 372 U.S. 528 . Apart from direct physical coercion, however, no single default or fixed combination of defaults guaranteed exclusion, and synopses of the cases would serve little use because the overall gauge has been steadily changing, usually in the direction of restricting admissibility. But to mark just what point had been reached before the Court jumped the rails in Escobedo v. Illinois, 378 U.S. 478 , it is worth capsulizing the then-recent case of Haynes v. Washington, 373 U.S. 503 . There, Haynes had been held some 16 or more hours in violation of state law before signing the disputed confession, had received no warnings of any kind, and despite requests had been refused access to his wife or to counsel, the police indicating that access would be allowed after a confession. Emphasizing especially this last inducement and rejecting some contrary indicia of voluntariness, the Court in a 5-to-4 decision held the confession inadmissible.

There are several relevant lessons to be drawn from this constitutional history. The first is that with over 25 years of precedent the Court has developed an elaborate, sophisticated, and sensitive approach to admissibility of confessions. It is "judicial" in its treatment of one case at a time, see Culombe v. Connecticut, 367 U.S. 568, 635 (concurring opinion of THE CHIEF JUSTICE), flexible in its ability to respond to the endless mutations of fact presented, and ever more familiar to the lower courts. [384 U.S. 436, 509]   Of course, strict certainty is not obtained in this developing process, but this is often so with constitutional principles, and disagreement is usually confined to that borderland of close cases where it matters least.

The second point is that in practice and from time to time in principle, the Court has given ample recognition to society's interest in suspect questioning as an instrument of law enforcement. Cases countenancing quite significant pressures can be cited without difficulty, 5 and the lower courts may often have been yet more tolerant. Of course the limitations imposed today were rejected by necessary implication in case after case, the right to warnings having been explicitly rebuffed in this Court many years ago. Powers v. United

States, 223 U.S. 303 ; Wilson v. United States, 162 U.S. 613 . As recently as Haynes v. Washington, 373 U.S. 503, 515 , the Court openly acknowledged that questioning of witnesses and suspects "is undoubtedly an essential tool in effective law enforcement." Accord, Crooker v. California, 357 U.S. 433, 441 .

Finally, the cases disclose that the language in many of the opinions overstates the actual course of decision. It has been said, for example, that an admissible confession must be made by the suspect "in the unfettered exercise of his own will," Malloy v. Hogan, 378 U.S. 1, 8 , and that "a prisoner is not `to be made the deluded instrument of his own conviction,'" Culombe v. Connecticut, 367 U.S. 568, 581 (Frankfurter, J., announcing the Court's judgment and an opinion). Though often repeated, such principles are rarely observed in full measure. Even the word "voluntary" may be deemed somewhat [384 U.S. 436, 510] misleading, especially when one considers many of the confessions that have been brought under its umbrella. See, e. g., supra, n. 5. The tendency to overstate may be laid in part to the flagrant facts often before the Court; but in any event one must recognize

how it has tempered attitudes and lent some color of authority to the approach now taken by the Court.

I turn now to the Court's asserted reliance on the Fifth
Amendment, an approach which I frankly regard as a trompe
l'oeil. The Court's opinion in my view reveals no adequate
basis for extending the Fifth Amendment's privilege against
self-incrimination to the police station. Far more important, it
fails to show that the Court's new rules are well supported,
let alone compelled, by Fifth Amendment precedents. Instead, the new rules actually derive from quotation and anal-
ogy drawn from precedents under the Sixth Amendment,
which should properly have no bearing on police interrogation.

The Court's opening contention, that the Fifth Amendment
governs police station confessions, is perhaps not an impermissible extension of the law but it has little to commend itself in the present circumstances. Historically, the privilege
against self-incrimination did not bear at all on the use of extra-legal confessions, for which distinct standards evolved;
indeed, "the history of the two principles is wide apart, differing by one hundred years in origin, and derived through separate lines of precedents . . . ." 8 Wigmore, Evidence 2266,

at 401 (McNaughton rev. 1961). Practice under the two doctrines has also differed in a number of important respects. 6 [384 U.S. 436, 511] Even those who would readily enlarge the privilege must concede some linguistic difficulties since the Fifth Amendment in terms proscribes only compelling any person "in any criminal case to be a witness against himself." Cf. Kamisar, Equal Justice in the Gatehouses and Mansions of American Criminal Procedure, in Criminal Justice in Our Time 1, 25-26 (1965).

Though weighty, I do not say these points and similar ones are conclusive, for, as the Court reiterates, the privilege embodies basic principles always capable of expansion. 7 Certainly the privilege does represent a protective concern for the accused and an emphasis upon accusatorial rather than inquisitorial values in law enforcement, although this is similarly true of other limitations such as the grand jury requirement and the reasonable doubt standard. Accusatorial values, however, have openly been absorbed into the due process standard governing confessions; this indeed is why at present "the kinship of the two rules [governing confessions and self-incrimination] is too apparent for denial." McCormick, Evidence 155 (1954). Since extension of the general principle has already occurred, to insist that the privilege applies as such serves only to carry over inapposite historical details and engaging rhetoric and to obscure the policy choices to be made in regulating confessions.

Having decided that the Fifth Amendment privilege does apply in the police station, the Court reveals that the privilege imposes more exacting restrictions than does the Fourteenth Amendment's voluntariness test. 8 [384 U.S. 436, 512] It then emerges from a discussion of Escobedo that the Fifth Amendment requires for an admissible confession that it be given by one distinctly aware of his right not to speak and shielded from "the compelling atmosphere" of interrogation. See ante, pp. 465-466. From these key premises, the Court finally develops the safeguards of warning, counsel, and so forth. I do not believe these premises are sustained by precedents under the Fifth Amendment. 9

The more important premise is that pressure on the suspect must be eliminated though it be only the subtle influence of the atmosphere and surroundings. The Fifth Amendment, however, has never been thought to forbid all pressure to incriminate one's self in the situations covered by it. On the contrary, it has been held that failure to incriminate one's self can result in denial of removal of one's case from state to federal court, Maryland v. Soper, 270 U.S. 9 ; in refusal of a military commission, Orloff v. Willoughby, 345 U.S. 83 ; in denial of a discharge in bankruptcy, Kaufman v. Hurwitz, 176 F.2d 210; and in numerous other adverse consequences. See 8 Wigmore, Evidence 2272, at 441-444, n. 18 (McNaughton rev. 1961); Maguire, Evidence of Guilt 2.062 (1959). This is not to say that short of jail or torture any sanction is permissible in any case; policy and history alike may impose sharp limits. See, e. g., [384 U.S. 436, 513]   Griffin v. California, 380 U.S. 609 . However, the Court's unspoken assumption that any pressure violates the privilege is not supported by the precedents and it has failed to show why the Fifth Amendment prohibits that relatively mild pressure the Due Process Clause permits.

The Court appears similarly wrong in thinking that precise knowledge of one's rights is a settled prerequisite under the Fifth Amendment to the loss of its protections. A number of lower federal court cases have held that grand jury witnesses need not always be warned of their privilege, e. g., United States v. Scully, 225 F.2d 113, 116, and Wigmore states this to be the better rule for trial witnesses. See 8 Wigmore, Evidence 2269 (McNaughton rev. 1961). Cf. Henry v. Mississippi, 379 U.S. 443, 451 -452 (waiver of constitutional rights by counsel despite defendant's ignorance held allowable). No Fifth Amendment precedent is cited for the Court's contrary view. There might of course be reasons apart from Fifth Amendment precedent for requiring warning or any other safeguard on questioning but that is a different matter entirely. See infra, pp. 516-517.

A closing word must be said about the Assistance of Counsel Clause of the Sixth Amendment, which is never expressly relied on by the Court but whose judicial precedents turn out to be linchpins of the confession rules announced today. To support its requirement of a knowing and intelligent waiver, the Court cites Johnson v. Zerbst, 304 U.S. 458 , ante, p. 475; appointment of counsel for the indigent suspect is tied to Gideon v. Wainwright, 372 U.S. 335 , and Douglas v. California, 372 U.S. 353 , ante, p. 473; the silent-record doctrine is borrowed from Carnley v. Cochran, 369 U.S. 506 , ante, p. 475, as is the right to an express offer of counsel, ante, p. 471. All these cases imparting glosses to the Sixth Amendment concerned counsel at trial or on appeal. While the Court finds no pertinent difference between judicial proceedings and police interrogation, I believe [384 U.S. 436, 514] the differences are so vast as to disqualify wholly the Sixth Amendment precedents as suitable analogies in the present cases. 10

The only attempt in this Court to carry the right to counsel into the station house occurred in Escobedo, the Court repeating several times that that stage was no less "critical" than trial itself. See 378 U.S., 485-488. This is hardly persuasive when we consider that a grand jury inquiry, the filing of a certiorari petition, and certainly the purchase of narcotics by an undercover agent from a prospective defendant may all be equally "critical" yet provision of counsel and advice on that score have never been thought compelled by the Constitution in such cases. The sound reason why this right is so freely extended for a criminal trial is the severe injustice risked by confronting an untrained defendant with a range of technical points of law, evidence, and tactics familiar to the prosecutor but not to himself. This danger shrinks markedly in the police station where indeed the lawyer in fulfilling his professional responsibilities of necessity may become an obstacle to truthfinding. See infra, n. 12. The Court's summary citation of the Sixth Amendment cases here seems to me best described as "the domino method of constitutional adjudication . . . wherein every explanatory statement in a previous opinion is made the basis for extension to a wholly different situation." Friendly, supra, n. 10, at 950.

III. POLICY CONSIDERATIONS.

Examined as an expression of public policy, the Court's new regime proves so dubious that there can be no due [384 U.S. 436, 515] compensation for its weakness in constitutional law. The foregoing discussion has shown, I think, how mistaken is the Court in implying that the Constitution has struck the balance in favor of the approach the Court takes. Ante, p. 479. Rather, precedent reveals that the Fourteenth Amendment in practice has been construed to strike a different balance, that the Fifth Amendment gives the Court little solid support in this context, and that the Sixth Amendment should have no bearing at all. Legal history has been stretched before to satisfy deep needs of society. In this instance, however, the Court has not and cannot make the powerful showing that its new rules are plainly desirable in the context of our society, something which is surely demanded before those rules are engrafted onto the Constitution and imposed on every State and county in the land.

Without at all subscribing to the generally black picture of police conduct painted by the Court, I think it must be frankly recognized at the outset that police questioning allowable under due process precedents may inherently entail some pressure on the suspect and may seek advantage in his ignorance or weaknesses. The atmosphere and questioning techniques, proper and fair though they be, can in themselves exert a tug on the suspect to confess, and in this light "[t]o speak of any confessions of crime made after arrest as being `voluntary' or `uncoerced' is somewhat inaccurate, although traditional. A confession is wholly and incontestably voluntary only if a guilty person gives himself up to the law and becomes his own accuser." Ashcraft v. Tennessee, 322 U.S. 143, 161 (Jackson, J., dissenting). Until today, the role of the Constitution has been only to sift out undue pressure, not to assure spontaneous confessions. 11 [384 U.S. 436, 516]

The Court's new rules aim to offset these minor pressures and disadvantages intrinsic to any kind of police interrogation. The rules do not serve due process interests in preventing blatant coercion since, as I noted earlier, they do nothing to contain the policeman who is prepared to lie from the start.

The rules work for reliability in confessions almost only in the Pickwickian sense that they can prevent some from being given at all. 12 In short, the benefit of this new regime is simply to lessen or wipe out the inherent compulsion and in-equalities to which the Court devotes some nine pages of description. Ante, pp. 448-456.

What the Court largely ignores is that its rules impair, if they will not eventually serve wholly to frustrate, an instrument of law enforcement that has long and quite reasonably been thought worth the price paid for it. 13 There can be little doubt that the Court's new code would markedly decrease the number of confessions. To warn the suspect that he may re-main silent and remind him that his confession may be used in court are minor obstructions. To require also an express waiver by the suspect and an end to questioning whenever he demurs [384 U.S. 436, 517]   must heavily handicap questioning. And to suggest or provide counsel for the sus-pect simply invites the end of the interrogation. See, supra, n. 12.

How much harm this decision will inflict on law enforcement cannot fairly be predicted with accuracy. Evidence on the

role of confessions is notoriously incomplete, see Developments, supra, n. 2, at 941-944, and little is added by the
Court's reference to the FBI experience and the resources
believed wasted in interrogation. See infra, n. 19, and text.
We do know that some crimes cannot be solved without confessions, that ample expert testimony attests to their im-
portance in crime control, 14 and that the Court is taking a
real risk with society's welfare in imposing its new regime on
the country. The social costs of crime are too great to call
the new rules anything but a hazardous experimentation.

While passing over the costs and risks of its experiment, the
Court portrays the evils of normal police questioning in terms
which I think are exaggerated. Albeit stringently confined by
the due process standards interrogation is no doubt often in-
convenient and unpleasant for the suspect. However, it is no
less so for a man to be arrested and jailed, to have his house
searched, or to stand trial in court, yet all this may properly
happen to the most innocent given probable cause, a warrant, or an indictment. Society has always paid a stiff price
for law and order, and peaceful interrogation is not one of
the dark moments of the law.

This brief statement of the competing considerations seems to me ample proof that the Court's preference is highly debatable at best and therefore not to be read into [384 U.S. 436, 518] the Constitution. However, it may make the analysis more graphic to consider the actual facts of one of the four cases reversed by the Court. Miranda v. Arizona serves best, being neither the hardest nor easiest of the four under the Court's standards. 15

On March 3, 1963, an 18-year-old girl was kidnapped and forcibly raped near Phoenix, Arizona. Ten days later, on the morning of March 13, petitioner Miranda was arrested and taken to the police station. At this time Miranda was 23 years old, indigent, and educated to the extent of completing half the ninth grade. He had "an emotional illness" of the schizophrenic type, according to the doctor who eventually examined him; the doctor's report also stated that Miranda was "alert and oriented as to time, place, and person," intelligent within normal limits, competent to stand trial, and sane within the legal definition. At the police station, the victim picked Miranda out of a lineup, and two officers then took him into a separate room to interrogate him, starting about 11:30 a. m. Though at first denying his guilt, within a short time Miranda gave a detailed oral confession and then wrote out in his own hand and signed a brief statement admitting and describing the crime. All this was accomplished in two hours or less without any force, threats or promises and - I will assume this though the record is uncertain, ante, 491-492 and nn. 66-67 - without any effective warnings at all.

Miranda's oral and written confessions are now held inadmissible under the Court's new rules. One is entitled to feel astonished that the Constitution can be read to produce this result. These confessions were obtained [384 U.S. 436, 519] during brief, daytime questioning conducted by two officers and unmarked by any of the traditional indicia of coercion. They assured a conviction for a brutal and unsettling crime, for which the police had and quite possibly could obtain little evidence other than the victim's identifications, evidence which is frequently unreliable. There was, in sum, a legitimate purpose, no perceptible unfairness, and certainly little risk of injustice in the interrogation. Yet the resulting confessions, and the responsible course of police practice they represent, are to be sacrificed to the Court's own finespun conception of fairness which I seriously doubt is shared by many thinking citizens in this country. 16

The tenor of judicial opinion also falls well short of supporting the Court's new approach. Although Escobedo has widely been interpreted as an open invitation to lower courts to re-write the law of confessions, a significant heavy majority of the state and federal decisions in point have sought quite narrow interpretations. 17 Of [384 U.S. 436, 520] the courts that have accepted the invitation, it is hard to know how many have felt compelled by their best guess as to this Court's likely construction; but none of the state decisions saw fit to rely on the state privilege against self-incrimination, and no decision at all has gone as far as this Court goes today. 18

It is also instructive to compare the attitude in this case of those responsible for law enforcement with the official views that existed when the Court undertook three major revisions of prosecutorial practice prior to this case, Johnson v. Zerbst, 304 U.S. 458 , Mapp v. Ohio, 367 U.S. 643 , and Gideon v. Wain-wright, 372 U.S. 335 . In Johnson, which established that ap-pointed counsel must be offered the indigent in federal crim-inal trials, the Federal Government all but conceded the basic issue, which had in fact been recently fixed as Depart-ment of Justice policy. See Beaney, Right to Counsel 29-30,

36-42 (1955). In Mapp, which imposed the exclusionary rule on the States for Fourth Amendment violations, more than half of the States had themselves already adopted some such rule. See 367 U.S., at 651 . In Gideon, which extended Johnson v. Zerbst to the States, an amicus brief was filed by 22 States and Commonwealths urging that course; only two States besides that of the respondent came forward to pro-test. See 372 U.S., at 345 . By contrast, in this case new re-strictions on police [384 U.S. 436, 521] questioning have been opposed by the United States and in an amicus brief signed by 27 States and Commonwealths, not including the three other States which are parties. No State in the country has urged this Court to impose the newly announced rules, nor has any State chosen to go nearly so far on its own.

The Court in closing its general discussion invokes the prac-tice in federal and foreign jurisdictions as lending weight to its new curbs on confessions for all the States. A brief re-sume will suffice to show that none of these jurisdictions has struck so one-sided a balance as the Court does today. Heaviest reliance is placed on the FBI practice. Differing cir-cumstances may make this comparison quite untrustworthy, 19 but in any event the FBI falls sensibly short of the Court's formalistic rules. For example, there is no indication that FBI agents must obtain an affirmative "waiver" before they pursue their questioning. Nor is it clear that one invoking his right to silence may not be prevailed upon to change his mind. And the warning as to appointed counsel apparently indicates only that one will be assigned by the judge when the suspect appears before him; the thrust of the Court's rules is to induce the suspect to obtain appointed counsel before continuing the interview. See ante, pp. 484-486. Apparently American military practice, briefly mentioned by the Court, has these same limits and is still less favorable to the suspect than the FBI warning, making no mention of appointed counsel. Developments, supra, n. 2, at 1084-1089.

The law of the foreign countries described by the Court also reflects a more moderate conception of the rights of [384 U.S. 436, 522]   the accused as against those of society when other data are considered. Concededly, the English experience is most relevant. In that country, a caution as to silence but not counsel has long been mandated by the "Judges' Rules," which also place other somewhat imprecise limits on police cross-examination of suspects. However, in the court's discretion confessions can be and apparently quite frequently are admitted in evidence despite disregard of the Judges' Rules, so long as they are found voluntary under the common-law test. Moreover, the check that exists on the use of pretrial statements is counterbalanced by the evident admissibility of fruits of an illegal confession and by the judge's often-used authority to comment adversely on the defendant's failure to testify. 20

India, Ceylon and Scotland are the other examples chosen by the Court. In India and Ceylon the general ban on police-adduced confessions cited by the Court is subject to a major exception: if evidence is uncovered by police questioning, it is fully admissible at trial along with the confession itself, so far as it relates to the evidence and is not blatantly coerced. See Developments, supra, n. 2, at 1106-1110; Reg. v. Ramasamy 1965. A. C. 1 (P. C.). Scotland's limits on interrogation do measure up to the Court's; however, restrained comment at trial on the defendant's failure to take the stand is allowed the judge, and in many other respects Scotch law redresses the prosecutor's disadvantage in ways not permitted in this country. 21 The Court ends its survey by imputing [384 U.S. 436, 523]   added strength to our privilege against self-incrimination since, by contrast to other countries, it is embodied in a written Constitution. Considering the liberties the Court has today taken with constitutional history and precedent, few will find this emphasis persuasive.

In closing this necessarily truncated discussion of policy considerations attending the new confession rules, some reference must be made to their ironic untimeliness. There is now in progress in this country a massive re-examination of criminal law enforcement procedures on a scale never before witnessed. Participants in this undertaking include a Special Committee of the American Bar Association, under the chairmanship of Chief Judge Lumbard of the Court of Appeals for the Second Circuit; a distinguished study group of the American Law Institute, headed by Professors Vorenberg and Bator of the Harvard Law School; and the President's Commission on Law Enforcement and Administration of Justice, under the leadership of the Attorney General of the United States. 22 Studies are also being conducted by the District of Columbia Crime Commission, the Georgetown Law Center, and by others equipped to do practical research. 23 There are also signs that legislatures in some of the States may be preparing to re-examine the problem before us. 24 [384 U.S. 436, 524]

It is no secret that concern has been expressed lest long-range and lasting reforms be frustrated by this Court's too rapid departure from existing constitutional standards. Despite the Court's disclaimer, the practical effect of the decision made today must inevitably be to handicap seriously sound efforts at reform, not least by removing options necessary to a just compromise of competing interests. Of course legislative reform is rarely speedy or unanimous, though this Court has been more patient in the past. 25 But the legislative reforms when they come would have the vast advantage of empirical data and comprehensive study, they would allow experimentation and use of solutions not open to the courts, and they would restore the initiative in criminal law reform to those forums where it truly belongs.

IV. CONCLUSIONS.

All four of the cases involved here present express claims that confessions were inadmissible, not because of coercion in the traditional due process sense, but solely because of lack of counsel or lack of warnings concerning counsel and silence. For the reasons stated in this opinion, I would adhere to the due process test and reject the new requirements inaugurated by the Court. On this premise my disposition of each of these cases can be stated briefly.

In two of the three cases coming from state courts, Miranda v. Arizona (No. 759) and Vignera v. New York (No. 760), the confessions were held admissible and no other errors worth comment are alleged by petitioners. [384 U.S. 436, 525] I would affirm in these two cases. The other state case is California v. Stewart (No. 584), where the state supreme court held the confession inadmissible and reversed the conviction. In that case I would dismiss the writ of certiorari on the ground that no final judgment is before us, 28 U.S.C. 1257 (1964 ed.); putting aside the new trial open to the State in any event, the confession itself has not even been finally excluded since the California Supreme Court left the State free to show proof of a waiver. If the merits of the decision in Stewart be reached, then I believe it should be reversed and the case remanded so the state supreme court may pass on the other claims available to respondent.

In the federal case, Westover v. United States (No. 761), a number of issues are raised by petitioner apart from the one already dealt with in this dissent. None of these other claims appears to me tenable, nor in this context to warrant extended discussion. It is urged that the confession was also inadmissible because not voluntary even measured by due process standards and because federal-state cooperation brought the McNabb-Mallory rule into play under Anderson v. United States, 318 U.S. 350 . However, the facts alleged fall well short of coercion in my view, and I believe the involvement of federal agents in petitioner's arrest and detention by the State too slight to invoke Anderson. I agree with the Government that the admission of the evidence now protested by petitioner was at most harmless error, and two final contentions - one involving weight of the evidence and another improper prosecutor comment - seem to me without merit. I would therefore affirm Westover's conviction.

In conclusion: Nothing in the letter or the spirit of the Constitution or in the precedents squares with the heavy-handed and one-sided action that is so precipitously [384 U.S. 436, 526] taken by the Court in the name of fulfilling its constitutional responsibilities. The foray which the Court makes today brings to mind the wise and farsighted words of Mr. Justice Jackson in Douglas v. Jeannette, 319 U.S. 157, 181 (separate opinion): "This Court is forever adding new stories to the temples of constitutional law, and the temples have a way of collapsing when one story too many is added."

[Footnote 1] My discussion in this opinion is directed to the main questions decided by the Court and necessary to its decision; in ignoring some of the collateral points, I do not mean to imply agreement.

[Footnote 2] The case was Bram v. United States, 168 U.S. 532 (quoted, ante, p. 461). Its historical premises were afterwards disproved by Wigmore, who concluded "that no assertions could be more unfounded." 3 Wigmore, Evidence 823, at 250, n. 5 (3d ed. 1940). The Court in United States v. Carignan, 342 U.S. 36, 41 , declined to choose between Bram and Wigmore, and Stein v. New York, 346 U.S. 156, 191 , n. 35, cast further doubt on Bram. There are, however, several Court opinions which assume in dicta the relevance of the Fifth Amendment privilege to confessions. Burdeau v. McDowell, 256 U.S. 465, 475 ; see Shotwell Mfg. Co. v. United States, 371 U.S. 341, 347 . On Bram and the federal confession cases generally, see Developments in the Law - Confessions, 79 Harv. L. Rev. 935, 959-961 (1966).

[Footnote 3] Comment, 31 U. Chi. L. Rev. 313 & n. 1 (1964), states that by the 1963 Term 33 state coerced-confession cases had been decided by this Court, apart from per curiams. Spano v. New York, 360 U.S. 315, 321 , n. 2, collects 28 cases.

[Footnote 4] Bator & Vorenberg, Arrest, Detention, Interrogation and the Right to Counsel, 66 Col. L. Rev. 62, 73 (1966): "In fact, the concept of involuntariness seems to be used by the courts as a shorthand to refer to practices which are repellent to civilized standards of decency or which, under the circumstances, are thought to apply a degree of pressure to an individual which unfairly impairs his capacity to make a rational choice." See Herman, The Supreme Court and Restrictions on Police Interrogation, 25 Ohio St. L. J. 449, 452-458 (1964); Developments, supra, n. 2, at 964-984.

[Footnote 5] See the cases synopsized in Herman, supra, n. 4, at 456, nn. 36-39. One not too distant example is Stroble v. California, 343 U.S. 181 , in which the suspect was kicked and threatened after his arrest, questioned a little later for two hours, and isolated from a lawyer trying to see him; the resulting confession was held admissible.

[Footnote 6] Among the examples given in 8 Wigmore, Evidence 2266, at 401 (McNaughton rev. 1961), are these: the privilege applies to any witness, civil or criminal, but the confession rule protects only criminal defendants; the privilege deals only with compulsion, while the confession rule may exclude statements obtained by trick or promise; and where the privilege has been nullified - as by the English Bankruptcy Act - the confession rule may still operate.

[Footnote 7] Additionally, there are precedents and even historical arguments that can be arrayed in favor of bringing extra-legal questioning within the privilege. See generally Maguire, Evidence of Guilt 2.03, at 15-16 (1959).

[Footnote 8] This, of course, is implicit in the Court's introductory announcement that "[o]ur decision in Malloy v. Hogan, 378 U.S. 1 (1964) [extending the Fifth Amendment privilege to the States] necessitates [384 U.S. 436, 512] an examination of the scope of the privilege in state cases as well." Ante, p. 463. It is also inconsistent with Malloy itself, in which extension of the Fifth Amendment to the States rested in part on the view that the Due Process Clause restriction on state confessions has in recent years been "the same standard" as that imposed in federal prosecutions assertedly by the Fifth Amendment. 378 U.S., at 7 .

[Footnote 9] I lay aside Escobedo itself; it contains no reasoning or even general conclusions addressed to the Fifth Amendment and indeed its citation in this regard seems surprising in view of Escobedo's primary reliance on the Sixth Amendment.

[Footnote 10] Since the Court conspicuously does not assert that the Sixth Amendment itself warrants its new police-interrogation rules, there is no reason now to draw out the extremely powerful historical and precedential evidence that the Amendment will bear no such meaning. See generally Friendly, The Bill of Rights as a Code of Criminal Procedure, 53 Calif. L. Rev. 929, 943-948 (1965).

[Footnote 11] See supra, n. 4, and text. Of course, the use of terms like voluntariness involves questions of law and terminology quite as much as questions of fact. See Collins v. Beto, 348 F.2d 823, 832 (concurring opinion); Bator & Vorenberg, supra, n. 4, at 72-73.

[Footnote 12] The Court's vision of a lawyer "mitigat[ing] the dangers of untrustworthiness" (ante, p. 470) by witnessing coercion and assisting accuracy in the confession is largely a fancy; for if counsel arrives, there is rarely going to be a police station confession. Watts v. Indiana, 338 U.S. 49, 59 (separate opinion of Jackson, J.): "[A]ny lawyer worth his salt will tell the suspect in no uncertain terms to make no statement to police under any circumstances." See Enker & Elsen, Counsel for the Suspect, 49 Minn. L. Rev. 47, 66-68 (1964).

[Footnote 13] This need is, of course, what makes so misleading the Court's comparison of a probate judge readily setting aside as involuntary the will of an old lady badgered and beleaguered by the new heirs. Ante, pp. 457-458, n. 26. With wills, there is no public interest save in a totally free choice; with confessions, the solution of crime is a countervailing gain, however the balance is resolved.

[Footnote 14] See, e. g., the voluminous citations to congressional committee testimony and other sources collected in Culombe v. Connecticut, 367 U.S. 568, 578 -579 (Frankfurter, J., announcing the Court's judgment and an opinion).

[Footnote 15] In Westover, a seasoned criminal was practically given the Court's full complement of warnings and did not heed them. The Stewart case, on the other hand, involves long detention and successive questioning. In Vignera, the facts are complicated and the record somewhat incomplete.

[Footnote 16] "[J]ustice, though due to the accused, is due to the accuser also. The concept of fairness must not be strained till it is narrowed to a filament. We are to keep the balance true." Snyder v. Massachusetts, 291 U.S. 97, 122 (Cardozo, J.).

[Footnote 17] A narrow reading is given in: United States v. Robinson, 354 F.2d 109 (C. A. 2d Cir.); Davis v. North Carolina, 339 F.2d 770 (C. A. 4th Cir.); Edwards v. Holman, 342 F.2d 679 (C. A. 5th Cir.); United States ex rel. Townsend v. Ogilvie, 334 F.2d 837 (C. A. 7th Cir.); People v. Hartgraves, 31 Ill. 2d 375, 202 N. E. 2d 33; State v. Fox, ___ Iowa ___, 131 N. W. 2d 684; Rowe v. Commonwealth, 394 S. W. 2d 751 (Ky.); Parker v. Warden, 236 Md. 236, 203 A. 2d 418; State v. Howard, 383 S. W. 2d 701 (Mo.); Bean v. State, ___ Nev. ___, 398 P.2d 251; State v. Hodgson, 44 N. J. 151, 207 A. 2d 542; People v. Gunner, 15 N. Y. 2d 226, 205 N. E. 2d 852; Commonwealth ex rel. Linde v. Maroney, 416 Pa. 331, 206 A. 2d 288; Browne v. State, 24 Wis. 2d 491, 131 N. W. 2d 169.

An ample reading is given in: United States ex rel. Russo v. New Jersey, 351 F.2d 429 (C. A. 3d Cir.); Wright v. Dickson, [384 U.S. 436, 520]   336 F.2d 878 (C. A. 9th Cir.); People v.

Dorado, 62 Cal. 2d 338, 398 P.2d 361; State v. Dufour, ____ R. I. ____, 206 A. 2d 82; State v. Neely, 239 Ore. 487, 395 P.2d 557, modified, 398 P.2d 482.

The cases in both categories are those readily available; there are certainly many others.

[Footnote 18] For instance, compare the requirements of the catalytic case of People v. Dorado, 62 Cal. 2d 338, 398 P.2d 361, with those laid down today. See also Traynor, The Devils of Due Process in Criminal Detection, Detention, and Trial, 33 U. Chi. L. Rev. 657, 670.

[Footnote 19] The Court's obiter dictum notwithstanding, ante, p. 486, there is some basis for believing that the staple of FBI criminal work differs importantly from much crime within the ken of local police. The skill and resources of the FBI may also be unusual.

[Footnote 20] For citations and discussion covering each of these points, see Developments, supra, n. 2, at 1091-1097, and Enker & Elsen, supra, n. 12, at 80 & n. 94.

[Footnote 21] On comment, see Hardin, Other Answers: Search and Seizure, Coerced Confession, and Criminal Trial in Scotland, 113 U. Pa. L. Rev. 165, 181 and nn. 96-97

(1964). Other examples are less stringent search and seizure rules and no automatic exclusion for violation of them, id., at 167-169; guilt based on majority jury verdicts, id., at 185; and pre-trial discovery of evidence on both sides, id., at 175.

[Footnote 22] Of particular relevance is the ALI's drafting of a Model Code of Pre-Arraignment Procedure, now in its first tentative draft. While the ABA and National Commission studies have wider scope, the former is lending its advice to the ALI project and the executive director of the latter is one of the reporters for the Model Code.

[Footnote 23] See Brief for the United States in Westover, p. 45. The N. Y. Times, June 3, 1966, p. 41 (late city ed.) reported that the Ford Foundation has awarded $1,100,000 for a five-year study of arrests and confessions in New York.

[Footnote 24] The New York Assembly recently passed a bill to require certain warnings before an admissible confession is taken, though the rules are less strict than are the Court's. N. Y. Times, May 24, 1966, p. 35 (late city ed.).

[Footnote 25] The Court waited 12 years after Wolf v. Colorado, 338 U.S. 25 , declared privacy against improper state in-

trusions to be constitutionally safeguarded before it concluded in Mapp v. Ohio, 367 U.S. 643 , that adequate state
remedies had not been provided to protect this interest so
the exclusionary rule was necessary.

MR. JUSTICE WHITE, with whom MR. JUSTICE HARLAN
and MR. JUSTICE STEWART join, dissenting.

I.

The proposition that the privilege against self-incrimination
forbids in-custody interrogation without the warnings speci-
fied in the majority opinion and without a clear waiver of
counsel has no significant support in the history of the privilege or in the language of the Fifth Amendment. As for the
English authorities and the common-law history, the privilege, firmly established in the second half of the seventeenth
century, was never applied except to prohibit compelled judicial interrogations. The rule excluding coerced confessions
matured about 100 years later, "[b]ut there is nothing in the
reports to suggest that the theory has its roots in the privilege
against self-incrimination. And so far as the cases reveal, the
privilege, as such, seems to have been given effect only in
judicial proceedings, including the preliminary examinations

by authorized magistrates." Morgan, The Privilege Against Self-Incrimination, 34 Minn. L. Rev. 1, 18 (1949).

Our own constitutional provision provides that no person "shall be compelled in any criminal case to be a witness against himself." These words, when "[c]onsidered in the light to be shed by grammar and the dictionary . . . appear to signify simply that nobody shall be [384 U.S. 436, 527] compelled to give oral testimony against himself in a criminal proceeding under way in which he is defendant." Corwin, The Supreme Court's Construction of the Self-Incrimination Clause, 29 Mich. L. Rev. 1, 2. And there is very little in the surrounding circumstances of the adoption of the Fifth Amendment or in the provisions of the then existing state constitutions or in state practice which would give the constitutional provision any broader meaning. Mayers, The Federal Witness' Privilege Against Self-Incrimination: Constitutional or Common-Law? 4 American Journal of Legal History 107 (1960). Such a construction, however, was considerably narrower than the privilege at common law, and when eventually faced with the issues, the Court extended the constitutional privilege to the compulsory production of books and papers, to the ordinary witness before the grand jury and to witnesses generally. Boyd v. United States, 116 U.S. 616, and

Counselman v. Hitchcock, 142 U.S. 547 . Both rules had solid support in common-law history, if not in the history of our own constitutional provision.

A few years later the Fifth Amendment privilege was similarly extended to encompass the then well-established rule against coerced confessions: "In criminal trials, in the courts of the United States, wherever a question arises whether a confession is incompetent because not voluntary, the issue is controlled by that portion of the Fifth Amendment to the Constitution of the United States, commanding that no person `shall be compelled in any criminal case to be a witness against himself.'" Bram v. United States, 168 U.S. 532, 542 . Although this view has found approval in other cases, Burdeau v. McDowell, 256 U.S. 465, 475 ; Powers v. United States, 223 U.S. 303, 313 ; Shotwell v. United States, 371 U.S. 341, 347 , it has also been questioned, see Brown v. Mississippi, 297 U.S. 278, 285 ; United States v. Carignan, [384 U.S. 436, 528] 342 U.S. 36, 41 ; Stein v. New York, 346 U.S. 156, 191 , n. 35, and finds scant support in either the English or American authorities, see generally Regina v. Scott, Dears. & Bell 47; 3 Wigmore, Evidence 823 (3d ed. 1940), at 249 ("a confession is not rejected because of any connection with the privilege against self-crimination"), and 250, n. 5 (particularly criticizing Bram); 8 Wigmore, Evidence 2266, at 400-401 (McNaughton rev. 1961). Whatever the source of the rule excluding coerced confessions, it is clear that prior to the application of the privilege itself to state courts, Malloy v. Hogan, 378 U.S. 1 , the admissibility of a confession in a state criminal prosecution was tested by the same standards as were applied in federal prosecutions. Id., at 6-7, 10.

Bram, however, itself rejected the proposition which the Court now espouses. The question in Bram was whether a confession, obtained during custodial interrogation, had been compelled, and if such interrogation was to be deemed inherently vulnerable the Court's inquiry could have ended there. After examining the English and American authorities, however, the Court declared that:

"In this court also it has been settled that the mere fact that the confession is made to a police officer, while the accused was under arrest in or out of prison, or was drawn out by his questions, does not necessarily render the confession involuntary, but, as one of the circumstances, such imprisonment or interrogation may be taken into account in determining whether or not the statements of the prisoner were voluntary." 168 U.S., at 558 .

In this respect the Court was wholly consistent with prior and subsequent pronouncements in this Court.

Thus prior to Bram the Court, in Hopt v. Utah, 110 U.S. 574, 583 -587, had upheld the admissibility of a [384 U.S. 436, 529] confession made to police officers following arrest, the record being silent concerning what conversation had occurred between the officers and the defendant in the short period preceding the confession. Relying on Hopt, the Court ruled squarely on the issue in Sparf and Hansen v. United States, 156 U.S. 51, 55 :

"Counsel for the accused insist that there cannot be a voluntary statement, a free open confession, while a defendant is confined and in irons under an accusation of having committed a capital offence. We have not been referred to any authority in support of that position. It is true that the fact of a prisoner being in custody at the time he makes a confession is a circumstance not to be overlooked, because it bears upon the inquiry whether the confession was voluntarily made or was extorted by threats or violence or made under the influence of fear. But confinement or imprisonment is not in itself sufficient to justify the exclusion of a confession, if it appears to have been voluntary, and was not obtained by putting the prisoner in fear or by promises. Wharton's Cr. Ev. 9th ed. 661, 663, and authorities cited."

Accord, Pierce v. United States, 160 U.S. 355, 357 .

And in Wilson v. United States, 162 U.S. 613, 623 , the Court had considered the significance of custodial interrogation without any antecedent warnings regarding the right to remain silent or the right to counsel. There the defendant had answered questions posed by a Commissioner, who had failed to advise him of his rights, and his answers were held admissible over his claim of involuntariness. "The fact that [a defendant] is in custody and manacled does not necessarily render his statement involuntary, nor is that necessarily the effect of popular excitement shortly preceding. . . . And it is laid down [384 U.S. 436, 530]   that it is not essential to the admissibility of a confession that it should appear that the person was warned that what he said would be used against him, but on the contrary, if the confession was voluntary, it is sufficient though it appear that he was not so warned."

Since Bram, the admissibility of statements made during custodial interrogation has been frequently reiterated. Powers v. United States, 223 U.S. 303 , cited Wilson approvingly and held admissible as voluntary statements the accused's testimony at a preliminary hearing even though he was not warned that what he said might be used against him. Without any discussion of the presence or absence of warnings, presumably because such discussion was deemed unnecessary, numerous other cases have declared that "[t]he mere fact that a confession was made while in the custody of the police does not render it inadmissible," McNabb v. United States, 318 U.S. 332, 346 ; accord, United States v. Mitchell, 322 U.S. 65 , despite its having been elicited by police examination, Wan v. United States, 266 U.S. 1, 14 ; United States v. Carignan, 342 U.S. 36, 39 . Likewise, in Crooker v. California, 357 U.S. 433, 437 , the Court said that "the bare fact of police `detention and police examination in private of one in official state custody' does not render involuntary a confession by the one so detained." And finally, in Cicenia v. Lagay, 357 U.S. 504 , a confession obtained by police interrogation after arrest was held voluntary even though the authorities refused to permit the defendant to consult with his attorney. See generally Culombe v. Connecticut, 367 U.S. 568, 587 -602 (opinion of Frankfurter, J.); 3 Wigmore, Evidence 851, at 313 (3d ed. 1940); see also Joy, Admissibility of Confessions 38, 46 (1842).

Only a tiny minority of our judges who have dealt with the question, including today's majority, have considered in-custody interrogation, without more, to be a violation of the Fifth Amendment. And this Court, as [384 U.S. 436, 531] every member knows, has left standing literally thousands of criminal convictions that rested at least in part on confessions taken in the course of interrogation by the police after arrest.

II.

That the Court's holding today is neither compelled nor even strongly suggested by the language of the Fifth Amendment, is at odds with American and English legal history, and involves a departure from a long line of precedent does not prove either that the Court has exceeded its powers or that the Court is wrong or unwise in its present reinterpretation of the Fifth Amendment. It does, however, underscore the obvious - that the Court has not discovered or found the law in making today's decision, nor has it derived it from some irrefutable sources; what it has done is to make new law and new public policy in much the same way that it has in the course of interpreting other great clauses of the Constitution. 1 This is what the Court historically has done. Indeed, it is what it must do and will continue to do until and unless there is some fundamental change in the constitutional distribution of governmental powers.

But if the Court is here and now to announce new and fundamental policy to govern certain aspects of our affairs, it is wholly legitimate to examine the mode of this or any other constitutional decision in this Court and to inquire into the advisability of its end product in terms of the long-range interest of the country. At the very least the Court's text and reasoning should withstand analysis and be a fair exposition of the constitutional provision which its opinion interprets. Decisions [384 U.S. 436, 532] like these cannot rest alone on syllogism, metaphysics or some ill-defined notions of natural justice, although each will perhaps play its part. In proceeding to such constructions as it now announces, the Court should also duly consider all the factors and interests bearing upon the cases, at least insofar as the relevant materials are available; and if the necessary considerations are not treated in the record or obtainable from some other reliable source, the Court should not proceed to formulate fundamental policies based on speculation alone.

III.

First, we may inquire what are the textual and factual bases of this new fundamental rule. To reach the result announced on the grounds it does, the Court must stay within the confines of the Fifth Amendment, which forbids self-incrimination only if compelled. Hence the core of the Court's opinion is that because of the "compulsion inherent in custodial surroundings, no statement obtained from [a] defendant [in custody] can truly be the product of his free choice," ante, at 458, absent the use of adequate protective devices as described by the Court. However, the Court does not point to any sudden inrush of new knowledge requiring the rejection of 70 years' experience. Nor does it assert that its novel conclusion reflects a changing consensus among state courts, see Mapp v. Ohio, 367 U.S. 643, or that a succession of cases had steadily eroded the old rule and proved it unworkable, see Gideon v. Wainwright, 372 U.S. 335 . Rather than asserting new knowledge, the Court concedes that it cannot truly know what occurs during custodial questioning, because of the innate secrecy of such proceedings. It extrapolates a picture of what it conceives to be the norm from police investigatorial manuals, published in 1959 and 1962 or earlier, without any attempt to allow for adjustments in police practices that may [384 U.S. 436, 533]   have occurred in the wake of more recent decisions of state appellate tribunals or this Court. But even if the relentless application of the described procedures could lead to involuntary confessions, it most assuredly does not follow that each and every case will disclose this kind of interrogation or this kind of consequence. 2 Insofar as appears from the Court's opinion, it has not examined a single transcript of any police interrogation, let alone the interrogation that took place in any one of these cases which it decides today. Judged by any of the standards for empirical investigation utilized in the social sciences the factual basis for the Court's premise is patently inadequate.

Although in the Court's view in-custody interrogation is inherently coercive, the Court says that the spontaneous product of the coercion of arrest and detention is still to be deemed voluntary. An accused, arrested on probable cause, may blurt out a confession which will be admissible despite the fact that he is alone and in custody, without any showing that he had any notion of his right to remain silent or of the consequences of his admission. Yet, under the Court's rule, if the police ask him a single question such as "Do you have anything to say?" or "Did you kill your wife?" his response, if there is one, has somehow been compelled, even if the accused has [384 U.S. 436, 534]   been clearly warned of his right to remain silent. Common sense informs us to the contrary. While one may say that the response was "involuntary" in the sense the question provoked or was the occasion for the response and thus the defendant was induced to speak out when he might have remained silent if not arrested and not questioned, it is patently unsound to say the response is compelled.

Today's result would not follow even if it were agreed that to some extent custodial interrogation is inherently coercive. See Ashcraft v. Tennessee, 322 U.S. 143, 161 (Jackson, J., dissenting). The test has been whether the totality of circumstances deprived the defendant of a "free choice to admit, to deny, or to refuse to answer," Lisenba v. California, 314 U.S. 219, 241, and whether physical or psychological coercion was of such a degree that "the defendant's will was overborne at the time he confessed," Haynes v. Washington, 373 U.S. 503, 513 ; Lynumn v. Illinois, 372 U.S. 528, 534 . The duration and nature of incommunicado custody, the presence or absence of advice concerning the defendant's constitutional rights, and the granting or refusal of requests to communicate with lawyers, relatives or friends have all been rightly regarded as important data bearing on the basic inquiry. See, e. g., Ashcraft v. Tennessee, 322 U.S. 143 ; Haynes v. Washington, 373 U.S. 503 . 3 [384 U.S. 436, 535] But it has never been suggested, until today, that such questioning was so coercive and accused persons so lacking in hardihood that the very first response to the very first question following the commencement of custody must be conclusively presumed to be the product of an overborne will.

If the rule announced today were truly based on a conclusion that all confessions resulting from custodial interrogation are coerced, then it would simply have no rational foundation. Compare Tot v. United States, 319 U.S. 463, 466 ; United States v. Romano, 382 U.S. 136 . A fortiori that would be true of the extension of the rule to exculpatory statements, which the Court effects after a brief discussion of why, in the Court's view, they must be deemed incriminatory but without any discussion of why they must be deemed coerced. See Wilson v. United States, 162 U.S. 613, 624 . Even if one were to postulate that the Court's concern is not that all confessions induced by police interrogation are coerced but rather that some such confessions are coerced and present judicial procedures are believed to be inadequate to identify the confessions that are coerced and those that are not, it would still not be essential to impose the rule that the Court has now fashioned. Transcripts or observers could be required, specific time limits, tailored to fit the cause, could be imposed, or other devices could be utilized to reduce the chances that otherwise indiscernible coercion will produce an inadmissible confession.

On the other hand, even if one assumed that there was an adequate factual basis for the conclusion that all confessions obtained during in-custody interrogation are the product of compulsion, the rule propounded by [384 U.S. 436, 536] the Court would still be irrational, for, apparently, it is only if the accused is also warned of his right to counsel and waives both that right and the right against self-incrimination that the inherent compulsiveness of interrogation disappears. But if the defendant may not answer without a warning a question such as "Where were you last night?" without having his answer be a compelled one, how can the Court ever accept his negative answer to the question of whether he wants to consult his retained counsel or counsel whom the court will appoint? And why if counsel is present and the accused nevertheless confesses, or counsel tells the accused to tell the truth, and that is what the accused does, is the situation any less coercive insofar as the accused is concerned? The Court apparently realizes its dilemma of foreclosing questioning without the necessary warnings but at the same time permitting the accused, sitting in the same chair in front of the same policemen, to waive his right to consult an attorney. It expects, however, that the accused will not often waive the right; and if it is claimed that he has, the State faces a severe, if not impossible burden of proof.

All of this makes very little sense in terms of the compulsion which the Fifth Amendment proscribes. That amendment deals with compelling the accused himself. It is his free will that is involved. Confessions and incriminating admissions, as such, are not forbidden evidence; only those which are compelled are banned. I doubt that the Court observes these distinctions today. By considering any answers to any interrogation to be compelled regardless of the content and course of examination and by escalating the requirements to prove waiver, the Court not only prevents the use of compelled confessions but for all practical purposes forbids interrogation except in the presence of counsel. That is, instead of confining itself to protection of the right against compelled [384 U.S. 436, 537]   self-incrimination the Court has created a limited Fifth Amendment right to counsel - or, as the Court expresses it, a "need for counsel to protect the Fifth Amendment privilege . . . ." Ante, at 470. The focus then is not on the will of the accused but on the will of counsel and how much influence he can have on the accused. Obviously there is no warrant in the Fifth Amendment for thus installing counsel as the arbiter of the privilege.

In sum, for all the Court's expounding on the menacing atmosphere of police interrogation procedures, it has failed to supply any foundation for the conclusions it draws or the measures it adopts.

IV.

Criticism of the Court's opinion, however, cannot stop with a demonstration that the factual and textual bases for the rule it propounds are, at best, less than compelling. Equally relevant is an assessment of the rule's consequences measured against community values. The Court's duty to assess the consequences of its action is not satisfied by the utterance of the truth that a value of our system of criminal justice is "to respect the inviolability of the human personality" and to require government to produce the evidence against the accused by its own independent labors. Ante, at 460. More than the human dignity of the accused is involved; the human personality of others in the society must also be preserved. Thus the values reflected by the privilege are not the sole desideratum; society's interest in the general security is of equal weight.

The obvious underpinning of the Court's decision is a deep-seated distrust of all confessions. As the Court declares that the accused may not be interrogated without counsel present, absent a waiver of the right to counsel, and as the Court all but admonishes the lawyer to [384 U.S. 436, 538] advise the accused to remain silent, the result adds up to a judicial judgment that evidence from the accused should not be used against him in any way, whether compelled or not. This is the not so subtle overtone of the opinion - that it is inherently wrong for the police to gather evidence from the accused himself. And this is precisely the nub of this dissent. I see nothing wrong or immoral, and certainly nothing unconstitutional, in the police's asking a suspect whom they have reasonable cause to arrest whether or not he killed his wife or in confronting him with the evidence on which the arrest was based, at least where he has been plainly advised that he may remain completely silent, see Escobedo v. Illinois, 378 U.S. 478, 499 (dissenting opinion). Until today, "the admissions or confessions of the prisoner, when voluntarily and freely made, have always ranked high in the scale of incriminating evidence." Brown v. Walker, 161 U.S. 591, 596 ; see also Hopt v. Utah, 110 U.S. 574, 584 -585. Particularly when corroborated, as where the police have confirmed the accused's disclosure of the hiding place of implements or fruits of the crime, such confessions have the highest reliability and significantly contribute to the certitude with which we may believe the accused is guilty. Moreover, it is by no means certain that the process of confessing is injurious to the accused. To the contrary it may provide psychological relief and enhance the prospects for rehabilitation.

This is not to say that the value of respect for the inviolability of the accused's individual personality should be accorded no weight or that all confessions should be indiscriminately admitted. This Court has long read the Constitution to proscribe compelled confessions, a salutary rule from which there should be no retreat. But I see no sound basis, factual or otherwise, and the Court gives none, for concluding that the present rule against the receipt of coerced confessions is inadequate for the [384 U.S. 436, 539] task of sorting out inadmissible evidence and must be replaced by the per se rule which is now imposed. Even if the new concept can be said to have advantages of some sort over the present law, they are far outweighed by its likely undesirable impact on other very relevant and important interests.

The most basic function of any government is to provide for the security of the individual and of his property. Lanzetta v. New Jersey, 306 U.S. 451, 455 . These ends of society are served by the criminal laws which for the most part are aimed at the prevention of crime. Without the reasonably effective performance of the task of preventing private violence and retaliation, it is idle to talk about human dignity and civilized values.

The modes by which the criminal laws serve the interest in general security are many. First the murderer who has taken the life of another is removed from the streets, deprived of his liberty and thereby prevented from repeating his offense. In view of the statistics on recidivism in this country 4 and of the number of instances [384 U.S. 436, 540] in which apprehension occurs only after repeated offenses, no one can sensibly claim that this aspect of the criminal law does not prevent crime or contribute significantly to the personal security of the ordinary citizen.

Secondly, the swift and sure apprehension of those who refuse to respect the personal security and dignity of their neighbor unquestionably has its impact on others who might be similarly tempted. That the criminal law is wholly or partly ineffective with a segment of the population or with many of those who have been apprehended and convicted is a very faulty basis for concluding that it is not effective with respect to the great bulk of our citizens or for thinking that without the criminal laws, [384 U.S. 436, 541] or in the absence of their enforcement, there would be no increase in crime. Arguments of this nature are not borne out by any kind of reliable evidence that I have seen to this date.

Thirdly, the law concerns itself with those whom it has confined. The hope and aim of modern penology, fortunately, is as soon as possible to return the convict to society a better and more law-abiding man than when he left. Sometimes there is success, sometimes failure. But at least the effort is made, and it should be made to the very maximum extent of our present and future capabilities.

The rule announced today will measurably weaken the ability of the criminal law to perform these tasks. It is a deliberate calculus to prevent interrogations, to reduce the incidence of confessions and pleas of guilty and to increase the number of trials. 5 Criminal trials, no [384 U.S. 436, 542]   matter how efficient the police are, are not sure bets for the prosecution, nor should they be if the evidence is not forthcoming. Under the present law, the prosecution fails to prove its case in about 30% of the criminal cases actually tried in the federal courts. See Federal Offenders: 1964, supra, note 4, at 6 (Table 4), 59 (Table 1); Federal Offenders: 1963, supra, note 4, at 5 (Table 3); District of Columbia Offenders: 1963, supra, note 4, at 2 (Table 1). But it is something else again to remove from the ordinary criminal case all those confessions which heretofore have been held to be free and voluntary acts of the accused and to thus establish a new constitutional barrier to the ascertainment of truth by the judicial process. There is, in my view, every reason to believe that a good many criminal defendants who otherwise would have been convicted on what this Court has previously thought to be the most satisfactory kind of evidence will now, under this new version of the Fifth Amendment, either not be tried at all or will be acquitted if the State's evidence, minus the confession, is put to the test of litigation.

I have no desire whatsoever to share the responsibility for any such impact on the present criminal process.

In some unknown number of cases the Court's rule will return a killer, a rapist or other criminal to the streets and to the environment which produced him, to repeat his crime whenever it pleases him. As a consequence, there will not be a gain, but a loss, in human dignity. The real concern is not the unfortunate consequences of this new decision on the criminal law as an abstract, disembodied series of authoritative proscriptions, but the impact on those who rely on the public authority for protection and who without it can only engage in violent self-help with guns, knives and the help of their neighbors similarly inclined. There is, of [384 U.S. 436, 543] course, a saving factor: the next victims are uncertain, unnamed and unrepresented in this case.

Nor can this decision do other than have a corrosive effect on the criminal law as an effective device to prevent crime. A major component in its effectiveness in this regard is its swift and sure enforcement. The easier it is to get away with rape and murder, the less the deterrent effect on those who are inclined to attempt it. This is still good common sense. If it were not, we should posthaste liquidate the whole law enforcement establishment as a useless, misguided effort to control human conduct.

And what about the accused who has confessed or would confess in response to simple, noncoercive questioning and whose guilt could not otherwise be proved? Is it so clear that release is the best thing for him in every case? Has it so unquestionably been resolved that in each and every case it would be better for him not to confess and to return to his environment with no attempt whatsoever to help him? I think not. It may well be that in many cases it will be no less than a callous disregard for his own welfare as well as for the interests of his next victim.

There is another aspect to the effect of the Court's rule on the person whom the police have arrested on probable cause. The fact is that he may not be guilty at all and may be able to extricate himself quickly and simply if he were told the circumstances of his arrest and were asked to explain. This effort, and his release, must now await the hiring of a lawyer or his appointment by the court, consultation with counsel and then a session with the police or the prosecutor. Similarly, where probable cause exists to arrest several suspects, as where the body of the victim is discovered in a house having several residents, compare Johnson v. State, 238 Md. 140, 207 A. 2d 643 (1965), cert. denied, 382 U.S. 1013 , it will often [384 U.S. 436, 544] be true that a suspect may be cleared only through the results of interrogation of other suspects. Here too the release of the innocent may be delayed by the Court's rule.

Much of the trouble with the Court's new rule is that it will operate indiscriminately in all criminal cases, regardless of the severity of the crime or the circumstances involved. It applies to every defendant, whether the professional criminal or one committing a crime of momentary passion who is not part and parcel of organized crime. It will slow down the investigation and the apprehension of confederates in those cases where time is of the essence, such as kidnapping, see Brinegar v. United States, 338 U.S. 160, 183 (Jackson, J., dissenting); People v. Modesto, 62 Cal. 2d 436, 446, 398 P.2d 753, 759 (1965), those involving the national security, see United States v. Drummond, 354 F.2d 132, 147 (C. A. 2d Cir. 1965) (en banc) (espionage case), pet. for cert. pending, No.

1203, Misc., O. T. 1965; cf. Gessner v. United States, 354 F.2d 726, 730, n. 10 (C. A. 10th Cir. 1965) (upholding, in espionage case, trial ruling that Government need not submit classified portions of interrogation transcript), and some of those involving organized crime. In the latter context the lawyer who arrives may also be the lawyer for the defendant's colleagues and can be relied upon to insure that no breach of the organization's security takes place even though the accused may feel that the best thing he can do is to cooperate.

At the same time, the Court's per se approach may not be justified on the ground that it provides a "bright line" permitting the authorities to judge in advance whether interrogation may safely be pursued without jeopardizing the admissibility of any information obtained as a consequence. Nor can it be claimed that judicial time and effort, assuming that is a relevant consideration, [384 U.S. 436, 545]   will be conserved because of the ease of application of the new rule. Today's decision leaves open such questions as whether the accused was in custody, whether his statements were spontaneous or the product of interrogation, whether the accused has effectively waived his rights, and whether nontestimonial evidence introduced at trial is the fruit of statements made

395

during a prohibited interrogation, all of which are certain to prove productive of uncertainty during investigation and litigation during prosecution. For all these reasons, if further restrictions on police interrogation are desirable at this time, a more flexible approach makes much more sense than the Court's constitutional straitjacket which forecloses more discriminating treatment by legislative or rule-making pronouncements.

Applying the traditional standards to the cases before the Court, I would hold these confessions voluntary. I would therefore affirm in Nos. 759, 760, and 761, and reverse in No. 584.

[Footnote 1] Of course the Court does not deny that it is departing from prior precedent; it expressly overrules Crooker and Cicenia, ante, at 479, n. 48, and it acknowledges that in the instant "cases we might not find the defendants' statements to have been involuntary in traditional terms," ante, at 457.

[Footnote 2] In fact, the type of sustained interrogation described by the Court appears to be the exception rather than the rule. A survey of 399 cases in one city found that in almost half of the cases the interrogation lasted less than 30 minutes. Barrett, Police Practices and the Law - From Arrest to Release or Charge, 50 Calif. L. Rev. 11, 41-45 (1962). Questioning tends to be confused and sporadic and is usually concentrated on confrontations with witnesses or new items of evidence, as these are obtained by officers conducting the investigation. See generally LaFave, Arrest: The Decision to Take a Suspect into Custody 386 (1965); ALI, A Model Code of Pre-Arraignment Procedure, Commentary 5.01, at 170, n. 4 (Tent. Draft No. 1, 1966).

[Footnote 3] By contrast, the Court indicates that in applying this new rule it "will not pause to inquire in individual cases whether the defendant was aware of his rights without a warning being given." Ante, at 468. The reason given is that assessment of the knowledge of the defendant based on information as to age, education, intelligence, or prior contact with authorities can never be more than speculation, while a warning is a clear-cut fact. But the officers' claim that they gave the requisite warnings may be disputed, and facts respecting the defendant's prior experience may be undisputed and be of such a nature as to virtually preclude any doubt that the defendant knew of his rights. See United States v. Bolden, 355 F.2d 453 [384 U.S. 436, 535] (C. A. 7th Cir. 1965), petition for cert. pending No. 1146, O. T. 1965

(Secret Service agent); People v. Du Bont, 235 Cal. App. 2d 844, 45 Cal. Rptr. 717, pet. for cert. pending No. 1053, Misc., O. T. 1965 (former police officer).

[Footnote 4] Precise statistics on the extent of recidivism are unavailable, in part because not all crimes are solved and in part because criminal records of convictions in different jurisdictions are not brought together by a central data collection agency. Beginning in 1963, however, the Federal Bureau of Investigation began collating data on "Careers in Crime," which it publishes in its Uniform Crime Reports. Of 92,869 offenders processed in 1963 and 1964, 76% had a prior arrest record on some charge. Over a period of 10 years the group had accumulated 434,000 charges. FBI, Uniform Crime Reports - 1964, 27-28. In 1963 and 1964 between 23% and 25% of all offenders sentenced in 88 federal district courts (excluding the District Court for the District of Columbia) whose criminal records were reported had previously been sentenced to a term of imprisonment of 13 months or more. Approximately an additional 40% had a prior record less than prison (juvenile record, probation record, etc.). Administrative Office of the United States Courts, Federal Offenders in the United States District Courts: 1964, x, 36 (hereinafter cited as Federal Offenders: 1964); Administrative [384 U.S. 436, 540] Office of the United States Courts, Federal Offenders in the United States District Courts: 1963, 25-27 (hereinafter cited as Federal Offenders: 1963). During the same two years in the District Court for the District of Columbia between 28% and 35% of those sentenced had prior prison records and from 37% to 40% had a prior record less than prison. Federal Offenders: 1964, xii, 64, 66; Administrative Office of the United States Courts, Federal Offenders in the United States District Court for the District of Columbia: 1963, 8, 10 (hereinafter cited as District of Columbia Offenders: 1963).

A similar picture is obtained if one looks at the subsequent records of those released from confinement. In 1964, 12.3% of persons on federal probation had their probation revoked because of the commission of major violations (defined as one in which the probationer has been committed to imprisonment for a period of 90 days or more, been placed on probation for over one year on a new offense, or has absconded with felony charges outstanding). Twenty-three and two-tenths percent of parolees and 16.9% of those who had been mandatorily released after service of a portion of their sentence likewise committed major violations. Reports of the

Proceedings of the Judicial Conference of the United States and Annual Report of the Director of the Administrative Office of the United States Courts: 1965, 138. See also Mandel et al., Recidivism Studied and Defined, 56 J. Crim. L., C. & P. S. 59 (1965) (within five years of release 62.33% of sample had committed offenses placing them in recidivist category).

[Footnote 5] Eighty-eight federal district courts (excluding the District Court for the District of Columbia) disposed of the cases of 33,381 criminal defendants in 1964. Only 12.5% of those cases were actually tried. Of the remaining cases, 89.9% were terminated by convictions upon pleas of guilty and 10.1% were dismissed. Stated differently, approximately 90% of all convictions resulted from guilty pleas. Federal Offenders: 1964, supra, note 4, 3-6. In the District Court for the District of Columbia a higher percentage, 27%, went to trial, and the defendant pleaded guilty in approximately 78% of the cases terminated prior to trial. Id., at 58-59. No reliable statistics are available concerning the percentage of cases in which guilty pleas are induced because of the existence of a confession or of physical evidence unearthed as a result of a confession. Undoubtedly the number of such cases is substantial.

Perhaps of equal significance is the number of instances of known crimes which are not solved. In 1964, only 388,946, or 23.9% of 1,626,574 serious known offenses were cleared. The clearance rate ranged from 89.8% for homicides to 18.7% for larceny. FBI, Uniform Crime Reports - 1964, 20-22, 101. Those who would replace interrogation as an investigatorial tool by modern scientific investigation techniques significantly overestimate the effectiveness of present procedures, even when interrogation is included. [384 U.S. 436, 546]

Anlage 7:

LGT: Illegal weitergegebenes Datenmaterial beschränkt sich auf die 2002 gestohlenen Kundendaten der LGT Treuhand

24. Februar 2008

Weitere Informationen zur Täterschaft und zum Hergang

Vaduz, 24. Februar 2008 - Wie schon in der ersten Medienmitteilung der LGT Group am 15. Februar 2008 vermutet, beschränkt sich das illegal an deutsche Behörden weitergegebene Datenmaterial, soweit es die LGT betrifft, mit an Sicherheit grenzender Wahrscheinlichkeit auf die 2002 bei der LGT Treuhand gestohlenen Kundendaten. Aufgrund der Indizienlage geht die LGT bezüglich des Datendiebstahls und der Datenweitergabe von derselben Täterschaft aus und richtet ihre zunächst gegen Unbekannt erstattete Anzeige nun auch direkt gegen den verurteilten Datendieb. Nach Erhärtung dieser Sachverhalte und aufgrund des grossen medialen Interesses publiziert die LGT zudem weitere Details zum Täter und zum Hergang des Datendiebstahls.

Für die LGT Group weist trotz teilweise gegenteiliger Aussagen aus angeblich BND-nahen Quellen nun alles darauf hin, dass sich das illegal an deutsche Behörden weitergegebene Datenmaterial, soweit es die LGT betrifft, auf die 2002 gestohlenen Kundendaten der LGT Treuhand beschränkt. Die LGT hatte am 15. Februar 2008 über den Datendiebstahl und den vermuteten Zusammenhang zu den Ereignissen in Deutschland informiert. Obwohl auch dazu zunächst andere Gerüchte in Umlauf gesetzt wurden, geht die LGT Group aufgrund zahlreicher Indizien davon aus, dass es sich bei der Person, welche die Daten illegal an den BND weitergegeben hat, um den ehemaligen Mitarbeiter der LGT Treuhand handelt, der 2002 den Datendiebstahl beging. Dabei wurden angeblich Anwaltskanzleien als Zwischenhändler eingeschaltet. Die LGT wird ihre Anzeige gegen Unbekannt nun auch direkt gegen den verurteilten Datendieb richten.

Offenbar wurde das gestohlene Datenmaterial direkt oder indirekt auch an andere Behörden illegal weitergegeben. Gemäß Medienberichten wurde die wegen mehrerer Delikte vorbestrafte Person dabei durch Zahlungen in Millionenhöhe abgegolten und mit einer neuen Identität versehen. Die LGT erachtet derartige Methoden als zutiefst befremdlich, zumal damit offenbar in Kauf genommen wird, dass diese Person die vertraulichen Kundendaten auch zu anderen kriminellen Zwecken missbrauchen könnte.

Bei den im Jahr 2002 gestohlenen Daten handelt es sich um Akten unterschiedlichster Natur. Sie betreffen ungefähr 1'400 Kundenbeziehungen der LGT Treuhand, die vor Ende 2002 eingegangen wurden. Davon ist der größte Teil, gegen 600 Kunden, in Deutschland wohnhaft. Bei der in den Medien kursierenden Zahl von 4'527 Datensätzen handelt es sich exakt um die Anzahl der Begünstigten aller Stiftungen, die sich auf dem 2002 gestohlenen Datenmaterial der LGT Treuhand befinden. Sie ist nicht zu verwechseln mit der Anzahl Kunden, welche Anlagen in eine oder mehrere Stiftungen mit jeweils einem oder mehreren Begünstigten einbringen. Im Übrigen ist der teilweise pauschalisierten Darstellung, es handle sich bei allen betroffenen Kunden um Steuersünder, entschieden entgegen zu treten.

Datendiebstahl 2002: Zur Täterschaft und zum Hergang im Einzelnen

Die LGT Group hat am 15. Februar 2008 in einer Medienmitteilung bekannt gegeben, dass ein ehemaliger Mitarbeiter der LGT Treuhand in Vaduz im Jahr 2002 Kundendaten gestohlen hat und in der Folge angezeigt sowie gerichtlich verurteilt wurde. Sie hat weiter darüber informiert, dass die Kundendaten im Zuge von Kontakten zwischen den Parteien vermeintlich zurückgegeben wurden und dass vom Datendiebstahl ausschließlich Kundenbeziehungen der LGT Treuhand betroffen sind, die bis Ende 2002 eingegangen wurden. Das Fürstliche Landgericht und die Liechtensteinische Staatsanwaltschaft haben die Kommunikation der LGT am 19. Februar 2008 mit Informationen zu den relevanten juristischen Aspekten ergänzt.

Inzwischen hat sich erhärtet, dass es sich bei dem verurteilten Datendieb ebenfalls um den so genannten „Informanten" des BND handelt, der die 2002 gestohlenen Kundendaten illegal weitergegeben hat. Deshalb, und aufgrund des grossen medialen Interesses, ist die LGT nun in der Lage, weitere - aus Kundensicht teilweise nicht relevante - Details zum Hergang des Datendiebstahls zu publizieren. Um einen umfassenden Überblick zu vermitteln, veröffentlicht sie dabei ausnahmsweise und in Absprache auch Informationen, die nicht die LGT Treuhand, sondern auch andere Instanzen betreffen.

Beim ehemaligen Mitarbeiter, der den Datendiebstahl begangen hat, handelt es sich um den Liechtensteinischen Staatsbürger Heinrich Kieber (HK). Er war ab Oktober 1999 als externer Mitarbeiter eines IT-Unternehmens und von April 2001 bis November 2002 als Angestellter bei der LGT Treuhand tätig. Seine Aufgabe bestand darin, im Zuge der Überführung der Datenbestände in ein elektronisches Archiv eingescannte Unterlagen zu überprüfen. Er war zum Zeitpunkt der Einstellung und während seiner Tätigkeit für die LGT Treuhand nicht vorbestraft. Hingegen bestand, wie später bekannt wurde, ein Haftbefehl gegen HK, der bei der standardmäßigen Überprüfung des neuen Mitarbeiters nicht zugänglich war.

Dieser Haftbefehl geht auf ein Immobiliengeschäft in Spanien im Jahr 1996 zurück, das HK mit ungedeckten Schecks finanziert haben soll, und wurde 1997 von den spanischen Strafverfolgungsbehörden zunächst auf nationaler und dann auf internationaler Ebene erlassen. Im Oktober 2001 wurde HK vom Fürstlichen Landgericht dazu verurteilt, dem Geschädigten rund CHF 600'000 zu bezahlen. Dagegen legte HK Berufung ein, die im Oktober 2002 vom Obergericht abgelehnt wurde. Im November 2002 brachte die Liechtensteinische Staatsanwaltschaft im Zusammenhang mit dem Immobiliengeschäft in Spanien Anklage wegen schweren Betrugs gegen HK ein. In demselben Monat verließ HK die LGT Treuhand und setzte sich ins Ausland ab. Wie sich später herausstellte, hatte er davor Kundendaten seines Arbeitgebers unrechtmäßig in seinen Besitz gebracht und auf vier DVDs kopiert.

Im Januar 2003 richtete HK ein Schreiben und eine Tonbandkassette an S.D. Fürst Hans-Adam von Liechtenstein. HK gab an, sich durch die Justiz ungerecht behandelt zu fühlen. Er forderte Unterstützung bei der Lösung seiner juristischen Probleme, was auch die Ausstellung zweier neuer Pässe beinhaltete, ansonsten er die gestohlenen Kundendaten an ausländische Medien und Behörden weitergeben würde. Diese Forderungen wurden abgelehnt, vom Landgericht wurde ein Haftbefehl erlassen, und die Staatsanwaltschaft brachte eine Anklageschrift gegen HK ein. Der LGT Treuhand gelang es, Kontakt mit HK herzustellen. Sie überzeugte ihn, im Mai 2003 nach Liechtenstein zurückzukehren und sich der Gerichtsbarkeit zu stellen. Das fürstliche Obergericht sicherte ihm dabei freies Geleit bis zum Prozess zu. Im Rahmen des gerichtlichen Verfahrens erhielt die LGT Treuhand die DVDs mit den gestohlenen Kundendaten vermeintlich zurück und vernichtete diese später. Die Kosten für den Rechtsbeistand von HK sowie für dessen Wohnung in Liechtenstein wurden durch die LGT Treuhand getragen.

HK - der geständig war und sich reuig zeigte - wurde im Oktober 2003 erstinstanzlich vom Kriminalgericht wegen schweren Betrugs, gefährlicher Drohung, Nötigung und Urkundenunterdrückung zu vier Jahren Haft verurteilt. Darauf wandte sich HK mit einem persönlichen Schreiben an S.D. Fürst Hans-Adam und bat ihn - im Hinblick auf eine Berufung gegen das Urteil - zu bekräftigen, dass er sich durch ihn nie bedroht gefühlt habe, was von Fürst Hans-Adam bestätigt wurde. Das rechtskräftige Urteil des Obergerichts vom Januar 2004 lautete schließlich auf schweren Betrug, Nötigung sowie Urkundenunterdrückung und beinhaltete eine Freiheitsstrafe von einem Jahr, die für eine Probezeit von drei Jahren bedingt nachgesehen wurde. Der Verurteilung wegen Betrugs lag das erwähnte Immobiliengeschäft in Spanien zugrunde; die versuchte Nötigung betraf die mit Schreiben gegenüber S.D. Fürst Hans-Adam ausgesprochenen Forderungen; und die Urkundenunterdrückung beinhaltete den Datendiebstahl bei der LGT Treuhand. Vom Verbrechen der Auskundschaftung eines Geschäfts- und Betriebsgeheimnisses wurde HK freigesprochen, weil die Gerichte davon ausgingen, dass er beim Diebstahl der Kundendaten noch nicht den Vorsatz hatte, diese dem Ausland preiszugeben. Der internationale Haftbefehl der spanischen Strafverfolgungsbehörden wurde im Oktober 2004 aufgehoben und das Strafverfahren in Spanien im November 2005 eingestellt.

Im April 2005 richtete HK ein erneutes Schreiben an S.D. Fürst Hans-Adam, in dem er um Begnadigung bat. Dieses Begnadigungsgesuch wurde von S.D. Erbprinz Alois in Übereinstimmung mit den zuständigen Behörden abgelehnt. Hingegen wurde im Mai 2005 das Recht auf Auskunft über das Strafregister von HK auf Strafverfolgungsbehörden beschränkt, was per Januar 2006 von Rechts wegen ohnehin eingetreten wäre. Wo sich HK heute aufhält, ist der LGT Group nicht bekannt. Laut Medienberichten soll er unter neuer Identität in Australien leben.

LGT in Kürze

LGT steht als Unternehmen im Besitz des Fürstenhauses von Liechtenstein für Wealth Management im ursprünglichen Sinn eines Privatbankiers. LGT ist mit rund 1500 Mitarbeitenden an 29 Standorten in Europa, Asien, dem Mittleren Osten und Amerika vor Ort präsent. Group CEO ist S.D. Prinz Max von und zu Liechtenstein. Per 30.6.2007 verwaltete die LGT Vermögenswerte von 99.7 Milliarden Schweizer Franken.

Über den Autor:

Torben Wissuwa ist seit mehr als zehn Jahren Lehrbeauftragter für Insolvenz- und Steuerrecht an der Hochschule für öffentliche Verwaltung und als Insolvenz- und Sanierungsberater sowie Insolvenzverwalter tätig. Schon seit Studientagen fasziniert ihn die Thematik um das Beschaffen und Verwerten von Beweisen.

CPSIA information can be obtained
at www.ICGtesting.com
Printed in the USA
BVHW031023150223
658562BV00004B/116

9 783347 170803